Mother-Teachers

Insights into inclusion

Barbara Ann Cole

David Fulton Publishers

David Fulton Publishers Ltd
The Chiswick Centre, 414 Chiswick High Road, London W4 5TF

www.fultonpublishers.co.uk

First published in Great Britain in 2004 by David Fulton Publishers

10 9 8 7 6 5 4 3 2 1

Note: The right of Barbara Cole to be identified as the author of this work has been asserted by her in accordance with the Copyright, Designs and Patents Act 1988.

Copyright © Barbara Ann Cole 2004

British Library Cataloguing in Publication Data
A catalogue record for this book is available from the British Library.

David Fulton Publishers is a division of Granada Learning, part of ITV plc.

ISBN 1 84312 179 4

Printed in Great Britain by Ashford Colour Press.

Contents

To Marie, Henry, Jemma and Graham

Acknowledgements

I would like to express my grateful thanks to a number of people for their help, support and encouragement during the writing of this book. I am completely indebted to Michael, Elizabeth, Christopher, Lara, Sally, John, Kirsty, Martin, Stuart and James, without whom the book would never have been written. I also want to thank their mothers, the six mother-teachers, who so willingly offered me their time and entrusted me with their experiences. I hope the book does them justice.

I would also like to express my thanks to my family, friends and colleagues who have been extremely understanding, supportive and patient during the whole process of the research: to my family for being there; to Mike Johnson for his constant willingness to listen, read drafts and discuss ideas; to Jerry Wellington and Derrick Armstrong for their constructive and encouraging comments on earlier drafts; to Miriam David for her strength and support during the research process; to Helen Gunter for her belief in me, friendship and enthusiasm; and to all the colleagues and friends whose work and support have inspired me and kept me going, particularly Jon Nixon, Pat Sikes, Peter Clough and Mike Calvert.

My thanks go to Molly, who has listened with patience, if little understanding, and walked every step of the way with me.

Finally and most importantly my thanks go to my own parents, for all their unquestioning love and care for a lifetime.

Preface

This book presents the stories of six women who are both mothers and teachers of children with special educational needs and/or disabilities. It sets the stories within relevant policy and sociological contexts which affect the lives of these women in their roles as mothers and teachers. It offers their experiences around a number of dichotomies, such as normality and difference, inclusion and exclusion, home and school, parent and professional, knowledge and experience.

It is not a 'how to do' book, but, rather through the stories, it seeks to offer to policy-makers and a broad range of educational, quasi-medical and even medical professionals, the lived experiences of the mother-teachers, with the intention of encouraging readers to reflect on their own professional understandings and practices in relation to children with special educational needs and disabilities. While the book acknowledges the wider policy and sociological context in relation to educational inclusion, it challenges professionals to explore the ways in which their own 'expert' processes and structures, 'knowledge' and understandings, might serve to maintain the reproduction of constructions of difference which exclude or 'other' some children and their families.

The stories draw on experiences from different sectors of education; mainstream primary and secondary; special day and residential schools and also initial teacher education. The children span a range of ages, from 3 to 24 years of age, and the experiences of the mother-teachers reflect this. Each story offers a section at the end of the chapter, which considers one aspect raised within the story for further discussion and reflection, but it is left to the reader to relate to the stories through the lens of personal experience. While the stories suggest many similarities of experience, they also challenge any notion of the women as a homogeneous group, as the discourses around them and their children might suggest. They hold different views on the meaning and nature of inclusion and special educational needs and their experiences reflect these different understandings. But what emerges from the stories is their belief that individual professionals can make a real difference to the lives of their children. All these women have changed their professional practice as a result of being the mothers of children with special needs/disabilities. They reflect the view that 'professional knowledge' needs to be based, at least in part, on personal understanding and experience, which they maintain can develop through listening to parents who have a particular knowledge of their children. The stories demonstrate the importance of this shared understanding, if all children are to be truly valued and 'included'.

Introduction

The greater the fear, the more thinking you do. Yet she came closer to the truth than anyone else. Maybe that's how it works – that whatever is closest to the truth, you do not think about; you cannot reach it by achievement; you can only feel it …

(Høeg 1996: 80)

The book and its context

This book is based on research with six women who are mothers of children with special educational needs/disabilities and who are also teachers of children with special educational needs (SEN). It contextualises their experiences of inclusion and exclusion against a political background of conflicting educational policies and a sociological background of powerful 'expert' discourses.

The last few years have seen the growth of policies aimed at raising the achievement of *all* children in mainstream educational settings. The most recent of these include the *Special Educational Needs Code of Practice* (DfES 2001), the Audit Commission's Report *Special Educational Needs: A Mainstream Issue* (DfES 2002), the Green Paper *Every Child Matters* (TSO 2003), and *Removing Barriers to Achievement: The Government's Strategy for SEN* (DfES 2004). All these documents state the government's commitment to safeguard and support the development and learning of all children wherever possible in mainstream educational contexts. The most recent of them (DfES 2004) commits the government to 'partnership working' to 'unlock the potential of the many children who may have difficulty learning, but whose life chances depend on a good education'. The Introduction makes clear that:

All teachers should expect to teach children with special educational needs (SEN) and all schools should play their part in educating children from their local community, whatever their background or ability. We must reflect this in the way we train our teachers, in the way we fund our schools, and in the way we judge their achievements.

(ibid.)

In the spirit of this continuing and indeed growing commitment to a more inclusive approach to education, this book exhorts policy-makers and all those professionals involved in supporting the education of children with special educational needs/disabilities to explore outside their own professional 'boxes' and listen to the voices of those who, through their personal experiences, have particular and significant insights into issues of inclusion and exclusion. This book considers the voices of mothers and offers their insights on two levels, as mothers *and* as teachers of children with special educational needs/disabilities. I argue that while the rhetoric of policy has moved inclusion into the mainstream, in reality, for many children and their families, the experience of inclusion is very different. If the policy commitment is to translate into reality in our schools and classrooms, then I would argue that policies relating to inclusion, such as the training of teachers, the funding of schools and the assessment of achievement, must be informed by these voices of experience.

This is a book about lived experiences of inclusion and exclusion. Since the early 1980s 'inclusion' has been one of the key initiatives in education policy, internationally and in the UK, and the principal policy imperative in relation to children with special educational needs (Lindsay 2003). Emerging from the growing demand for equity and social justice, inclusion requires changes in the structures and processes of mainstream educational institutions to meet the needs of all children within an educational system which values and respects difference as diversity rather than deviance. It also requires the support and determination of parents and professionals if it is ever to become a reality for thousands of children in the UK.

Within the official discourse of inclusion, the development of home–school relations has been signalled in the official discourse as a significant way to ensure a more equal partnership between parents and professionals. Indeed, since the 1981 Education Act, numerous policy documents (e.g. DfEE 1994, 1997a, 1997b, 1997c, 1998a, 1998b, 1999, DfES 2001, 2004) have called for partnership between parents and professionals in relation to children perceived as having special educational needs. During that time a number of books and articles exploring issues related to parent–professional partnership (e.g. Armstrong 1995, Dale 1996, Wolfendale 1997, 2002, Swain and Walker 2003) have highlighted the need for a greater understanding of how meaningful partnerships might be developed for the benefit of the children. The suggestion in the literature is that despite the legislation increasing parental rights, there remains an imbalance between parents and professionals (Fulcher 1989, Armstrong 1995, Wolfendale and Cook 1997, Todd 2003), although Armstrong (1995: 27) maintains that parents are not perceived as passive participants. Liz Todd (2003: 294) argues that current policy and practice offer a 'complex mixture' in which there is 'respect for parents as equals' but there remains a 'continuing deficit discourse', especially in relation to the assessment of special needs, evidenced by the renewed call for the active involvement of parents in the Code of Practice (DfES 2001).

This complexity merits further examination if we are to gain new insights into how inclusion might be moved forward. This book argues that listening to the experiences of mothers who are also professionals in a related field is an important and relevant way of gaining new understandings and exploring the perceived imbalance of power. Only by professionals setting aside the powerful and constraining discourses, which divide and boundary professionals and parents, can they really begin to give credence and significance to the voices of 'others'. Some nine years after Derrick Armstrong's study (1995) this book considers aspects of both power and partnership in relation to SEN. It explores experiences of inclusion and exclusion from both the professional and the personal perspective and offers the experiences of six women who are mothers of children perceived as having special needs/disabilities. These women are also involved in the education of children who in some way or other present a challenge to the education system as it stands at the beginning of the twenty-first century.

The stories of the mother-teachers span 20 years or more and cross two continents. Two of the children are now in their late teens and one is now an adult; one is just embarking on her school career; one has experience of two education systems 3,000 miles apart, and two will always need the constant support of both their parents and a range of professionals. Although there are similarities, the stories of the children and their families represent unique and singular experiences, reflecting considerable differences in degrees of inclusion and support. They offer different perspectives on parental and professional approaches and should alert the reader to an awareness of the many differences of meaning and experience of both inclusion and exclusion. But the stories also reflect many similarities in relation to issues of power, partnership and the construction of 'knowledge' in the area of special educational needs.

Inclusion and exclusion

Inclusion and exclusion take place on many different levels within different contexts. While policy offers a macro-context, internationally, nationally and locally, experience offers insights into how that policy impacts on individual lives in both the public and the private domains. The book explores some of these experiences of SEN/disability in relation to inclusion, exclusion and parent–professional relationships through the stories of women who have experience of both sides of the personal/professional boundary. The main tenet of the book is that while a plethora of policies have been developed which support parent partnerships in SEN and educational inclusion, there still remains a 'real' gap between theory and practice. This may be an uncomfortable thought for practitioners but, far from seeking to lay blame, the book exhorts professionals to listen to parents and to examine how they, as professionals, might address some of the issues within their own practice. These stories are not written by either 'disgruntled' parents or by 'disillusioned' professionals. They are told by supportive parents who are also active practitioners working in both roles as agents for change who also have agency on behalf of 'their' children. Through a different and unique perspective, these mother-teachers have reflected on their practice, values and approaches and in many cases have redefined their own understandings of terms such as inclusion, exclusion and special educational needs.

Special educational needs and terminology

Writing a book about special educational needs, disability, inclusion and exclusion is problematic in relation to terminology. As support and funding have historically been associated with the identification and categorisation of need, parents have, not unreasonably, sought to use SEN terminology to argue their case for educational support for their children. The 2001 SEN Code of Practice (DfES 2001: sections 7.52–7.67) redefines the categories of SEN in an attempt to engage with the complexity of categorisation and the barriers which can emerge through the labelling of children. The use of terminology to refer to the different aspects of disability and learning difficulty is in itself a challenge, for, in condensing the multiplicity of issues to a single term, there is always the danger of reductionism. In this book I will adopt the meanings and definitions offered in the 2001 DfES SEN Code of Practice which are outlined in Figure 1.1.

Knowledge, experience, research

These stories are not intended as statements of 'how things *really* are' (Allan 1999: 1) but rather as insights into what Allan refers to as a 'complex power/knowledge knot, which is not supposed to be unravelled' (*ibid.*). As with the pupils' voices in Allan's book, the voices of these mother-teachers challenge the binaries, the related divisions used to boundary children and their families in relation to special educational needs; binaries such as inclusion/exclusion; normal/special; parent/professional; home/school; experience/ expertise; powerful/powerless. What the book aims to do by presenting the stories in some of their complexity through the eyes of the parent-professionals is to reopen or at least blur the boundaries between parents and professionals; and to recreate a 'listening space' from which a renewed understanding might develop. Thomas and Glenny suggest that such arguments for inclusion

> have to emerge less out of the kind of supposed knowledge so respected by 20th-century educators, less out of notions of success and failure (of children or of schools) and more out of ideas about social justice and human rights.
>
> (2002: 345)

If SEN and disability are considered within this context of rights, then the question must be asked about the nature of the evidence used to make judgements on SEN, for rational enquiry and empirical studies do not always appear to support the notion of inclusion with regard to effectiveness and learning (Lindsay 2003, Thomas and Glenny 2002, Wilson 2000). But as Lindsay (2003) argues, we need to consider rights

> Children have special educational needs if they have a *learning difficulty* which calls for *special educational provision* to be made for them (original emphasis).
>
> Children have a *learning difficulty* if they:
>
> a) have a significantly greater difficulty in learning than the majority of children of the same age; or
>
> b) have a disability which prevents or hinders them from making use of educational facilities of a kind generally provided for children of the same age in schools within the area of the local education authority;
>
> c) are under compulsory school age and fall within the definition at (a) or (b) above or would do so if special educational provision was not made for them. (DfES 2001: 6, section 1.3)
>
> A child is disabled if he is blind, deaf or dumb or suffers from a mental disorder of any kind or is substantially and permanently handicapped by illness, injury or congenital deformity or such other disability as may be prescribed (Section 17(11), Children Act 1989, quoted in DfES 2001: 7).
>
> A person has a disability for the purposes of this Act if he has a physical or mental impairment which has a substantial and long-term adverse effect on his ability to carry out normal day-to-day activities. (Section 1(1), Disability Discrimination Act 1995, quoted in DfES 2001: 7)

Figure 1.1 Definition of Special Educational Needs (DfES 2001: 6–7, section 1.3)

as well as efficacy and to this end qualitative research has much to offer. This book endorses the view that there needs to be 'a new epistemology' around issues related to educational inclusion; a 'reappraisal of the precepts, presumptions, tenets and methods of inquiry' which supported the framework of SEN in the twentieth century (Thomas and Glenny 2002: 346).

There is now a growing literature which offers 'insider perspectives' and lived experiences around aspects of disability, SEN and learning difficulties, inclusion and exclusion (e.g. Clough and Barton 1998, Moore *et al.* 1998). The stories told here are from two very particular insider perspectives. The lived experiences reflect the range and complexity of issues and ideas; of what counts as inclusion and what matters to these mothers and teachers. It is not just about the ideology of inclusion but about the reality, experienced in different ways and on many different levels. It is interesting to compare two levels of inclusion: on the one hand there is the National Study of Inclusive Education (Lipsky and Gartner 1998), which covers 1,000 school districts and which identified seven factors contributing to inclusive schools; on the other there is the voice of Julia (see Chapter 9) celebrating the 'inclusion' of her son Martin as he walks across the playground, head held high with pride having been trusted to take the register back to the school office. If we are ever to achieve 'meaningful' inclusion surely both kinds of evidence must have their place. While the macro-level and meta-analysis offer an important overview, we must keep a space in which we can listen to the voices of individuals and their experiences. This book is about that space and some of those voices. The stories are lived within both a policy and a sociological context. Without some understanding of these contexts, the stories remain the tales of individual lives; fascinating and provoking but impossible to bring into political and sociological relief. For this they need to be considered against the broader canvass of their times.

Policy and sociological contexts

Conflicting policies? Raising standards, SEN/disability and inclusion

The last 30 years of the twentieth century saw enormous challenges to 'traditional' ways of understanding society. Postmodernism and feminism explored dominant, patriarchal constructions of the social order and challenged 'the way things were'. In education policy, too, these years saw considerable changes involving the gradual and continual erosion of professional teacher autonomy and the removal of Local Education Authority control of education through policies which, at the same time, centralised the control of education in the national government and decentralised budgets to schools. Parental choice and performance indicators such as league tables, seen as the way to raise educational standards, worked to create a quasi-market in education (Barton 1998) and from the mid-1970s onwards there was a marked shift from notions of social equity, as set out in the 1944 Education Act, to those of standards and excellence.

Alongside policies aimed at raising standards were placed those supporting the rights of children with SEN and policies which purported to promote educational inclusion for all children. Against the backcloth of league tables, parental choice and 'failing schools', policies promoting inclusion, particularly of children who present behavioural challenges to the school, are, it is argued, destined to fail (Barton 1998, Gewirtz *et al.* 1995). Many teachers feel that the government is sending out 'mixed messages' with policies of inclusion within the general context of an education market, which, they argue, creates tensions in many schools (Birkett 2000).

There is competition for funding both between schools and within individual schools, and provision for SEN can often depend on the level of parental advocacy: the more vocal the parent, the more resources the child may receive. Such competition and inequity of provision places great pressure on SEN professionals who, as well as having to work within the general education market, 'have to work within the internal market of the school to secure policy commitment and resources' (Bines 2000: 22). They have to ensure that they meet the needs of the children and their parents, for inclusion means more than 'integration' into mainstream classrooms of pupils defined as having special educational needs. It involves policies of entitlement, rights and the recognition and valuing of diversity (Barton 1998, Armstrong and Barton 1999).

Many argue that a relationship between the market ethos and inclusion is incompatible (e.g. Armstrong 1998, Barton 1998, Warnock 1996, Gewirtz *et al.* 1995) and that there will inevitably be winners and losers. It is suggested that the losers could well be children with SEN and/or disabilities (Slee 1996, Warnock 1996, Armstrong 1998). It is against the emerging tensions from this seemingly incompatible policy context that the stories are told. Within these tensions, teachers and parents have to try to negotiate a relationship between the private space of home and the public arena of the school. For children with SEN and disabilities, this is seen as especially important and is increasingly recognised in policy documents (e.g. DfES 2001).

Home–school relations/partnership

Relations between home and school have been brought into a more formal, public arena since 1981 through the introduction of policies designed to improve home–school relations especially in the area of special educational needs. In 1978 the Warnock Report (DES 1978: 151) stated:

> Parents can be effective partners only if professionals take notice of what they say and of how they express their needs, and treat their contribution as intrinsically important.

The need for partnership was also recognised in the Code of Practice (DfEE 1994: 12, section 2.28), which states:

> Children's progress will be diminished if their parents are not seen as equal partners in the educational process with unique knowledge and information to impart.

> Professional help can seldom be wholly effective unless it builds upon parents' capacity to be involved and unless professionals take account of what they say and treat their views and anxieties as intrinsically important.

The more recent SEN Code of Practice (DfES 2001: 12, section 2.2) offers an even stronger rationale for partnership with parents:

> Parents hold key information and have a critical role to play in their children's education. They have unique strengths, knowledge and experience to contribute to the shared view of the child's needs and the best ways of supporting them. It is therefore essential that all professionals (schools, LEAs and other agencies) actively seek to work with parents and value the contribution they make. The work of professionals can be more effective when parents are involved and account is taken of their wishes, feelings and perspectives on their children's development. This is particularly so when a child has special educational needs. All parents of children with special educational needs should be treated as partners.

The next section (2.3) adds:

These partnerships can be challenging, requiring positive attitudes by all, and in some circumstances additional support and encouragement for parents.

Since 1999, the Schools Standards and Framework Act (DfEE 1998c) has required all schools in England and Wales to have signed home–school agreements which are to be drawn up in consultation with parents. There are differences in meaning, however, between the terms relationship and partnership, but I consider Pugh *et al.*'s definition of the word partnership to be a useful way of conceptualising both:

A working relationship that is characterised by a shared sense of purpose, mutual respect and the willingness to negotiate. This implies a sharing of information, responsibility, skills and decision making and accountability.
(Pugh *et al.* 1987: 5)

While the government acknowledges that the 'best results are achieved where parents, schools and LEAs work in partnership' (DfEE 1998a: 12), such relationships are not easily achieved and depend on the collaboration of both parents and professionals and the weaving together of their worries, concerns, responsibilities and priorities (Dale 1996). A number of things may contribute to the tensions and possible conflict between parents and professionals: competition for resources; greater expectations of parents; increasing legal power of parents; difference between parental expectations and professional achievements; greater division and competition among professionals; parental stress and family conflict; lack of empathy and, perhaps most notably, poor communication skills and an unwillingness to share power on the part of the professionals (Dale 1996). Hood (1999) argues that the unequal balance of power between professionals and parents is certainly a factor here. Indeed, the National Association for Special Educational Needs (NASEN 2000) expressed concern over the draft of the 2001 Code of Practice, maintaining that it still did not reflect equality in the partnership.

The power of the professional lies in the possession of a 'specialised body of knowledge and skills' which has usually been achieved after a period of prolonged training and:

although frequent rhetoric has been made of the immense importance of parenting, minimum practical recognition has been given to the validity and usefulness of their expertise and experiences. The unpaid and unlimited hours of parenting contrast with the professional's role where there is remuneration for specific hours of employment.

(Dale 1996: 5)

Parents and professionals may have similar 'knowledge', but it is their positioning in the system that renders their perspectives and personae very different from each other. Despite the notion that parents and professionals may appear 'on the same side', i.e. that of the child, there are important differences. The parent wants what is 'right' for the child 'exclusively'; the professionals want 'what is right for him in a context' (Todd and Higgins 1998: 229). Professionals may regard parents as 'resources' in their children's education, expecting them to follow the goals of the professionals rather than act as partners with shared aims. Recent research supports the view that parents are more usually seen not as consumers or partners but rather as supporters or, even worse, as problems, and that despite the rhetoric, the home–school divide seems as wide as ever (Ouston and Hood 2000).

Armstrong (1995: 1) raises some interesting questions in relation to the role of professionals and partnership. He maintains that there is a 'contradiction in the professional-client relationship in special education assessments between benevolence and control which the concept of partnership does little to address'. From the outset, professionals 'define' the needs of others through their assessment of children with SEN, which contrasts with the 'humanitarian principles' often expressed by professionals when they theorise their own practice (ibid.). He argues that the relationship is further complicated by the vested interest of professionals in the outcomes of assessment procedures. While he is not suggesting that there is a 'conspiracy theory of professional activity' (ibid.: 147), he does maintain that professional interests, values, ethics and pressures may differ from those of other professionals and may even 'sit uneasily with an ethic of professional service governed solely by the interests of the children' (ibid.: 148). He draws on Fulcher's notion of 'entrenched professionalism' (1989: 165) by which the 'parents as partners model ... incorporates parents into the bureaucratic procedures' to illustrate how such partnerships remove the 'genuine' power of parents, allowing them merely to 'facilitate the smooth operation' of the procedures (Armstrong 1995: 144).

This is an extremely complex area where it is evident that power relations cannot easily be explained by a simple dichotomy of powerful professionals and powerless parents (Armstrong 1995, Todd and Higgins 1998). Parents are often presented as a unified group who support the aims and ethos of the school without question (Vincent 1996); but this does not appear to be the case (Hanafin and Lynch 2002). There are differences ascribed to social class, which appears to emerge as an issue in two ways: from a cultural deficit model in relation to working-class parents perceived as 'on the periphery'; and also in relation to perceptions of parental involvement as an important influence on children's learning (Hanafin and Lynch 2002: 34–5).

The discourse of home–school relations is another important factor. The separation of 'home' and 'school' puts mothers in the external environment in relation to the school and its management and therefore on the other side of the boundary from the teachers. School can be seen as representative of the divide between public and private, between professional knowledge and personal experience. For their part, mothers soon begin to perceive schools as the 'public settings' in their children's lives (Ribbens McCarthy 2000). Ribbens McCarthy maintains that there is an important and unequal power divide here between the public and the private:

> *In order to understand what is going on between mothers and schools we have to recognise this boundary and the various associated and extensive differences in terms of the values and concerns that are relevant on each side. I would argue, however, that the values and concerns to be found on the public side of the boundary, are manifested in very powerful social practices including the dominance of the 'psy' public discourses and ideas about 'child development' that underpin the work of schools.*
>
> (ibid.: 11)

The use of the term 'parent' in the home–school literature disguises the very gendered nature of the responsibility for schooling. Such literature on home–school relations talks about 'parental' involvement despite the evidence that it is mothers who for the most part take on that responsibility (David 1993a, 1993b, 1998, Hanafin and Lynch 2002). This responsibility affects women's roles in other areas of their lives (David 2000b: 12), as the stories in this book suggest. David argues that the mother's responsibilities in relation to school are increasing, for schools now expect children to have acquired certain knowledge and skills before they come to school. Failure to acquire such knowledge reflects on mothers, especially if the mother is herself a teacher. In reality, parental choice means mother's choice (David *et al.* 1997), but mothers' voices are not heard as women because of this 'un-gendering' of the term 'parent'.

The sociological context

Discourses and constructions of 'others'

Powerful discourses appear to permeate through society, encouraging us to see things, often groups of 'other' people, in a particular way, making it difficult for us not to refer to them as if they were 'really' thus (Parker 1992). Discourses help to form our notions of how 'others' are, and what it should mean to be a part of a particular group, for example single mothers, black youths, gay men, disabled people, mothers of, or teachers of, children with SEN/disabilities.

Such discourses work to support the social status quo through what comes to be accepted practices or 'common understandings' (Gramsci 1971: 326). Within discourse lies an 'understanding' of how these different groups, or 'others', should play their part within the scheme of things (Fulcher 1999). Discourses are constructed through ways of talking about and conceptualising 'others'. Through academe, the media, government policy, social practices, linguistic rules and the language of the powerful, often patriarchal groups, these constructions come into play. Discourses are powerful, for they can shape our actions, thoughts and even our perception of ourselves as successes or failures.

Often discourses work through the concept of deviance (Giroux 1991), marking some groups out as 'different'. They 'homogenize' people within a group (Pratt 1985: 138), creating an 'ideal' or 'norm'. Hidden within these discourses are the privileged perspectives and interests of certain groups representing the 'articulate, professional voice' which assumes 'legitimacy' over others (Fine 1998: 136), for example professionals involved in the assessment of children with SEN/disabilities. Control of the dominant discourses in any area affects the distribution of resources and therefore the material success of one group over others. Within these powerful discourses, the voice of individual experience is frequently silenced within the generality of meaning that discourses create. Through the silencing of the language of experience, discourse objectifies individuals (Corker and French 1999) and removes their private voice, the voice of experience.

The lives of the mother-teachers are constructed by a number of dominant discourses, including those around motherhood, working mothers, SEN and disability, teachers, and teachers of children with special needs/disability. However, it is argued that the creation of a dominant discourse also allows for the development of 'counter' discourses, which can 'compete' within the public domain (Corker and French 1999: 8). Certainly hegemonic discourse is being challenged in a number of areas now, such as race, gender and sexuality. In the field of special educational needs and disability, the social construction model is a good example of the re-authoring of discourse (Moore *et al.* 1998, Corker and French 1999). How these women position themselves within dominant discourses and offer resistance to them emerges through their stories, along with the ways in which discourses can shift to retain control.

The mother-teachers are clearly actors in both the political and the social fields and the complexity of the issues, which form the background to the book, are mirrored in the lived complexities emerging from the stories. My aim is to offer the women's narratives in such a way as to retain some of the interaction, intersubjectivity and interrelatedness of lives; to create stories which suggest the messy, ongoing and unresolved nature of life as it is lived; a challenge to the discourses which appear to constrain their lives. A qualitative, personal experience, narrative approach seemed to be the most appropriate methodology.

The search for the stories

Identifying teachers of children with special educational needs, who were also mothers of children with special educational needs, was not an easy task at first. How to identify this select group without seeming to be asking personal and possibly sensitive questions needed to be carefully considered. Letters were sent to the head teachers of all the schools (mainstream primary, secondary and special) within five LEAs, explaining the research and enclosing a separate envelope for the SENCO (Special Educational Needs Co-ordinator), which contained a covering letter. It was then up to the mother-teachers to make contact with me and enclose their own contact details only if they chose to do so.

The final six stories for inclusion in the research were selected for the diversity of their experiences both personally and professionally. The stories were usually told over several sessions and all began with the same question: 'How and why did you become a teacher?'

A number of replies were also received from men who were fathers and teachers of children with SEN and/or disabilities and who wanted their stories to be included in the study. Regrettably their stories could not be told here, for the research was about *mother*-teachers and there are, arguably, 'major differences' between mothers and fathers in their involvement with their children's school life (David 2000b: 11):

> *Mothers ... assume the main responsibility for all aspects of child care, including education, whether they are lone mothers, working class mothers or middle class, employed or at home. They invest resources and time, just as official and normative discourses would have us believe.*
> (David 1998: 1)

As mothers, the women in this book inhabit the private sphere, the domestic domain where women and young children live their experiences. As teachers, they move into the public world; the professional world of expert knowledge. If, as is claimed (David 1993a, Sikes 1997, Ribbens McCarthy 2000), school is where these two worlds meet, then the stories told here span that boundary.

Introducing the mother-teachers

As mother-teachers of children with special educational needs and/or disabilities, the women included in this book share certain common life experiences, although, as the stories demonstrate, there is a wide range of diversity in their experiences. They span a generation of women. But their temporal, social and cultural location, along with their 'special' roles as both mothers and teachers, gives them a very particular positionality. The mother-teachers are all fully qualified teachers with a range of teaching experience, which includes mainstream primary, mainstream secondary, special schools, special residential schools and higher education. All the women are white and, although some of them describe their origins as working class, they would all now consider themselves middle class. They are all in long-standing, married relationships (none of them are single parents), although this only emerged through the subsequent interviews. It is my regret that none of the mothers represents any other ethnic or single-parent group. This reflects the fact that in the original search for participants it was felt that there were already two limiting variables; to introduce a third or fourth might have made the task too difficult. However, while I acknowledge this omission and the possibility that mother-teachers from different groups may have different perceptions, I hope they will relate to some of the experiences and perspectives described here.

All names are pseudonyms and some dates and place names have been changed to protect anonymity further.

Sonia teaches in the primary department of a residential special school and long-stay centre for pupils and adults with epilepsy. Her son Christopher has autism and profound and multiple learning difficulties and disabilities.

Deborah is a SENCO in a mainstream secondary school. She has two daughters, Sally (aged 15) and Lara (aged 13), both of whom have dyslexia.

Truda is a teacher educator from the USA who is trained as a 'special educator' for children with hearing impairment and language difficulties. She has an adopted son John (aged 10) who has learning difficulties and emotional and behavioural difficulties.

Kate is the youngest of the mother-teachers. She is a SENCO in a mainstream primary school and has a daughter Kirsty (aged 3) who has cystic fibrosis.

Joan works at a special school and has a senior management post with responsibility for inclusion. James, her son of almost 19, has a rare condition, Cornelia de Lange syndrome, which has left him with profound learning difficulties.

Julia teaches in a special secondary school for SLD (severe learning difficulties) pupils where she supports and promotes inclusive practices between mainstream and special schools whenever possible. She has a son, Martin (aged 17), who has Down's syndrome.

Structure of the book

The book seeks to encourage 'other' ways of conceptualising issues often presented within dominant discourses as dichotomies such as inclusion–exclusion, public–private, knowledge–experience. I hope that it will encourage professionals in education and related fields to reflect on their own thinking and practice; their role within the construction of power relations and the ways in which these are embedded within social structures to 'exclude' rather than 'include' children with SEN/disabilities and their families. The stories in this book are representations of experience, single accounts, moments in time. They are not presented as 'true' and defining statements, but as lenses for personal reflection set within particular contexts at particular times. I hope that they will in some way resonate with the reader's own experiences and that through them practitioners will consider issues such as:

- the dominant discourses around the exclusion–inclusion of certain groups and how these discourses shift to retain control within their own professional context;

- the power relations between parents and professionals and the ways in which professional processes and practice reproduce and maintain these;

- the small, everyday, seemingly unimportant interactions which can marginalise, make difficult and exclude the lives and meanings of others;

- the ways in which they as professionals can offer resistance to the dominant discourses drawing on the experiences of parents/ mothers to support the development of inclusive practices.

The first two chapters outline the political and sociological contexts. Chapter 1 offers the policy context in relation to the developing tensions between the two key policy initiatives of recent governments, i.e. raising standards and inclusion. It considers these tensions in relation to teachers in mainstream and special schools, particularly SENCOs in mainstream schools, who are often expected to balance the needs of children with SEN and policies aimed at promoting inclusion within the context of a competitive market ethos.

Chapter 2 considers the sociological context and examines the ways in which powerful discourses can create 'boundaries' which are difficult to challenge. The rhetoric of home–school relations and the 'contested terrain' of school are explored along with the role of mothers in the private, personal domain and that of teachers placed within the public, expert sphere. The chapter goes on to consider how discourses construct and maintain these boundaries and work to 'other' usually less powerful groups such as people with disabilities and children with SEN before examining how challenges to these powerful discourses are emerging through feminist research.

Chapter 3 offers my own personal and professional story from which the study began. The story moves from my own development as a teacher; through the births of my two children and early years of motherhood, to my personal and professional experiences of inclusion and exclusion as competing policies began to impact on schools. It outlines my family's struggles to have its voice heard by professionals as decisions were made about the future of our son. The chapter closes by signposting some of the issues which will be explored in other stories.

The following six chapters offer the stories of the mother-teachers. Chapter 4 tells Sonia's story and reflects discourses of difference and normality. It suggests that notions of inclusion and exclusion operate at many levels not just in relation to mainstream or special schools but also within special schools. The story challenges the medical model of disability and SEN which presents the birth of a child with profound and multiple disabilities as a tragedy for the whole family, particularly the mother.

Deborah's story is told in Chapter 5, in which she talks about her experiences as a mother and teacher in relation to children with dyslexia at a time and in a particular context when dyslexia was not always recognised as a learning difficulty. The inter- and intra-relationship between the personal and professional are highlighted in this story in which the mother uses her professional role to gain support for her daughters both within her family and in the public arena. Also illuminated here are some of the difficulties in relation to the delicate balance for teachers and schools between policies of inclusion and competition.

Chapter 6 offers Truda's account and tells the story of a woman who makes challenges to exclusion within a number of different contexts as a professional woman in two different patriarchal communities, and as a mother on behalf of her adopted son. Truda is a professor in an American university, where she trains teachers of children with hearing impairments. She and her husband adopt a boy of four with learning difficulties. John offers challenges to Truda both as a mother and as a professional. Coming from a very particular social context within 'gendered' America, her story also offers insights into the ways in which lived experience challenges and resists dominant discourses around women, mothers, special educational needs, inclusion and professional knowledge.

Chapter 7 tells the story of Kate, a SENCO in a mainstream primary school, a professional with particular professional knowledge. Her story illustrates the need for both professional 'understanding' as well as knowledge, and highlights how drawing on and acknowledging personal 'moral experience' can offer professionals a means of developing this understanding. It offers a particular lens through which to view what might otherwise become the certainty and 'orthodoxy' of professionals (Sikes 1997).

Chapter 8 follows Joan's story, giving insights into the struggles and resistance of mothers to dominant constructions of women as selfless, unpaid carers of dependent young adults. The notion of them and their children as independent beings who can lead separate lives does not appear in the discourses around mothers or disability, making it difficult for such women to work outside the home, or for their children to have any degree of independence or social interaction with others outside the family. The story highlights the difficulties of matching the needs of mother and child. For working mothers such as Joan, there remain barriers to working outside the home unless there is considerable family support, and her story corroborates other evidence which suggests that many families with children with SEN and/or disabilities may consequently be economically disadvantaged.

The last story is that of Julia in Chapter 9 and illustrates many of the potential issues faced by children with Down's syndrome, and their parents, particularly their mothers, when they try to access mainstream education. Julia's story highlights the dominance of the medical model of disability and learning difficulty and the construction of need through the discourses of 'experts' and professionals. The story makes visible the ways in which professionals take control and construct difference in both child and family. However, Julia's story also signals how small acts of inclusion can make a great deal of difference to children with SEN and their families.

The final chapter explores some of the emerging contexts, contra-dictions and complexities, and reflects on possible 'conclusions' in relation to the continual resistance by these mother-teachers to dominant professional and medical discourses which appear to construct, constrain and define them and their children. Emerging through the individual life stories is a sense of what inclusion means to these women and their children.

These mother-teachers are at the very intersection between many issues and tensions related to educational inclusion and exclusion, on many different levels. They are at the junction where policy meets practice; where public meets private; where home meets school. They are in a position to act as agents of change for their own children and the children they meet in their professional lives. They have agency in the sense that they can change their own practice and influence the practice of others. Their stories have much to offer other professionals by way of reflection and consideration. In what can be argued to be a less flexible professional culture within education today, these stories have an important contribution to make with regard to constructions of difference, inclusion and exclusion, resistance, power relations and, not least, the very real contribution parents can make. The processes of change are inevitably 'messy', as Charles Handy acknowledges when he writes about 'the importance of "the various stages of in between-ness"' (Handy 1995: 271), and we are certainly at such a stage in relation to educational inclusion at present. But Handy offers words of encouragement to those who strive to challenge the reproduction of processes, practices and power relations which may exclude certain groups. They are words I find encouraging:

Change comes from small initiatives which work, initiatives which, imitated, become the fashion. We cannot wait for great visions from great people, for they are in short supply at the end of history. It is up to us to light our own small fires in the darkness.

(ibid.)

1 Contradictions of principle: the policy context

How could she know that they had never been able to prove that one thing is better than another?

(Høeg 1996: 80)

This chapter considers the policy background against which the stories are set. It outlines the historical changes in education policy since 1944 and the development of policies of special educational needs since the Warnock Report (DES 1978). The two key education policy initiatives of the last two decades of the twentieth century are examined, namely raising standards and inclusion. The 'contradictions of principle' emerging from the interaction of these two policies and the resulting tensions for many parents and professionals involved in the education of children with SEN/disabilities are considered, for they contribute to the personal and professional contexts in which the mother-teachers live and work.

Introduction

Having a child with perceived learning difficulties/disabilities can bring about profound changes in a mother's private life. If the mother is also a teacher of children with special educational needs there can be significant changes in her professional life as well. Few would deny that such an event affects one's philosophy of life in some way, or that it changes the lens through which the mother and ultimately the teacher experiences the world. The impact of our private experiences on our professional lives is something which is increasingly being explored through feminist methodology (David 2003). The experiences of the mother-teachers need to be contextualised against the policy, which, in part, informs them. Changes in the welfare state are a part of the context within which national education policy is made. In Britain, national education policy is an important part of social policy, and education and family matters are at the forefront of the government's policy priorities (David 1993a) as we begin the twenty-first century.

Education reforms affect not only children but also their families, and in particular their mothers (ibid.).

The 'reforms' in education focusing on raising standards, parental rights and the reconstruction of the teacher's professional role have been underpinned by a competitive market ideology. Schools are judged on the published results of their children in tests measured against national norms, with implications for recruitment and funding. The introduction of a National Curriculum and a government inspection service, Ofsted (Office for Standards in Eduction), with a remit to 'name and shame' schools perceived as failing, has ensured greater government control over education, despite the introduction of more decentralised local management of schools (LMS). Within the official rhetoric, the development of home–school relationships has been signalled as a way to ensure a more equal partnership between parents and professionals.

However, as I suggested in the introductory chapter, the restructuring of education since 1986 by both Conservative and Labour governments along market lines has produced a 'potentially hostile context for the development of policies of inclusion' (Fulcher 1999: 151). The creation of a 'quasi education market' (Le Grand and Bartlett 1993, Gewirtz *et al.* 1995, Barton 1998), 'generally equated with measurable outcomes' (Gilbourne and Youdell 2000: 20), and the development of inclusive education policies (Bines 2000) have also created tensions for many teachers and parents in the field of SEN. These two policy strands will now be considered in more detail.

'Standards, Standards, Standards'

Historical overview

The 1944 Education Act
While the 1944 Education Act allowed for parental 'choice' across a range of options (state or private), there was a clear aim to uphold the principle of equality of educational opportunity and to promote a system based on merit rather than on the parent's socio-economic circumstances (David 1993a). The 1944 Education Act created a 'partnership' in education between 'the centre, the locality and

institutions', with no single partner having a monopoly of power in the decision-making (Ranson and Tomlinson 1986: 3). The Act extended the spirit of partnership to parents who were required by law to ensure that their child received:

efficient full-time education suitable to … [the] age ability and aptitude, either by regular attendance at school or otherwise.

(Part 11: 36)

It gave nominal acceptance of the power of parental choice (Part 1V, 76). Teachers were seen as an important part of the partnership, and control of the curriculum was left to them with only minimum restrictions concerning religious education. This 'Golden Age of teacher control of the curriculum' (Lawton 1980: 22) did not give teachers complete freedom, for they had to work within the demands of wider influences such as public examinations and the different types of education (grammar, etc.) (Helsby and McCulloch 1996). Tensions did exist, however, concerning the balance of power between local and central government which were to have long-term effects on the education system (Ranson and Tomlinson 1986).

The breakdown of the 1944 settlement

By the 1960s and early 1970s the partnership envisaged by the 1944 Act was breaking down. Changes in economic and social conditions in the 1960s placed increasing demands on the education system while funding declined due to a worsening world economic situation. The education system had largely developed at local and regional levels (the case of comprehensivisation Circular 10/65 was a case in point, where there was little coherent national development). There seemed to be no national response to the claims being made from all sides, that education was no longer meeting the needs of the country or the individual. The lack of a national and relevant curriculum to meet the increasing demands of the technological revolution appeared to support the argument that 'the professionally dominated education service anxious to preserve standards and keep philistines at bay' was seen as a 'dead hand on national development' (Dale 1989: 102).

During the 1950s the campaign for civil rights had grown in the United States and, although fought initially over race, it had raised issues related to the exclusion of groups of children from certain educational opportunities. By the mid-1960s an investigation into equal educational opportunities was taking place (David 1993a). In Britain, the Plowden Report (DES 1967) recommended more parental involvement and positive discrimination in funding and resources for deprived areas. The development of 'educational priority areas' (EPAs) meant that a range of local strategies was introduced, aimed at involving parents in home–school schemes. Indeed, 'making schooling more effective through the relationships with families became a major public policy issue of the 1970s' (David 1993a: 50). Parents were not represented in the decision-making processes although it was argued that this was the way to make education more effective (ibid.).

However, the recommendations of the Plowden Report, which appeared to be advocating a more progressive style of education in primary schools in England and Wales, were coming under increasing criticism. By the mid-1970s there were calls for the Department of Education and Science (DES) to take greater control over education and 'irresponsible' and 'unaccountable' teachers. Critics argued that a more national and centralised system was needed if the economy was to develop and technological change to take place. The Black Papers (See Cox and Boyson 1975, 1977) began the pressure to increase 'standards' and allow parents more choice in their children's schooling. In 1974 the Bullock Committee on Reading and the Use of English continued this attack and the Assessment of Performance Unit (APU) was set up (1974), under the auspices of the DES, to monitor pupil performance in certain areas of the curriculum. Teachers were increasingly being seen as a part of the problem, a view which was made explicit in October 1976 by the famous speech, at Ruskin College Oxford, of the then Prime Minister, James Callaghan. The Green Paper, Education in Schools (1976), made a direct attack on the professional right and indeed suitability of teachers to control the 'secret garden' of the curriculum. By 1979 there was little in British educational policy which promoted social equality, despite the emergence of the Commission for Racial Equality (CRE) (1976) and the Equal Opportunities Commission (1975) (David 1993a), or the publication of the Warnock Commission's Report (DES 1978), which related to special educational needs.

The battle over autonomy in the classroom became enmeshed with the battle between the national government and the local authorities over spending, and as education came within the remit of the Local

Education Authority (LEA), cuts in funding were inevitable. After 1979, the Conservative government of Margaret Thatcher became increasingly at odds with local authorities. Central government felt it timely to combine attacks on the control of education with attacks on the inefficiency of the service and ineptitude of the teachers. Falling standards were held to be partly responsible for Britain's economic decline and calls for accountability and responsibility in education were whipped up by the media. Dale (1989) notes that, by 1984, LEAs and teachers were 'in a state of shock'; the LEAs were being 'squeezed' and teachers were constructed as 'problems'. The dominant discourse held that there was something wrong with schools and the teachers in them.

Parents, on the other hand, were evolving as natural experts and moral guardians (Dale 1989), although it is interesting to note that in the home–school relationship discourse it is the parents who, by the 1990s, are perceived as the problem. This 'ideology of parentocracy' (Brown 1990: 66), where the 'child's education is increasingly dependent upon the wealth and wishes of parents rather than the ability and efforts of pupils' (ibid.), marked a shift from social equity to standards and excellence determined through parental choice. During the 1970s educational priorities were directed away from equal opportunities for children from 'disadvantaged' backgrounds to the training of manpower for new technologies (Silver 1990).

Education 'reform' and parents 1979–88
The 1979 Education Act reversed earlier legislation which had required LEAs to reorganise their schools along comprehensive lines, although few authorities did revert to selective education (David 1993a). The Education Act of 1980 aimed to make schools more accountable to parents and the public. It required LEAs and schools to publish a prospectus and annual report making known examination results and HMI (Her Majesty's Inspectorate) reports. Parents were allowed to state their preference in choice of school, although this did not guarantee a place for their child; to complain about procedures; and to have representation on school governing bodies. Falling numbers of pupils were creating organisational problems for schools which, it was argued, could be solved by open enrolment. This would allow popular and successful schools to expand.

The 1981 Education Act implemented many of the recommendations of the Warnock Report (DES 1978) in relation to children with special educational needs. It required all LEAs to follow a formal, staged assessment procedure to identify and assess special educational needs and to issue a Statement of Special Educational Need for schools and parents. There was also a limited commitment to integrate children with SEN into mainstream schools.

However, the major changes were to appear in the two Acts of 1986 and 1988. The 1986 Education Act and the 1988 Education Reform Act (ERA) together marked the beginning of a period of turbulence and change in English and Welsh education policy, designating the move from equality to quality and making a 'radical break with the past':

> With the passing of the 1988 Education Reform Act, no longer do a concern for equality of opportunity and the ideals of a fully comprehensive system of state education figure highly in national educational programmes and initiatives. Instead, the emphasis has come to be placed on parental choice and competition, the management of resources, people and institutions in an increasingly cost-conscious environment, and the extension of a new battery of central controls that establish a strong regulatory framework for state education.
>
> (Flude and Hammer 1990: vii)

The rationale for the changes lay in the belief that the 'market led assumption of demand and supply relationships' would necessarily lead to the improvement of school-based education and result in the closure of schools which did not meet consumer demand (Gilbourne and Youdell 2000: 18).

The 1986 Education Act gave parents a more significant role to play on governing bodies, providing them with the majority vote and requiring an annual parents' meeting to discuss school business. But it was the 1988 Education Reform Act which 'was unique in the history of British educational legislation in many senses' (David 1993a: 64). It affected schools and higher education, increased parental choice and 'allowed educational institutions to be removed from state financial control with impunity' (ibid.). As a means of increasing the choice of schools, the 1988 ERA introduced different ways of funding educational institutions independent of the LEAs. City Technology Colleges (CTCs) and grant-maintained schools offered a challenge to comprehensive schools. The stated aim, according to the right-wing pressure group, the Hillgate Group (1987: 1–2), was to make an 'independent education' available to all through parental choice. It is interesting to note that, despite a decade of Labour government, the debate about selection by ability on entry has not yet gone away completely (Gilbourne and Youdell 2000). The legislation also introduced open enrolment and LMS, which involved the devolution of the majority of school funding from the LEA to the school. Funding was worked out on a formula based on the number of pupils on the school roll, the more pupils the bigger the budget. But even so, many schools have shown no wish to increase their numbers by taking in pupils whose education might place

> unusual or 'excessive' demands on school budgets – such as those with special learning needs, minority pupils for whom English is an additional language, and homeless pupils whose parent(s)/carer(s) have no stable shelter.

> (ibid.: 19)

The effect of the two Acts (1986 and 1988) changed the nature of the role of parents, creating them as 'consumers' of education and emphasising not collective welfare but private interests and rights (Munn 1993). Hardly surprisingly, surveys of parental opinions suggest that many parents welcomed the increased powers given to the Secretary of State for Education by clause 4 of the 1988 Education Reform Act (Batho 1989). But, as Gilbourne and Youdell (2000) note, the notion of parental 'choice' of school, while supported by both of the major political parties, in reality means a right to state 'preference' for a particular school with no guarantee of a place. In 1991 a Parent's Charter (later to form the basis for the 1992 Education (Schools) Act) was introduced by John Major's government, making mandatory parents' rights of access to their children's schools and progress. Parents were also given increased powers over budgetary control and inspection. By the early 1990s the shift from equity to parental rights began to include parental responsibilities for ensuring their child's success in examinations (David 1993a). 'Raising standards' became the rallying cry for politicians.

The National Curriculum and the 'deprofessionalisation' of teachers

The introduction of a National Curriculum, introduced in the first clauses of the ERA 1988, set out the curriculum for all pupils from the ages of 5 to 16 in state schools. To support the National Curriculum and the struggle for 'standards', the ERA laid out plans for the testing of pupils at the ages of 7, 11 and 14 in the form of Standard Attainment Tests (SATs) and at 16 through the General Certificate of Secondary Education (GCSE). Many teachers argued that this seriously undermined their professionalism. Helsby and McCulloch (1996: 59) commented that:

> The State had moved in on the classroom, hitherto regarded as the province of the teacher, with the effect of downgrading the teacher's role to that of merely implementing decisions reached elsewhere.

The 1988 Education Act set out a direction for the content of the curriculum for schools to follow but it did not attempt to tell teachers how it should be taught. The Act explicitly excluded the allocation of time to be spent on different subjects. Kenneth Baker stated, in a speech to the House of Commons in December 1987, that neither then nor in subsequent legislation did the government intend to lay down the specific amount of time to be spent on each subject, although he felt it would take at least 70 per cent of the available time to deliver the National Curriculum (Davies *et al.* 1998). Although initial plans for the National Curriculum have been modified there is still a high degree of control over the curriculum especially in secondary schools. The National Curriculum has been criticised for its somewhat narrow content and colonial perspective based on a 'traditional' and academic approach (David 1993a) and a 'general failure to engage with issues of cultural diversity and social inequality' (Gilbourne and Youdell 2000: 20).

The amount of prescription appears to be increasing, for the literacy strategy (DfEE 1998d) and numeracy strategy (DfEE 1998e) do prescribe the amount of time. The pedagogy of the two strategies is said to be based on research from within the school effectiveness literature, which pointed to the concept of the effectiveness of teachers as instructors rather than as organisers and facilitators. A policy of 'zero tolerance' of failure and school effectiveness research encouraged the idea that schools should not be allowed to fail; they needed to have 'high reliability' (Davies *et al.* 1998: 6). The publication of the results of national tests in league tables forms part of the policy discourse of 'accountability' but for many teachers this translates as 'surveillance and control' (Gilbourne and Youdell 2000: 21).

The 1988 Act brought to an end the relative freedom which teachers had experienced since the early post-war years (Helsby and McCulloch 1996). The 1990s saw the replacement of this freedom with control by central government in both the 'what' and the 'how' of teaching (Ranson and Tomlinson 1986). There is evidence that many teachers did not support the changes (Helsby and Saunders 1993), feeling that much of their flexibility to make and act upon professional judgement had been removed. There was also a suggestion that the role of the teacher was being reduced to that of technician, delivering standardised programmes divided into 'units', and 'inspected by outside efficiency experts and finally judged by consumers' (Helsby and McCulloch 1996: 65) rather than by teachers.

It is argued that, for many teachers, the combination of imposed change, lack of support and planning time has resulted in the loss of a considerable amount of professional confidence (Helsby 1999). It is not just policy content that has affected teachers but:

> the sheer cumulative impact of multiple, complex non-negotiable innovations on teachers' time, energy motivation, opportunities to reflect and their very capacity to cope.
>
> (Hargreaves 1994: 6)

The need for a balance between an 'increased trust in teachers ... matched by accountability to parents and society' has been noted by Dearing (1994: 25), who called for increased scope for teachers to use their professional judgement. Even the former Chief Inspector of Schools in England and Wales has been forced to admit that it is 'only teachers in classrooms who can really make the difference' (Chris Woodhead, quoted in Helsby 1999: 28).

Parental choice, league tables and SEN

The accountability of teachers is still largely measured by the percentage of pupils gaining five or more GCSEs grades A to C, despite the addition of various 'value-added' indicators by the government.

This 'crude and misleading data' is the basis for the 'hierarchical ranking of individual schools and LEAs nation-wide' (Gilbourne and Youdell 2000: 22). Although the results tables do reflect some degree of 'value-added' achievement, they still make little allowance for social and cultural differences in schools and their environments, with the result that 'the long-established association between socio-economic status and educational attainment is free to distort the figures without control' (ibid.). This contributes to the fostering of what Corbett (1998: 2) refers to as a 'cruel hierarchy in the state sector' in which many working-class parents have no choice but to send their children to the local schools. In these areas the exercise of parental 'choice' merely confirms existing class and ethnic divisions (Gilbourne and Youdell 2000). It increases the possibility of the development of 'sink' schools (Gewirtz *et al.* 1995), which results in:

> The least marketable schools ... finding themselves with higher proportions of children labelled as 'SEN'. These schools often struggle to cope with a disproportionate number of children who require additional help with literacy and numeracy, and are themselves labelled as 'failing schools' by the current inspection regime.
>
> (Corbett 1998: 2)

The league tables do not allow for those children for whom success cannot be measured in examination results and who find it difficult to relate to a curriculum which is often culturally exclusive. Children who experience learning difficulties, for whatever reason, may not be considered of value to schools who have to publish their examination results, as the league tables do not offer any indication of the range of learning difficulties within a school. Birkett (2000: 3) argues that league tables only paint half the picture:

> They should put results into context a bit more. When you present league tables or other performance indicators, you can say there are 31 Statemented children, but you can't say the nature of their difficulties. A bright child with physical disability is not the same as a child with severe learning difficulties. The simple numbers don't explain the impact.

The identification of a 'failing school' results from inspections and from the failure of schools to perform to a required standard at certain stages. David Blunkett, then the Secretary of State for Education, called for 'absolute standards' to be met in skills such as numeracy and literacy (DfEE 1997c). These standards must be reached regardless of the social background of the pupil (Davies *et al.* 1998: 4).

While national targets appear to recognise Warnock's '20 per cent' (children who have SEN), this percentage may be much higher in many schools but may not always be in evidence due to the nature of the special educational need. This can result in great stress and tension for those teachers working with children with SEN, in schools perceived as 'failing'. 'Such is the very harsh climate in which Special Educational Needs Coordinators (SENCOs) must operate' (ibid.: 4):

> There is already anecdotal evidence of schools rejecting pupils who they think may adversely affect their KS1 and 2 assessment averages, because they have either learning difficulties or behavioural difficulties. SENCOs are likely to be placed in a position of being the advocate for such children, putting themselves in professional – and possibly personal conflict with their colleagues.

(ibid.: 5)

The ERA, special educational needs and inclusion

The 1988 Education Reform Act claimed that it would:

> raise the expectations of all pupils, including those with statements. Built into the Act are provisions to ensure that these expectations are appropriate so that all children, including those with special educational needs, can benefit to the best of their ability.

(DES 1988)

But the changes brought about by the Education Acts of 1986 and 1988 have considerably affected the cultural climate within which SEN reform and policies of inclusion take place. Sheila Brown, a former Chief Inspector (quoted in Russell 1990: 208), voiced the concerns of many when she claimed that the development of a balanced curriculum to promote the broad development of all pupils 'is light years away' from the attainment targets and assessment procedures mentioned above. For teachers and children this undoubtedly causes stresses and strains as they try to achieve imposed targets and meet prescribed assessment procedures.

SEN and inclusion

In this context 'inclusion' refers to the education of all children, particularly those with SEN, in mainstream classes and requires schools to consider their systems, structures, teaching approaches and use of support in order to respond to the needs of all children.

Recent notions of segregated provision emanate from the 1944 Education Act, which while offering on one level an opportunity for social inclusion that would have otherwise been denied, did so through structures which excluded many children from mainstream education (Armstrong 1998). Originally developed through the Church and various charities, the concept of special education has grown through this separate and segregated provision. Before examining recent policy developments towards inclusion, it is important to understand the context within which the concept of special educational need has arisen.

SEN: a historical overview

Chapter 2 of the Warnock Report (DES 1978) outlines the historical development of special education in this country and illustrates how it grew as a separate part of the education system in the not too far distant past. I find the following passage worth quoting at length, for it neatly summarises the nature of this development.

> The very first schools for the blind and deaf were founded in the life time of Mozart; those for the physically handicapped awaited the great Exhibition; day schools for the mentally handicapped and epileptic arrived with the motor car; while special provision for the delicate, maladjusted and speech impaired children is younger than living memory. Even so the early institutions were nothing like the schools we know today and they were available only to the few. As with ordinary education, education for the handicapped began with individual and charitable enterprise. There followed in time the intervention of government, first to support voluntary effort and make good deficiencies through state provision and finally to create a national framework in which public and voluntary agencies could act in partnership to see that all children, whatever their disability received a suitable education. The framework reached its present form only in this decade.
>
> (ibid.: 8)

The 1944 Education Act placed the responsibility for 'handicapped' children on the LEAs and set out how they were to be provided for 'in special schools or otherwise' and by 1955 there were approximately 52,000 'handicapped' children being educated in 623 special schools in

England and Wales. The Handicapped Pupils and Special School Regulations, 1959, listed ten categories of pupils needing to attend special schools. By 1977 the number of children had risen to 135,261 in 1,653 special schools with some 21,674 children in 'special' classes in mainstream schools. Another 500,000 children with learning difficulties were being educated in mainstream classes, but with little help. By 1979, 19 categories of school existed for 'handicapped' children (Rogers 1984). The Education Act of 1970 ensured that all children, however severe the handicap, would come within the framework of the LEA's education department. In September 1974 the first Committee of Enquiry to be set up in Britain began its review of the educational provision for all children with disabilities and special educational needs and in 1978 the Warnock Commission presented its report.

Although Armstrong (1998) suggests that there were tensions and contradictions developing in special education even before the 1944 Education Act, it is true to say that until the last 20 years of the twentieth century, special education was largely neglected and marginalised at national policy level (Bines 2000). The publication of the Warnock Report (DES 1978) brought SEN into the 'mainstream' of British education policy.

The Warnock Report (1978)

The Warnock Report was commissioned by Margaret Thatcher (as Secretary of State for Education) in 1974. The Committee, chaired by Mary Warnock, was to review the provision for children with disabilities in response to growing criticism of the 1944 Education Act. In 1978, the Committee issued their findings on the educational provision for children with special educational needs (DES 1978), the terms of which were to form the basis of the 1981 Education Act. Since then, successive governments have gradually increased the number of policy initiatives which support the inclusion of all children into mainstream educational institutions at all levels.

It was not until the 1970 Education Act removed the notion that some children were 'ineducable', that responsibility for these children was transferred from the Department of Health to the Department of Education. This marked a move away from segregated provision for children with special needs even before the Warnock Report (Fulcher

1999). However, there can be little doubt that the Warnock Commission's Report was in some ways a watershed in the history of the education of children with special educational needs. The term 'special educational needs' was first used in the Report, which recognised a continuum of need. This was later incorporated into the 1981 Education Act, the 1993 Education Act, the Code of Practice (DfEE 1994), and the Code of Practice (DfES 2001).

The Warnock Report maintained that all children were 'educable' and should have the right to education. Education was seen as a journey on which all children should set out. Some children would need considerable support and might not get as far along the road as others but that should not prevent them from embarking on the journey. The Report stated that up to 18 per cent of children would have special educational needs at some time during their school life. A further 2 per cent of children would have more serious and long-term special educational needs and would need support for most, if not all, of their school life. Such support might come from segregated special provision.

Disability and special educational need have long been thought to be the concern of the individual, a matter of personal tragedy, a deficit 'within', which could only be addressed by medical attempts at 'normalisation'. The medical model places responsibility, and often blame, firmly on individuals or their families. In 1982, Tomlinson published an alternative theoretical perspective of special educational needs and disability, which sought to explore the role of external factors in the construction of SEN (Tomlinson 1982). This is explored in more detail in Chapter 3.

The Warnock Report did not directly challenge the medical discourse on disability (Fulcher 1999), but it did offer a framework from which future policies might be developed. While not claiming to espouse complete inclusion, it offered support for the notion of inclusion by encouraging the idea that, wherever possible, children should be educated along with their peers. However, its significance lies in the fact that it recognised the concept of 'educational' need, the notion that many children experience difficulties with learning at some point in their school life. The Warnock Committee recommended the abolition of the old categories of disability and replaced them with a more generic concept of SEN that laid emphasis on educational criteria, although it was still based on the idea that the fault or deficit lay with the child rather than the system. All aspects of a child's educational needs were to be taken into account but there was to be no labelling of children according to their disabilities. The Warnock Report also recommended that parents be considered as full partners with the range of professionals involved in the assessment process. This has recently been reaffirmed and strengthened in the SEN Code of Practice (DfES 2001).

Although Mary Warnock (1996) later denied that the Report was recommending inclusion *per se*, the structures set up through the 1981 Education Act encouraged many parents to seek financial support through the system of Statementing for their children to be educated in mainstream schools and classrooms. The 1981 Education Act, which implemented many of the recommendations of the Warnock Report, left the financial responsibility for special educational needs with LEAs. The five-stage process of gaining a Statement of Special Educational Need involved parents, teachers and support agencies as well as educational psychologists, who were often regarded by LEAs and teachers as the 'gatekeepers' of scarce resources. The Statement was a declaration of the educational needs of the child, which once specified must be met by the LEA and the school and financed accordingly. For both pupils and schools, the Statement was a way of assuring funding, the idea being that pupils took their Statements with them if they moved around the country, thus ensuring continuity of provision.

Parents who felt that their child had been wrongly assessed by the process could appeal to a Special Educational Needs Tribunal, which could decide not only the level of support but also the nature of the schooling, i.e. mainstream or special school. However, the staged provision of SEN and the linking of resources to the acquisition of a Statement led to an increase in the number of Statements and a corresponding increased demand on SEN budgets in most LEAs. In reality this did little to improve the interaction or the relationship between mainstream and special provision (Bines 2000), for LEAs were very reluctant to put funding into mainstream schools when they were already funding places in special schools. It was envisaged that policies of inclusion would be set against a reduction in the number of special schools (Baker 1988). Many special schools have felt threatened by moves towards the inclusion of children with special educational needs and/or disabilities into mainstream schools, and some have already closed (Croll and Moses 2000), restricting parental choice in some areas. But fear of scarce resources and the workings of the education market have meant that many parents still want what they perceive as the 'sanctuary' of special schools for their children (Russell 1990). In reality there has been no significant reduction in the number of special schools, although there are regional differences with some authorities, such as the London Borough of Newham, closing all special schools within the borough. Correspondingly, there has been no significant demand for places in mainstream schools (Croll and Moses 2000).

Research indicates that inclusion has become the norm in primary schools (ibid.). However, in their study, Croll and Moses spoke to teachers in 48 schools who 'virtually unanimously' supported a continuation of the role of special schools, particularly for children perceived as having emotional and behavioural difficulties. A significant number of these teachers felt that more children should be in segregated provision. Changes in recent legislation make clear the policy support for children with SEN and disabilities in mainstream schools (e.g. the Special Educational Needs and Disability Act 2001, which 'prohibits all schools from discriminating against disabled children in their admissions arrangements'). But there are serious concerns among many teachers about their own ability to deal adequately with inclusion (Croll and Moses 2000, Birkett 2000, Clough 1998b) especially within the present competitive market ethos. As I noted in the opening chapter, the concept of SEN may in some ways work against the inclusion of children who may experience learning difficulties for the very reason that their needs are seen as above the 'norm', requiring 'specialist' teaching and support (Corbett 1996).

Criticism of the Warnock Report

A number of criticisms have been levelled against the Warnock Report. It implied that the answer to the 'core' question, 'why do children fail in school?' was because they were disabled or had special educational needs (Fulcher 1999: 155). There was no consideration of the causes of 'special' educational needs and how and why these might arise. While recognising that SEN was relative, the Report failed to challenge the 'political logic of disability for twenty percent of the school population' and did not question existing school practices and pedagogy (ibid.: 156).

Mary Warnock (1996) herself has many criticisms of the Committee's Report. The aim of the Committee was to ensure that funding would be protected for the education of children, 'whose education will inevitably be expensive, of infinite value to them, but of little or no value to the national economy' (ibid.: 59). Yet the Conservative government set aside no extra resources for the implementation of the 1981 Education Act. Warnock condemned the Committee's 'absurd naiveté' for being so short-sighted in failing to see the way general education policy was developing. Eighteen years later, she reflected on the Report (ibid.: 60) and the 'contradictions of principle' between the Committee's recommendations and the Conservative government's policies supporting competition and choice. She describes the 1988 Education Act as emanating from a 'different world', likening her Committee's Report to a 'fish out of water':

> *Competition between schools and value for money are the key concepts and the whole vocabulary of education has suddenly been borrowed from that of manufacturing industry. No one within the management of a school will be willing to allow money to be spent on anything but that which will enhance the market-value of the school.*

> (ibid.: 59)

Warnock reserves her main criticism of her Committee's report for the 'real evil' of Statementing. She argues that not only could LEAs avoid specifying need but, by the issuing of Statements, other children were deprived of resources. As resources became less plentiful so parents became more concerned about ensuring that their own children received adequate support through the due processes of law (Wedell *et al.* 2000). By the mid-1980s the process of Statementing was taking over 12 months in some areas, reflecting the diversity of provision between LEAs as a result of the ambiguity in Circular 8/81 (DES 1981), which allowed LEAs to adopt their own interpretation of the procedures for Statementing (Fulcher 1999). The diversity of provision added to the developing tension and struggle at the local level, with some LEAs giving inadequate information to parents while some withheld relevant information (ibid.).

Education professionals criticised the bureaucracy attached to these practices, regarding them as time-consuming and too formal (ibid.). For many professionals involved in the process, such as the educational psychologists, this was a time of great stress and many found themselves under considerable pressure from LEAs. But the number of Statements rose steadily up to the end of the last century; the proportion of pupils with Statements rose between 1997 and 1999 from 1.4% to 1.6% in primary schools and from 2.3% to 2.5% in secondary schools (Bowers 2000: 203).

With the Special Educational Needs and Disability Discrimination Act (2001) and the SEN Code of Practice (2001), a number of changes have taken place with a view to reducing the number of Statements. There is now an expectation that:

> *The special educational needs of the great majority of children should be met effectively within mainstream settings through Early Years and Early Years Action Plus or School Action and School Action Plus without the local education authority needing to make a statutory assessment.*
>
> (DfES 2001: 74)

It is envisaged that only 'a very small number of cases' will require statutory assessment. However, funding for SEN remains a somewhat contentious issue. There was some opposition from parents at the earlier suggestion that Statements could be removed completely. They feared that this would mean less funding being safeguarded for SEN in schools. The delegation of budgets to schools (LMS) brought with it some extra funding for schools although it reduced the funding available for delegation by the LEA (Lunt and Evans 1991, Bines 2000). It also means that SEN is competing for funding with many other areas of the curriculum within schools. Vocal, parental advocacy can have a profound effect on the allocation of scarce resources (ibid.).

But as I argued in the opening chapter, competition and inequity of provision add considerably to the pressure on professionals working with children with SEN. They have to work not only within the general education market but they also have to negotiate the 'internal market' of the school if they are to secure support and funding (ibid.). It remains to be seen how the latest policy document from the Department for Education and Skills (DfES 2004) will impact on the priorities of schools and the allocation of resources. The document acknowledges research carried out by the Department for Education and Employment (DfEE) and the National Association for Special Educational Needs (NASEN) in 2000, which suggests that increased delegation of SEN funding has 'eroded the availability of support in some areas and that learning and behavioural support were most affected'. But it continues in a somewhat ambiguous way: 'We want to see further delegation but not at the cost of SEN support services, which play a key role in supporting the development of inclusive practice' (DfES 2004: 48). We await the outcome with interest.

In 1981 the use of the term 'special educational needs' was a move towards the recognition that many children experienced learning difficulties. Today, terms such as SEN and indeed the whole notion of 'special' needs may be considered a barrier to inclusion (Barton 1999, Corbett 1996). The categorising of children as having 'special' needs still relies on the deficit, medical model of assessment and the notion of 'treating' the difficulties 'within' the child, rather than addressing profound changes in the systems and structures of the environment. Against the background of the continuance of this medical model of disability and special educational needs, the move towards a more inclusive education system is heralded as the second key principle in the present government's stated policy agenda.

Educational inclusion: developing tensions and conflicts

Inclusion is most usefully regarded as a process rather than an event (Booth *et al.* 2000) and raises challenges concerning the nature and management of change for both schools and teachers in relation to school improvement and effectiveness (Sebba and Ainscow 1996). But there are concerns as to whether present strategies for improving school effectiveness are supportive of inclusion (Slee *et al.* 1998). It is suggested that, despite the Labour government's policy commitment to SEN, inclusion and social inclusion, there still appears to be a very considerable gap between the rhetoric and the reality (Tomlinson 2001).

A series of policy documents (e.g. DfEE 1997c, 1998a, TSO 2003, DfES 2004) recommend strategies aimed at supporting inclusion through home–school partnerships, early intervention, staff training and development, revision of the Code of Practice (see DfES 2001), changes in the nature of LEA support, as well as research support for 'best practice'. Within these changes the redefining of the role of SEN professionals, especially SENCOs (Special Educational Needs Co-ordinators), is an important feature. Staff development at all levels from newly qualified teachers to SENCOs is claimed to be an important aspect of increasing a school's ability to accept a wider range of pupils.

The Programme of Action (DfEE 1998a) states: 'We recognise the case for more inclusion where parents want it', but it adds ominously, 'and appropriate support can be given'. Resources have to be secured and in the present educational climate there are no guarantees that these will go towards implementing policies of inclusion. As Bines (2000) notes, there are aspects for concern in these new policy initiatives, which stem from the policy legacy, namely the continued use of parental choice, greater diversity of schools with particular specialisms, and the continued use of the 'business ethic' and 'managerialism' in the management of 'failing' schools. The introduction of the literacy and numeracy strategies suggests that 'prescriptive control' of both pedagogy and curriculum will continue through target setting, based on 'normative criteria' monitored by Ofsted to ensure 'standardisation of both outcomes and processes' (ibid.: 26–7). Within such a context, the struggle to secure resources and the gradual erosion of teaching flexibility will not help the implementation of inclusive policies.

The Special Educational Needs (SEN) and Disability Act came into force with a view to extending the existing Disability Discrimination Act (1995) to schools and educational institutions. It reaffirmed the government's commitment to the principle of inclusion and 'delivered a stronger right to mainstream education, making it clear that where parents want a mainstream place for their child, everything possible should be done to provide it' (DfES 2004: 24). The Act states that all schools must 'plan' for the inclusion of all children, the underlying assumption being that all children will ultimately attend mainstream schools. It was warmly received (Birkett 2000) by many groups fighting for the inclusion of children with SEN. Many teachers still feel that they need further training to deal adequately with issues of inclusion (ibid., Clough 1998b). Despite the fact that the Disability Discrimination Act included training for business, the new Act:

has no staff training that goes along with it. There's nothing to help schools in how they might implement it, so schools are trying as they go along, and making mistakes that get the publicity. They create a wariness of taking children with disabilities … Seventy percent of teachers will teach a child with autism; only 5% have had autism specific training.

(Birkett 2000: 2)

The most recent policy document (DfES 2004: 17) offers LEAs some funding for training particularly in early years settings (through the SEN and Disability strand of the Early Years and Childcare Grant). There is also commitment to improving specialist advice and support for schools. How far this will go to addressing the concerns of teachers in mainstream schools, particularly secondary schools, remains to be seen. The tension between a market ethos and policies that purport to promote the inclusion of all pupils is not conducive to the kind of culture which supports real inclusion and, despite the rhetoric, schools may increasingly lack the flexibility to create cultures that can (Bines 2000).

As I have already noted, many teachers feel that government policies of inclusion in the general context of an education market are contradictory (Birkett 2000), creating conflict in many schools. Such an uneasy relationship may ultimately prove incompatible, with the 'losers' being the children with SEN (Slee 1996, Armstrong 1998, Barton 1998, Davies *et al.* 1998). Now that SEN has been brought into the same budgetary framework, curriculum and assessment, and market forces as mainstream schools, there are many who maintain that children who experience learning difficulties will still be marginalised (e.g. Gewirtz *et al.* 1995, Gilbourne and Youdell 2000). The joint effect of the education market and the difficulties experienced by many schools in meeting the demands of new policy initiatives in inclusion and SEN has led to a continuation of the demand for Statements and resources by parents, and no significant decrease in segregation (Bines 2000).

The main concerns of advocates of inclusion centre around two issues. Firstly, how mainstream schools might change to provide for a broader range of educational needs and, secondly, how all teachers can be supported to accept responsibility for all children when for many teachers these tensions and conflicts have caused considerable pressure and stress. It is argued that the range of centrally generated policy initiatives has been particularly severe for teachers and SENCOs working within special and inclusive education (Davies *et al.* 1998). Davies *et al.* attribute this to the two parallel thrusts of government policies, legislation and administrative orders around raising standards, and the ideological debate surrounding the moves towards the inclusion, a debate which, they argue, has taken the moral high ground.

The tension may be exacerbated by the pressure to ensure an effective home–school partnership between, on the one hand, parents constructed as consumers and 'moral guardians' of educational standards (Dale 1989) and, on the other, the professionals–teachers who feel they will be blamed in the event of any failure (Hartnett and Carr 1995). There is a belief that teachers find central policies remote with little real impact on their everyday teaching and learning (Archbald and Porter 1994). But there seems little doubt that the impact of central policies can be plainly heard in the voices of teachers who find the tensions between the two major policy initiatives extremely difficult to manage. Teachers who ideologically support inclusion feel that there are growing pressures on them to exclude some pupils, usually those who challenge the school's learning environment (Clough 1998a). There are 'whispers' which suggest that there is almost a hierarchy for inclusion, suitable children who will 'fit' into mainstream contexts. It has also been suggested to me (in one case by the head of a special school) that the nature of special schools is changing and that they may be taking more children with behavioural difficulties and 'losing' children with disabilities such as cystic fibrosis or cerebral palsy to mainstream schools. Hence, while it may appear that the need for special schools remains, it seems probable that the nature of their 'clientele' may be changing.

Contradictions of principle? Reflections

This chapter has considered the two main strands of education policy since the early 1980s. It has highlighted the developing tensions for teachers, especially SENCOs, and for parents of children with SEN around issues related to the inclusion of these children into mainstream schools within the context of a quasi-market in education. While policies of inclusion were intended to be implemented in the light of a reduction in the number of special school places, there is no evidence that this is happening on a national scale. Rather, there is a suggestion that the nature of the SEN of children attending special schools is changing, with those who present challenging behaviour being increasingly likely to be excluded from mainstream settings.

Billington argues that:

> power relations are reproduced within everyday acts and interactions, no matter how inconsequential they may seem, and that they can be reproduced also, not only within the more clearly recognizable professional processes and practices (for example, such as those performed by teachers, psychologists and social workers) but also in all of the social relations which are generated by forms of institution and government.

(2000: 4)

Bearing this in mind, and reflecting on the contradictions of principle outlined in this chapter, I would like to bring the chapter to a close by highlighting three possible areas for reflection as the stories unfold:

1 the ways in which these two policies interact to identify, pathologise, marginalise and exclude certain groups;

1 the ways in which the processes and structures within both society and schools support this marginalisation;

1 the ways in which professionals, through these processes and structures and the implementation of policy into practice, might problematise and reconceptualise these issues.

2 Discourses and challenges

'It's something to do with time,' she said. 'You got a star because you had spent more time on the second drawing. And spent the time in a particular way. We think they have a plan, and that it has to do with time.'
'So the second one wasn't any better?' ...
'There's no such thing as better,' she said. 'The second one just fitted in better with their plan.'

(Høeg 1996: 77)

This chapter begins with an examination of the developing feminist literature around issues of inclusion, disability and learning difficulty, motherhood and teaching. It highlights the gap between dominant discourses and how these construct 'others' through the creation of 'common-sense notions', and the lived experiences of the mother-teachers. A number of discourses are examined: SEN and disability; motherhood; teachers, especially those working with children with SEN; and inclusion. There is also a consideration of the rhetoric of home–school relations and the 'contested terrain of school', the space in which the private and personal domain of home meets the public and professional one that is school. The chapter concludes with a brief consideration of how feminist research can offer insights into the experiences of individuals, particularly in marginalised groups, through methodologies such as narrative.

Introduction

How far is there any scope for mothers to build on their privately based experiences to resist dominant discourses and organisational imperatives around the schooling of their children?

(Ribbens McCarthy 2000: 2)

Few of us would deny the very close relationship between our public and our private lives. In the postmodern era, many academic research projects have emerged from the personal experiences of the researchers particularly in relation to women's lives both inside and outside the family. Such research (e.g. Sikes 1997, David 2003) considers the role of women as mothers, workers and professionals. Feminist approaches have slowly gained acceptance in the academy, enabling 'new' methodologies such as autobiography, narrative, critical reflection and reflexivity to be recognised. Reflection and reflexivity about one's location, position and perspectives are vital for feminist research which considers how policy and its context relates to family and personal life, and constrains it (David 2000a).

Despite education having transformed women's lives during the latter part of the last century, women's voices have not been reflected in public policies and in employment and have been generally missing from the public forum (ibid.). Capitalism and the industrial revolution changed the nature of social relations and prioritised the public rather than the private domain. The separation of the worlds of work and the home placed men firmly in the former and women in the latter. This has resulted in the creation of discourses, usually created by 'experts', which acted as controls and regulators through their constructions of 'norms'. These expert discourses effectively silenced the voices of women even in what were perceived to be the traditional areas of concern for women such as motherhood and childcare. This 'historical silencing of women' has been challenged by writers such as Dorothy Smith (1987: 9) who are calling for the voices of women to remove the boundaries relating to the separation of public and private life; the personal from the professional; experiential knowledge from the 'knowledge' of experts.

The role of women as mothers and the nature and meaning of motherhood are also being challenged. Motherhood is changing from what was previously felt to be a private and personal responsibility to a more public and political responsibility, and the responsibilities of motherhood are becoming more complex. Recognition is being given to the fact that mothers are 'pre-eminently responsible for their children's upbringing and education'. This responsibility affects women's roles in other areas of their lives. Nor is the changing nature of motherhood just about women taking responsibility for their own and their children's lives. Feminists such as Oakley (1979, 1980, 1986), Ehrenreich and English (1978), and Kaplan (1994) argue that there is a 'medicalisation' of mothers and motherhood, through the increasing control by medical and quasi-medical experts in relation to conception, childbirth and child rearing. Through this medical-expert model, the experiences of women are relegated almost to folklore and legend and therefore rendered powerless. The boundaries between expert knowledge and personal experience are perceived by feminist writers to be artificial and constructed. They usually relate to areas of 'ambiguity, tension and danger' (Ribbens McCarthy 2000: 7). School is perceived as such a boundary; a social setting which represents the division between public and private, the professional and the personal and as such can be regarded as a contested terrain (David 1993a).

The creation of 'norms' through oppositions or dichotomies can be seen in other areas such as disability and special educational needs. 'Common dichotomies' (Stanley 1992) of inclusion and segregation, of normality and difference, where difference is viewed as deviance, support the construction of disability as a negative experience, a private grief, rendering the individual powerless and needy (Oliver 1996a, Barton 1996). It is perceived as a deficit within the individual to be addressed, where possible, by medical efforts at 'normalisation'. Within these divisions, the knowledge of the professional is given more weight than the experience of the individual.

While the growth of feminist research has led to the growth of challenges to dominant discourses in a number of areas in relation to the lives of the mother-teachers, first it is important to consider how dominant discourses appear to construct their lives.

Dominant discourses and the mother-teachers

In the opening chapter I considered the meaning of 'discourse' and how dominant discourses could become accepted as 'common-sense' knowledge through the constructions of powerful groups. Such dominant constructions of the world often rely on the division between public construction and private reality. The language of powerful discourses represents the public rather than the personal, reflecting the 'expert' model in motherhood, in SEN/disability and increasingly in the developing discourse on teachers of children with SEN. These dominant discourses suggest a commonality of experience which may be very different from the lived experience of individuals.

The discourse of care is very prominent in the three areas considered here: SEN, motherhood and teaching. Caring for children has been seen as apolitical and a 'safe haven' for educational practice (Blackmore 1999). It idealises women as carers, and nurtures and supports the dominant discourses on mothering and motherhood which conceptualise women as strong in the face of adversity, emotionally resilient (ibid., Mirza 1993), while at the same time nurturing and caring for others. The discourse of care emerges in the area of SEN and disability in a number of ways. Not only does it construct mothers as caring and self-sacrificing, but it also carries over the notion of 'sentimental' care to SEN professionals and teachers. Yet within the field of SEN and disability the discourse of professional 'care' pathologises the individual. These complexities are now considered more closely as they form an important context for the stories.

Many children with disabilities do not have any special educational needs. Access may be their main concern. On the other hand many children defined as having SEN may have no physical impairment. In considering SEN and disability together, I acknowledge the danger of reductionism, but for the purposes of this book they will be considered together within the developing discourse of inclusion.

SEN and disability

The discourses around SEN have developed from models of disability constructed outside education. Before 1970 many children were confined in long-stay hospitals with no access or right to education. Their lives were controlled through doctors and the Department of Health. The language identified them as 'deficient', 'deviant', 'handicapped', 'educationally subnormal' and in need of 'remedial' treatment to address the deficit within the child.

While the Warnock Report (DES 1978) was still based on a discourse of individual needs rather than of rights and entitlements, the work of Tomlinson (1982) was to prove a watershed in the development of a different discourse on special educational needs. Tomlinson argued that SEN and disability were social constructions and that the deficit lay not with the individual but with society. This 'social construction' perspective opened up the first real challenge to the dominant medical model of learning difficulty and disability and although the medical model still dominates, we have seen this challenge developing since the early 1980s (e.g. Oliver 1996a, Armstrong and Barton 1999, Tomlinson 2001).

Three main theoretical approaches to SEN and disability are now generally identified: the medical model, the social construction or social creation model, and the interactional model offering a 'middle way' (Skidmore 1996).[1] There is little disagreement that the medical model is still dominant, individualising disability and learning difficulties, and the language remains one of the 'treatment' being in the 'best interests of the patient' (Fulcher 1999: 27). This language of persuasion can make it more difficult for some groups, such as working-class parents, to negotiate with professionals (Bagley and Woods 1998, Hanafin and Lynch 2002). As a consequence of this continued dominance, much teaching practice is still aimed at 'normalisation' as opposed to education (Corker and French 1999). This makes the whole notion of difference problematic, because it is always perceived in relation to some 'implicit norm' which 'perpetuates the illusion that individuals are measured from some universal standard of objective authority' (Peters 1996: 231).

Who counts as an 'educational' expert is significant. Doctors still play an important role in the 'diagnosis' and assessment of children perceived as having SEN. The whole process of providing a Statement of Special Educational Need perpetuates the medical model. Moves to reduce Statementing through School Action and School Action Plus (along with Early Years Action and Action Plus) (DfES 2001) place more emphasis on school interventions, but the demand from parents to secure scarce resources through the provision of a formal Statement may undermine these processes. Physical needs are often seen as the most important consideration in determining the educational placement, and meeting medical or physical requirements remains a frequently cited reason for not allocating a place in a mainstream school.

The medical treatment of certain behavioural 'conditions' is increasingly causing concern. The prescription of methylphenidate (Ritalin) to children diagnosed as suffering from Attention Deficit

---

[1] Fulcher (1999: 25) offers five discourses on disability – the medical, charity, lay, rights and a corporate approach – which commodifies disability and SEN.

Hyperactivity Disorder (ADHD) is a significant example of the intervention of medical experts in the education of children perceived as having a very particular learning difficulty (Norris and Lloyd 2000). The use of a class A drug with young children is highly controversial, and yet there is considerable evidence of its growing use in both Britain and the United States. Between 1991 and 1996, in England alone, there was a 2,000 per cent increase in the number of prescriptions for methylphenidate and the figures suggest a continuing, strong upward trend (ibid.).

The education of children defined as having SEN often involves other 'quasi'-medical experts such as speech therapists, physiotherapists, occupational therapists and educational psychologists whose role is often to carry out assessment tests and recommend appropriate educational placement. While there is documentary support for the involvement of parents in the process (DES 1988, DfEE 1997b, 1998a, DfES 2001), in reality the experts still have considerable responsibility for the decisions. Although parents have to be consulted, or at least 'told', and have recourse to the SEN Tribunal should they wish to challenge the decision (ibid.), many parents, particularly working-class parents, may feel unable to present a challenge to professionals (Bagley and Woods 1998), despite increasing levels of support in the process.

Such a model perpetuates the notion that children with special needs are somehow less than perfect and of less value than other, 'normal' children (Murray and Penman 2000). The testing of pregnant women for foetal abnormalities, and abortion for conditions such as Down's syndrome, reinforces the lower value of children who are not 'perfect'. The birth of such a child, or the discovery of learning difficulties, is often regarded as their personal tragedy, the occasion for sympathy for parents as indeed a number of the stories in this book suggest (e.g. Sonia, Chapter 4; Joan, Chapter 8; and Julia, Chapter 9).

The education and welfare of children with disabilities and learning difficulties has largely been regarded as a matter of private concern and charitable interest. Until well into the 1970s there were few statistics available about these children and their families (Glendinning 1983, Beresford 1995, Read 2000). However, in the latter half of the twentieth century media interest in the scandal of thalidomide, the issues over vaccine damage and the revelation of the appalling conditions in some long-stay hospitals for disabled children increased the awareness of the problems of these children and their families (Read 2000). The literature, which began to grow in the 1970s, was written largely by experts about the children and their families from a professional perspective. It concentrated on the psychological and psychoanalytical aspects and parents were often all but blamed and pathologised in relation to their children's disabilities (Roll-Petterson 2001), particularly in the case of children perceived as being on the autism spectrum. Parents might be regarded as 'overprotective, symbiotic, indecisive, lacking dominance and showing "perplexity" or psychic "paralysis"' (Cantwell *et al.* 1978: 273–4). Chapter 6 tells the story of Truda, who adopted her son John. In it she raises some interesting issues in relation to notions of 'guilt' associated with the birth of children with disabilities and learning difficulties from the perspective of an adoptive mother.

Mothers who could cope with their disabled children were open to criticism every bit as much as those who felt that they were unable to cope. Phrases such as 'well-disguised rejection' and 'over-normalisation' were not uncommon among experts about such mothers (Read 2000). Olshansky (1962) describes the parents' 'natural' responses to the 'tragic' birth of a 'mentally defective' child as 'chronic sorrow', which could go on all their lives. Other professionals argued that parents went through a staged response which included 'denial, isolation, reaction formation, projection and regression' (Roll-Petterson 2001: 2). If they didn't, they were perceived as dysfunctional. Certain ages and stages were seen as particularly critical, but Roll-Petterson suggests that professionals tended to underestimate the complexity of the parents' feelings as the children grew older, having overestimated them when they were young, as is suggested in the story of Joan (Chapter 8). The early literature has been much criticised, with critics claiming that it created misconceptions about the lives of these children and their families which were then adopted by the experts (e.g. Glendinning 1983, Read 2000, Roll-Petterson 2001). The story of Sonia (Chapter 4) offers some interesting insights which challenge such misconceptions.

The use of terms such as 'special' create considerable unease in some, who like Corbett argue that: 'if "special" is so positive, why is it not usurped by the patriarchy and widely employed to define power and status?' (1996: 49). Yet discourses of special needs have worked to preserve this 'specialness', helping SEN to 'reinvent itself in order to stake its claim in the so-called era of inclusion' (Slee 1998: 126). Perceived as a commodity by government, professionals and parents alike in the struggle to gain resources amidst an increasingly competitive state system, the discourse of SEN forms a significant part of the contextual setting for the mother-teachers.

While guilt and blame are constructed as a significant part of the discourse for the families and particularly the mothers, they also appear in the dominant and public discourses surrounding the construction of mothering and motherhood. There may be some differences in the upbringing of disabled children and non-disabled children, but there are also many commonalties in both the patterns of mothering and the ways of seeing mothers (Read 2000).

Discourses of motherhood

The history of motherhood is directly connected with the history of women and with women being seen to have the sole responsibility for the care of children (Oakley 1974). It was not until the mid-1980s that 'mothers' were perceived in the literature as a subject in their own right. Until then mothers were considered from the point of view of the child (Kaplan 1992). The discourses were 'about' mothers rather than 'by' them.

Becoming a mother is described by many women as a life-changing experience, a key life event which, along with death, 'influence[s] the ways in which we make sense of the world' (Sikes 1997: 1). Being a mother can directly change a woman's values, her relationships within her intimate family circle and the way she relates to, and is perceived by, society as a whole. The woman's public role may change and may become more limited (Wearing 1984). As a mother, she may now be expected to reinforce 'traditional' notions of motherhood contained within dominant discourses (see Chapter 6, Truda's story). The legacy of Freud has been substantial in the development of these discourses (Mitchell 1975, Sayers 1991, Chodorow 1989). Many works on women's attitudes to child bearing and rearing in the 1960s and 1970s were approached from a psychoanalytic perspective which then passed into popular literature as self-evident 'truths' (Read 2000).

Defining such terms as 'mothering' and 'motherhood' is not easy, for they are located within culturally specific contexts. Through literature and popular culture, Kaplan (1992) identifies three main representations of mothers: the self-sacrificing, saintly carer in the house; the selfish, over-indulgent woman; and the sinister, evil, all-possessing monster. This illustrates just some of the complexity and contradictory nature of the discourses on mothering and motherhood, which either idealise the mother for her selfless service to, and nurturing of, her family, or attack her for contributing to the ills of both the individual and the society (Glenn 1994).

Mothering is 'a socially constructed set of activities and relationships' (Glenn *et al.* 1994: ix) and can be 'produced and regulated, correct and incorrect, normal and abnormal' (Walkerdine and Lucey 1989: 30). Mothering is often presented as a 'labour of love', constructed in a romantic, altruistic way, where issues of power are regarded as irrelevant or are invisible. But these issues of power are very important, for mothering affects the power relations between the genders, races, economic and political groups and therefore is very much an 'arena of political struggle' (Glenn 1994: 17). The hidden use of power to control mothers is made visible by Smart (1996), who examines the extension of what was classed as 'good mothering' from the provision of physical requirements such as food, warmth and clothing, to include both physical development and the psychological care of the child. Much of the work of mothering appears to involve the more informal caring assumed to be 'natural' to women whether mothers or not (Read 2000). Yet feminists argue that this is not the whole picture since, although mothering concerns nurturing, and many feminists acknowledge that female values are often about caring for others, 'maternal thinking', according to Ruddick (1982), develops through mothers practising 'mothering', bringing together thought, emotion and judgement.

'Motherhood' is regarded as the institution embodying the norms through which mothers understand what they are and how they are constituted within their social, cultural and historical contexts (Rich 1976). Oakley (1979: 1) defines it as the 'way in which women become mothers in industrialised societies today'. Women have been under considerable pressure to become mothers and in many cultures it is the only way for women to gain status. The dominant model of motherhood prioritises the white, Anglo-American middle-class model (Collins 1994), and appears to date back to the white bourgeoisie in Western Europe and North America towards the end of the eighteenth century. Industrialisation took production out of the home and into factories leaving the home as the private, less important sphere where women and children were based. The division of public and private also created a construction of 'social childhood', which in turn required a different construction of motherhood (Glenn 1994: 14). For working-class women, the separation of home and production meant that work had to be found outside the home, and children had to be left with either an older child or an older family member. For Victorian middle-class women, the notion of working outside the home was unthinkable unless they were impoverished and even then there were only certain occupations considered suitable, such as governess or companion. The labour of working-class women was needed in the factories; that of the middle-class 'lady' was not. Her role was increasingly seen as that of supporter of her husband and children. The construction of the woman as the passive homemaker became one of the main concepts upon which the dominant discourse of mothering was constructed. The other was the subordination of women to men, a view supported by philosophers such as Locke, John Stuart Mill and Rousseau, on the grounds of a man's 'rationality' and a woman's 'irrationality'.

The differences between women in different social classes were not made visible in the construction of the dominant discourse which totally omitted diversity (Oakley 1979, Collins 1994, Glenn 1994). Such a model presented a very idealised image of motherhood. The Victorian ideal of 'sanctified domesticity' required a pure and self-sacrificing mother. After the Second World War, the work of Bowlby (1963), around theories of maternal attachment, reinforced the notion of the 'good' mother remaining at home to meet the needs of her children.

The last 50 years have seen three major 'waves' in relation to feminist thinking around the dominant discourse of motherhood. Early liberal feminists (e.g. Friedan 1963, Millet 1970, Mitchell 1975) criticised the Freudian view that being a woman meant aspiring to being a housewife and mother, who was ultimately to blame for the ills which might befall the children. Marxist feminists (e.g. Firestone 1970, Mitchell 1971) attacked the dominant discourses as supportive of state capitalism through the reproduction of gendered family values. The division of labour was seen as a sexual division between men and women, with women taking the subordinate position because they were regarded as the primary childcarers. Feminists highlighted the fact that, in meeting the needs of children, women often ignored their own needs.

The major division among feminists in the 1960s and 1970s centred on equality and greater autonomy for women, with the main issues being about mothering (Everingham 1994) and the politicisation of the domestic, private and personal sphere (Read 2000). While liberal feminists sought equality with men through the workplace, a third wave of feminist 'motherists' felt that this would be achieved with the loss of the 'values of nurturance and connectedness associated with mothering', which they were reluctant to relinquish (Everingham 1994: 3). Writers such as Ruddick (1989) maintain that women have a central role to play in raising children, for they offer a different ethical framework from men, which should be equally valued and celebrated along with women's 'mothering' qualities of care and nurturing. This was seen by some as an argument for the return to the patriarchal system and values, which merely romanticised mothering and negated the woman.

Since the 1990s feminists generally seem to agree that women need to 'construct a specifically women centred perspective', a 'value system strongly associated with mothering' (Everingham 1994: 4). But the dominant discourse still assumes that mothering is natural for all mothers and those who do not wish to mother are in some way perceived as 'unnatural'. For a woman to remain within the domestic and private sphere at the heart of the nuclear family appears to reinforce the 'traditional' dominant values, leaving her in the subordinate position. A recent study of social mobility reported that 'All women's gains can be lost when they have children if they cannot afford nannies' (Elliot and Iredale 2003: 6). The report suggests that career women almost always come from 'well-to-do backgrounds', suggesting a class division between them and 'stay-at-home mums'. Family support from relatives is less available than it once was due to greater social mobility, and for many women who choose to or have to return to work, their only option is to take part-time employment or less responsible positions in order to balance home and work.

Class is an issue which has caused much disagreement between feminists, with some arguing that many theories are based on the narrow class experience of white middle-class women in particular, and narrow social contexts (e.g. Firestone 1970, MacDonald 1981). Most feminists agree that the dominant model excludes many groups and so women constantly have to negotiate and construct their own identities, against the dominant model (e.g. Glenn 1994, Nelson 1994). For this reason Glenn suggests that there is a dominant discourse of mothering but with 'variations at the edges' insofar as 'mothering is differentially constructed for women of different races, ethnicities and classes' (Glenn 1994: 20).

There are indeed many dimensions to the dominant discourse of motherhood today, hence its complexity (DiQuinzio 1999). One of these dimensions, according to Oakley (1986), is that, as the accepted perception of the nuclear family changes, the nature and centre of control has moved from the family to the experts and in particular to medical professionals. During the last century there has been a tremendous expansion in what may be termed 'professional expertise' in many areas of life. Education, the medical profession and the social services have all been affected by advances in scientific and technological knowledge. The increase in 'expert' knowledge has not only affected childbirth but also approaches to child health, psychological and social development, well-being and education. From the moment of conception, care is dominated by experts, with the focus on the foetus rather than the mother (Kaplan 1994). Mothers who reject the advice on offer risk being regarded as irresponsible or uncaring. There are cultures which have even reached extremely invasive forms of control over female fertility against some groups, such as those with learning difficulties/disabilities (Glenn 1994). Many women in other cultures struggle to gain the right to control their own fertility (socially, politically and scientifically) through the right to contraception and abortion.

In the UK, hospitalisation for childbirth ensures that, for many women, the processes of childbirth are controlled by medical experts and this makes it hard for women to avoid what Foucault (1973) refers to as 'the gaze'; the deliberate use of medical skill to obtain power. Mothers can find this threatening and feel objectified by it when medical professionals talk 'at' them 'as if you weren't there' (Sikes

1997: 40). Childbirth has come to be seen as a medical procedure rather than a natural event, with many of the procedures creating distance between mother and child. Although the risk of a woman dying in childbirth today is the lowest ever, and women expect to be delivered of a healthy baby in hospital with medical staff present, Oakley (1979) warns that this is only part of the picture. Her words, written 25 years ago, have almost certainly been fulfilled and continue to sound a warning:

> *This colonisation of birth by medicine is a thread in the fabric of cultural dependence on professional health care. People are not responsible for their own health, their own illnesses, their own births and deaths; doctors are saviours, miracle-workers, mechanics, cultural heroes ... From being necessary to the cure of illnesses, they have been given responsibility for all illnesses and anything to which, like birth, the label of illness can be attached.*

> (ibid.: 15)

What Oakley refers to as 'debilitating deference to medical authority' makes it difficult for women to regard themselves as at the centre of their experiences. This relationship of control and dependency is not limited to childbirth, for bringing up children is now regarded as being 'technical, where the rational superiority of ... pediatric science' ultimately de-skills the mother (Oakley 1974: 274). Health professionals are now perceived as an inevitable part of the 'transition to motherhood' (ibid.) during which mothers may feel vulnerable and unable or unwilling to question the professionals.

Within this discourse of mothering is the discourse of normalisation (Foucault 1973, 1979, Donzelot 1979), which is used to separate what is perceived as different or deviant from what is classed as normal (Urwin 1985). On the one hand, 'normal' child development is regarded as 'natural' while, on the other, it is seen as the mother's responsibility. This can create fear, especially in young and first-time mothers, that they are doing something wrong. Professional advice can problematise the issue because it creates the choice between a 'normal' or a 'problem' family (ibid., Carpenter 2000). Normalising processes include infant testing and health clinic checks to record 'normal' progress. Such processes also produce a discourse of the 'normal' mother. Urwin (1985) argues that these tests and the whole modern notion of child development constructs mothering in a way which is totally child-centred. This perception is reinforced through the childcare literature, which emphasises the idea that the woman's place is in the home and not in the workplace, often creating feelings of guilt for working mothers (Sharpe 1984, Spain 1996), even where economic necessity dictates otherwise. The mothers of both working and middle classes are still equally held to be responsible for producing the 'right kind of child' (Steedman *et al.* 1985: 3).

Mothers of children with SEN/disabilities seem to be missing from the literature on the public discourse of motherhood. While race, gender, ethnicity and sexuality are increasingly a part of that discourse, these 'other' mothers are still, on the whole, invisible. According to Read, the discourse of 'normality' places the mothers of children with SEN and disabilities firmly on the 'other side of the track' (2000: 115).

Mothers of children with SEN

Where these mothers do emerge is in the *public* discourses of SEN and disability and through the expert and professional discourses on their children. As I have already noted, they do not even appear in government education policy documents concerning home–school partnerships and inclusion (DfEE 1997c, 1998a, 1999, DfES 2001). In all these public discourses, the voices are not those of the women themselves but of the professionals, usually experts in medicine, social services or education.

The changes in theoretical approaches to disability and SEN through a social construction perspective, research by academics with disabilities and the development of alternative research methodologies allowed a challenge to the public discourse to emerge slowly through the literature. The developing discourse was located in one of rights rather than needs and sought to hear the voices of both the children and their parents. The normality of the lives of many families with children with SEN and disabilities began to emerge through the work of people such as Thomas (1982) and research done by the Family Fund research team during the 1970s and 1980s. Other researchers (e.g. Baldwin and Glendinning 1981) challenged the notion that disability necessarily meant problems. They also highlighted the individuality of the families and their children, noting that as with any children there were strains and stresses but there was also happiness and joy.

Within the dominant discourses around motherhood, 'normality' means mother with 'normal' baby. There is little suggestion of 'difference' or 'difficulty'. The increasing 'medicalisation' of childbirth and motherhood and the resulting emphasis within that discourse for the need for expert attention and care means that mothers of children who may be seen as 'failures' of the professional system are unlikely to emerge in the public discourse. With the increasing number of pre-natal tests for an ever-widening range of disabilities and the increasing call by women for abortion on demand, bringing a disabled child into the world may appear as evidence of failure on behalf of the mother and/or the professionals. As the cost of caring for children with disabilities rises and a perfect baby becomes the expected norm, disability may be seen as even more undesirable. Certainly we are beginning to witness in the USA claims against mothers whose actions or habits during pregnancy go against professional advice. Within this pathologising of mothers, the notion that mothers may value their 'imperfect' child may seem a strange one indeed.

For many mothers, the birth of a disabled baby may mean a sense of exclusion, which begins almost at once (Julia's story in Chapter 9 offers some insights into this issue). Journals and parents' guides largely ignore the possibility that children can be born with disabilities or learning difficulties. The attitude of friends and relatives may not help as they offer well-intentioned sympathy or, worse, say nothing. By presenting a perfect image, the discourses of motherhood help to maintain society's fear of disability and impairment. As Glendinning (1983), Roll-Petterson (2001) and Carpenter (2000) show, many mothers do not feel this sense of disaster when they find they have a child with SEN/disabilities, although much depends on the support they receive as well as their previous personal experiences.

For the parents, the birth of a baby with disabilities can mean a different identity from other parents (Bryne *et al.* 1988). Research in the 1970s upheld the view that many families with disabled children received little support, were under considerable pressure and felt very isolated (Hewett 1970, 1976). While it cannot be denied that services for disabled children and their parents have been significantly improved since the early 1980s through changes in legislation, it is also suggested that this has not necessarily proved a positive benefit for all families and that services are at best 'patchy and under funded' over the country (Read 2000: 8). Read maintains that the families of disabled children need to be 'predominantly reliant on their own personal coping resources and strategies for much of what they need' (ibid.). This inevitably means that different families are left to deal with this in their own way and that there are considerable individual as well as contextual, cultural and social variations in the lived experiences.

The working mother

In 1931 women accounted for 31 per cent of the labour force in the UK; by the end of the twentieth century, the number of women equalled men (Lewis 1992). The reasons for this increase are complex: smaller families; better health and longer life expectancy; better housing and household technology; changing views of the family; changes in legislation; changes in the nature of work; and the emergence of state education and welfare provision. The views of women themselves have also been important. Feminist theories and constructions have opened up different ways of conceiving the role of women, rather than purely as determined by the ability to bear children. Indeed, as I noted earlier, the lives of working-class and certain other groups of women have never been constructed other than as part of the workforce. The 'working mother' has been of increasing interest to feminist researchers in the latter part of the last century. As more middle-class women have gone out to work, the dominant discourse has had to change to take account of this and what has been done for years by working-class women and been ignored within the patriarchal discourse now had to be addressed.

The term 'working mother' came into use after the Second World War (ibid.) and marked a dramatic change in the number and status of women who worked after marriage, and who returned to work having had children. It was used to signify a threat to the social and educational well-being of many children, which was based on what Lewis calls 'a remarkably consistent set of assumptions about the proper activities of men and women' (ibid.: 8). After the war, the development of the Welfare State, in particular the National Health Service, the extension of state education, the creation of a Social Services Department and the need to support these departments administratively, required an increase in the workforce of large numbers of doctors, nurses, social workers, welfare officers, teachers and secretarial support. Such employment was regarded as suitable employment for women, for it could be argued that it was an extension of the 'caring' and nurturing role which women did so well in the home. The dominant discourse began to accommodate the need for many married middle-class women to return to what was considered 'respectable' employment within the 'caring' professions such as teaching, and in 1944 the marriage bars, which had operated in some parts of the country, were removed for teachers, enabling married women to return to the classroom. However, despite the need for women to be part of the workforce and legislation making sexual discrimination in the workplace illegal, there are many issues in relation to pregnancy and employment which still affect the position of women (Glenn *et al.* 1994).

For many women there is little economic option but to return to work, despite the 'middle-class' discourse of what counts as 'natural mothering'. In her study on parent-teachers, Sikes (1997) notes that many mothers did not want to return to work after the birth of their babies, while others felt the need to extend themselves beyond their own children. In both cases there was a sense of 'doing the right thing' by staying at home with the children, with those mothers returning to work often feeling guilty. Despite the improvement in maternity benefits and conditions, many women on returning to work face scepticism from colleagues and employers about the difficulties of working, especially in full-time employment, and having children to look after (ibid.). However, it is interesting to note that, despite this criticism, research suggests that, far from resulting in stress and depression, paid work for women has 'by far the strongest and most consistent tie to women's good health' (Coward 1992).

Discourses of teachers and teaching

The growth of the Welfare State meant that there was a need for women to enter the 'caring' professions and by the second half of the twentieth century, the dominant discourse around teaching had changed to accommodate the view that the profession was appropriate for women because it allowed them to do what it was argued they did best, which was to 'mother'. The female teacher could make a reasonable contribution to the family's income, while still meeting all her commitments to family and home. Teaching allowed working-class women to move to the middle class (Sikes 1997) and the hours and holidays fitted in well with those of their children and therefore placed no extra demands on the working father. Steedman (1987: 120–1) argues that the hours and holidays were not the only reasons for women entering teaching. There were a number of 'societal shifts' which changed earlier views that what children needed was a firm hand, that only a man could give. This notion of the 'mother made conscious' (ibid.) presents the roles of mother and teacher (especially primary teacher) as similar and therefore 'appropriate'; indeed, Benn (1989) separates teaching into two areas: the 'mothering' done by women; and the teaching done by men, which has more to do with power and authority.

The discourse may be more complex than this today. Changes in education since the Education Reform Act (1988) are leading to a focus on notions of performance rather than on the education of the whole child, with a resulting 'shift in emphasis ... from the primary teacher as mother, to the primary teacher as teacher' (Sikes 1997: 69). There are a number of trends emerging which reflect this, such as the developing focus on performance; the intensification of testing; a demand for teachers to specify what is being done; the use of business competencies for teachers; payment by results; defining 'good' teaching through league tables and other performance indicators; competition and marginalisation of teachers as 'self interested producers' and a 'favouring' of consumers, vaguely defined as parents and employers (Smyth 1995: 1). Smyth regards these trends as worrying because of the comment they make about the work of teachers. Indeed, teachers themselves express concern about the National Curriculum, the pressure of SATs and the effects of both on young children (Sikes 1997).

The language that constructs the discourses of teachers and teaching is regarded as crucial to the ways in which they are conceptualised, and since the changes in educational policy, there has been an increasing emphasis on the discourse of derision (Hartnett and Carr 1995). This discourse blames teachers for the perceived failure of the educational system to produce young adults able to function in a rapidly changing technological and economic world. This has led to growing government control over the curriculum and increasingly over teaching methods (Lawn 1990: 389).

The increasing concentration on 'performance' means that other more social aspects of the curriculum are being pushed aside with the result that there is now a demand for 'good' parenting in relation to children's behaviour, with the blame being laid on parents whose children do not conform (Sikes 1997). When this is considered in the way that David (1993a) views the gendered nature of parenting, the question must be asked as to whether or not the demand is for 'good mothering' with mothers held responsible for the good behaviour, academic success and general well-being of their children.

While the trends outlined earlier have had some effect, the discourse of teacher as mother still remains in some areas of teaching. The emotional aspects of 'good mothering' – 'attention, identification, empathy with the child' – have been encouraged in teaching since the nineteenth century (Steedman 1987: 122–3), based on the work of Froebel and Pestalozzi, who saw mothers as educators from whom teachers could learn. Others have also made this connection between the roles of mother and teacher. Steedman *et al.* (1985) note that there is a 'remarkable congruity' in the roles of the teacher and the mother, who by 'passivity' and nurturance ensures the 'unfolding development of the child'. Sikes quotes a female teacher who said: 'We're their mothers while they are in school'. Sikes continues:

What has happened is that notions of what constitutes a 'good' mother (i.e. a 'good' woman) and a 'good' primary-school teacher have intertwined and 'fed' each other with the outcome being almost identical dominant ideologies of mothering and of teaching.

(1997: 68)

There is here almost a notion of the 'professionalisation' of mothering, which appears in Deborah's story (Chapter 5). It also acknowledges the emotional involvement within teaching, which emerges from the stories told here. Yet within the discourse of 'teacher as mother' there appears to be very little real value given to the experiences of teachers who *are* mothers or to the emotional aspects of teaching (ibid.). Without understanding their values and beliefs, their emotional responses and reactions, Nias argues that teachers cannot develop the necessary skills or their 'unique sense of self' which is socially grounded (1996: 294). By ignoring the personal 'mother and child' relationship from the public discourses of educational theory, we risk denying 'our own experience and our own knowledge. Our silence certifies the system' (Grumet 1988: xvi). The acknowledgement of the emotional 'professionalism' of teaching appears to be missing from the ever-growing discourse on teaching, which separates knowledge from emotion, knowing from experience, and prioritises what Lawn and Grace refer to as 'particular interpretations of professionalism' (1987: viii).

Relationships between teachers and parents appear to form a growing part of the public discourse on teachers and there is increasing reference to this in government education policy. While this forms part of such policies, it has been seen as particularly important for the educational development of children with SEN and disabilities. However, the presentation of the professional and the parent in policy documents still suggests that the balance of power remains with the professionals and it is the parent or mother who may be regarded as potentially deficient and damaging to the child (Sikes 1997).

For teachers working with children with SEN and disabilities, either in special or mainstream schools, many of these issues are intensified by the two key strands of government educational policy (discussed in Chapter 1), which have placed these teachers into a very public and challenging role.

Teachers of children with special educational needs and/or disabilities

As I noted earlier, legislation passed since the mid-1970s has drastically changed the educational provision for children now perceived as having SEN (Acts 1981, 1988, 1993, 1994, 1996). Before these changes, the public discourse was of care, which was seen as more important than education and qualifications. Until the Warnock Report (DES 1978) the education of children with SEN was largely based on what Tomlinson (1982) refers to as 'benevolent humani-tarianism'. Since then, changing theoretical perspectives on SEN and disability, the developing discourse of equity and rights, the government's policy drive towards inclusion and the resulting changes in legislation have altered the role of the SEN teacher. Such a role is no longer one of simply offering care. Particularly within mainstream settings, there is a need to meet the entitlement and rights of a number of different stakeholders and this is seen as creating considerable stress for teachers working in the area of SEN, especially where there are serious resource implications as well (May 1996, Upton and Varma 1996).

Government policy has created a public discourse of professionalism around special educators, which is reflected in the production of National Standards for Special Educational Needs Co-ordinators (TTA 1998) and the National Special Educational Needs Specialist Standards (TTA 1999). These standards for SENCOs and SEN specialists are two of five such National Standards (the others being for Head Teachers, Newly Qualified Teachers and Subject Leaders). The language used in this discourse focuses on:

> *Professional knowledge, understanding, skills and attributes necessary to carry out effectively the key tasks of that role. It is the sum of these aspects which defines the expertise demanded of the role, in order to achieve the outcomes in the standards.*
>
> (TTA 1998: 1)

Fulcher (1999: 150) considers this discourse of professionalism as the 'key discourse' in the struggle for the control of a profession or occupational group and defines it as a discourse in which the 'expert knows best'. The introduction of these National Standards for Special Educational Needs Co-ordinators was a recognition of the growing importance of the role of the SENCO in mainstream schools as expressed in a number of government policy documents (DfES 2001, 2002, 2004). This is especially important given the changing role for many SENCOs and learning support teachers in the light of the government's focus on inclusion. Many SEN teachers found themselves in a position of considerable ambiguity. They were at the juncture of a number of discourses around 'specialness-ordinariness', 'special teaching techniques' and 'discourses of commonality', which produced notions of different sets of 'common knowledge' in relation to the teaching of children with SEN and created conflict and stress for teachers (Dyson 1993). They were being given increased responsibility not only for ensuring that the legal educational requirements of children with SEN were met, but also for promoting inclusive practices within the school. This can mean that SENCOs are placed in an extremely difficult position with regard to performance targets and league tables for the school as a whole. Two pressures in particular are seen as significant for special needs teachers in both mainstream and special schools:

> First, the demand that the majority of pupils reach exactly the same standards and second, a requirement that these standards be delivered using similar pedagogies – that will cause most concern for SENCOs.
>
> (Davies *et al.* 1998: 11)

This takes us back to Dyson's argument that within the discourse of 'specialist' teaching for SEN lies the discourse of 'just good teaching'. SENCOs in mainstream schools and teachers in special schools are seen as a 'source of specialist knowledge which can be drawn on by class teachers' (ibid.: 10). Yet the source of this 'expert' knowledge is often unclear for many of these teachers have no specialist training in SEN, or feel that their training is insufficient to meet the needs of these children in mainstream settings (Daniels and Norwich 1996). Davies *et al.* note that over the years this expertise has 'developed' through 'liaison with external services in both assessment of pupils' needs and the writing of IEPs (Individual Education Plans) and analogous action plans'. Clough (1998b: 64) maintains that teacher education in England and Wales is in 'confusion if not crisis', despite policies designed to remedy this, and Slee critically observes:

> Teacher education is currently about acquiring fragmented knowledge. National frameworks for teacher training are not framed to produce the critically reflective practitioners or cultural workers who ought to teach in inclusive schools.
>
> (1999: 204)

The question must be asked as to what such teachers feel is wanted as well as needed in relation to teacher education in the field of SEN? What do SENCOs think counts as professional expertise in relation to SEN and inclusion?

The stresses for teachers in special schools are 'unusual' and are being increased by the changing population of special education (Ashdown 1996: 203). While classes may be smaller than in mainstream schools, the range and nature of the disabilities 'demand exceptional organizational skills' which 'requires good support for staff from their line managers (e.g. through mentoring and appraisal), together with an effective programme of staff induction and subsequent INSET' (ibid.:

203). Staff in special schools work very closely with other staff in team-teaching situations, which Ashdown (ibid.) believes can impose additional strains. Also, these teachers have to accommodate the values and ideas of other professionals (e.g. educational psychologists, speech therapists, etc.) as well as parents. The physical space in special schools may not meet the requirements of guidelines and, given the increase in the number of children with emotional and behavioural difficulties, may add to the pressures. Many staff in special schools may also be affected by the deaths or the progressive degeneration of some of their students and may have to support distressed or grieving parents. Ashdown argues that:

> *The problem for most staff is that they have never been given the opportunity to develop the skills needed for this kind of work with parents, or perhaps worse, they may not realise the limitations of what they can offer. In both cases the outcome can create undue pressure for the staff unless there is some recognised system for supporting them by involving senior staff in schools and external agencies with special skills and resources (e.g. clinical psychologists, respite care providers, community nurses etc.).*

(ibid.: 204–5)

Sonia's story in Chapter 4 raises many of these issues in relation to notions of expertise, respite care, relationships with parents, appropriate curriculum, space and, not least, the effects of the loss of a child in the professional context and its impact on her own private role as a mother. Her story reflects very poignantly the fact that, for many SEN teachers coping with the increasing tension and rising levels of stress, 'personal resources are the individual's own attitudes and methods for coming to terms with stressful situations' (ibid.: 207). The discourse of care features more prominently than the public discourse of professionalism in many special schools, which may account for the fact that closure of special schools has not gone ahead as predicted (Croll and Moses 1998). For mothers such as Sonia, this discourse of care is an important one which seems to have been excluded from the 'expert' discourse.

Despite the use of the TTA National Standards to create notions of professionalism, the professional role of SEN teachers is challenged on a number of levels, for example through the role of the educational psychologist and other quasi-medical 'experts' within the assessment and Statementing process. Lack of status for many special needs teachers in both mainstream and special schools reflects the marginal nature of SEN not only in the national context but also in the local context, in that such teachers are mainly women, work part time or have other roles within the school, despite recent guidelines which state otherwise (DfES 2001).

The creation of the special educator as a professional or expert is under construction; but who will decide what this professionalism will contain? The new SEN Code of Practice (DfES 2001) does not diminish the role; far from it. There is every reason to believe that within the new Code of Practice, the role of the SENCO will be stretched even further, with increased responsibilities, including legal obligations particularly in mainstream schools where the whole area of SEN is likely to become more contentious. There is recognition of the heavy workload of SENCOs in the recent DfES (2004) *Removing Barriers to Achievement: The Government's Strategy for SEN*, but it remains to be seen how this will help in reality. The inclusion of children with certain special educational needs, particularly behavioural ones, may come to dominate the political agenda as parents and many mainstream teachers object to their inclusion in the classroom. In both the United States and Australia policies of inclusion have been severely tested over the question of children with challenging behaviour (Kauffman and Hallahan 1995, Slee 1996).

The development of professional expertise in special educators is certainly political and will have to address the issues related to the concerns of 'other' parents and teachers. There may be a case for arguing that the role of the special educator as a professional may never be completely clear, for not only would it give status to an area of education which is, at present, still marginal but also it would become less flexible and be unable to meet any new challenge arising from changes in government policy. At present the content of any development is unresolved and, it is argued, negotiable (Clough 1998b).

Experience: different ways of knowing

The development of feminist qualitative research methodologies designed to access the voices of hitherto marginalised groups is enabling different 'ways of knowing' to emerge and the experiences of individuals and groups to be heard. Experiential accounts offer an opportunity to reflect on the emerging gap between the rhetoric of the dominant discourses and the private reality. By questioning what has been held to be 'natural' and 'self-evident' and deconstructing dominant discourses, such research opens up 'the agency of women' within social contexts, and particularly those who undertake mothering (Everingham 1994: 6). A growing number of writers note the significance of agency and the mother's role, perceiving mothers as active shapers and creators of values for themselves and others (e.g. Bortolaia Silva 1996, Read 2000). Women have to negotiate with and for their child but they also have a need for their own voice to be heard.

Being their child's ally is perceived by them as an extremely important role (Mayall 1996), whereby mothers and children share a common cause, with the mother acting as an intermediary between the child and the world at large. For mothers of children with SEN/disabilities this can be important but even more difficult. As Read (2000: 84) argues:

> Mothers become their children's advocates formally and informally. Doing so can be enormously difficult as they are often negotiating with others in contexts where a different morality, a different view of the world evidently holds sway.

This in itself can be a problem as there may be situations in which there is a conflict of interest between the mother and her child, which is not easily resolved. Then the question is whose voice shall be heard. The working mother may easily find herself in this position, as indeed does Joan (Chapter 8) when her own role as a working mother conflicts with the needs and wishes of her teenage son.

Since the 1970s there has been a growth in literature based on empirical evidence gained from parents about their own and their children's lives, which places their experiences at the centre. This emerging literature (e.g. Newson 1981, Murray and Penman 2000, Read 2000, Roll-Petterson 2001, McIntyre 2004) may help to narrow the gap between theoretical understandings of disability and SEN and the practical lived experiences. One important aspect of talking to mothers of children with SEN/disabilities has been a growing awareness of the many aspects of normality in the lives of these families, something which was ignored in most earlier studies but which comes over very strongly in the experiences related in this book. Read warns against the professional 'assumption(s) about the impossibility of disability ever existing with things ordinary' (2000: 10–11). There is no denying that for some women the shock and distress of having a disabled child are considerable. Joan (Chapter 8) and Julia (Chapter 9) were both devastated at first but they soon grew into a loving relationship with their children and at the same time changed their approach to many aspects of disability. However, along with this may come the realisation that:

> *The two of them [mother and child] are not seen as having a rightful place in the world to which she [the mother] had hitherto assumed that she belonged. The things that many others do and take for granted no longer seem to apply ... they begin to find themselves in the category of the marginal and the exceptional in almost all respects.*

(ibid.: 116)

Clearly parental responses to having a child with disabilities vary considerably and this can make it more difficult for professionals to make judgements or predictions. In her study, Roll-Petterson (2001) found that professionals tended to overestimate the problems experienced by parents in coming to terms with their children's needs as well as the problems that the parents may be experiencing in their marriages. It is important to note that many disabled children are cared for in single-parent families with the mother being the sole carer and provider (Read 2000). While there is some evidence to show that disabled children place considerable pressure on two-parent family relationships and the risk of family breakdown is higher (ibid.), Roll-Petterson casts doubt on this. However, she does argue that there is a greater risk of individual breakdown for the main carer. She suggests that professionals may view the parents from a 'dysfunctional or pathological perspective' (2001: 11), and that mothers may put on a 'brave face' for others. The stories here reflect the importance of the support the mothers felt they received from their partners, who in some cases (see Truda, Chapter 6) took the main responsibility for looking after the child on a day-to-day basis. It is also clear from the stories that, despite their professional roles, almost all the mothers in this study felt unable to cope with other professionals at some time or other.

Recent research based on the experiences of families with children with SEN shows that such families can experience a range of inequalities and outcomes, such as financial hardship and stress caused by social barriers and a reduction in the quality of family life (Dowling and Dolan 2001). That is not to say that it is the child with disabilities who disables the whole family unit, but rather society's construction of disability. According to Dowling and Dolan the causes of stress stem from 'lack of funding, inflexible care arrangements and the prejudices of others' (ibid.: 24). All the mother-teachers illustrate this in different ways: for example, Joan needs respite care for James when he finishes school. Respite care is often a cause of disagreement between professionals and parents as there may be conflicting views about the nature of the provision and who it is at the centre of the process – the child, or the mother as in Joan's case.

It is not caring for the child that causes the stress but the processes which the families have to go through, such as applying for services, the nature and organisation of the provision and the time and effort spent in accessing it. There are implications here for the wider family. The range of clinics which one family may have to attend can include speech therapy, hydrotherapy, physiotherapy, psychotherapy, occupational therapy, hearing, sight, dietary therapy and review sessions. While attendance at such clinics may be for the child's well-being, there is a great cost in terms of time and effort required by other members of the family. Public intolerance and disapproval of particular behaviours or disruption may also mean that the family avoids visits to cinemas, parks or restaurants. While not seeking to pathologise the families of children with disabilities as 'disabled families', Dowling and Dolan (2001) note that many such families 'do not have enough money to care for their child'. They quote research for the Department of Health, which maintains that it costs £20 per week more to keep a child with disabilities (at 1996 prices for middle-income families).

Families of disabled children are often considered the smallest units of analysis. Like David (1993a), Read (2000) maintains that the term 'parent' 'masks' the very gendered nature of care giving and hides the differences in experiences of mothers and fathers. Read noted that, in general, it was the mothers who had to 'extend' themselves when anything new had to be done; the mothers who had to juggle all their responsibilities. Where there was sharing of responsibilities, there was a division of the tasks with the mother taking the more intimate and personal ones, although, as with the women in this study, some mothers claimed that their partners supported them both emotionally and practically (Beresford 1995).

Mothers of children with SEN and/or disabilities have to negotiate with professionals of all kinds. Such negotiations are seen as crucial to the well-being of their children, and yet they can be one of the most difficult aspects of being such a mother (Read 2000, Dowling and Dolan 2001, Roll-Petterson 2001). This brings their lives, which would otherwise have been private, under the public scrutiny of the professionals. It has been likened to an invasion of the home (Read 2000). I certainly felt this as did Julia and Sonia. It is even worse when you realise that they are making judgements about the quality of your 'mothering'. This can depend on whether or not the mother is doing as the professionals decree, even if this is in opposition to what the mother feels is in the best interests of her child *and* the rest of her family.

In this situation, even mothers who are themselves professionals may not want to risk offending other professionals who may have considerable power over the lives of their children; indeed, they may have a sense of needing support from these professionals (Davis 1998). The irony here appears to be that many 'experts' are relatively untrained in working together, let alone working with families of children with SEN/disabilities. As a result, mothers often feel that it is up to them to ensure that the relationship produces the desired result for the child (McConachie 1997) and they may end up resenting this (Read 2000). When mothers do demand services and take control they risk being classed as 'pushy', selfish and depriving others of vital services (ibid.: 120). The challenges presented by disabled people today and the focus on rights may mean that mothers are criticised for doing the very thing which a few decades ago would have made them 'good' mothers (ibid.: 110). Changing professional notions and ideologies can result in different perceptions of mothers and what constitutes 'good mothering'; for instance, changing attitudes to inclusion may mean that a professional will support a mother's request for a mainstream educational placement today, whereas in the early 1990s such a request may have been regarded as 'unrealistic'.

Sometimes mothers may feel that the barriers against herself and her child are too strong or that she does not have the resources to meet the challenge. If the mother does not mediate for the child, there are few alternatives available. Truda's story (Chapter 6) offers very particular insights into how mothers may carry out this mediation. It takes time and energy to develop the skills to mediate and can take years to know the processes that must be gone through in order to gain access to rights and benefits.

Discourses and challenges: reflections

This chapter has explored aspects of the public and professional discourses which appear to construct the lives of the mother-teachers whose stories are told here. Through these discourses their lives are presented as separate and distinct, on different sides of the public-private divide. There appears little room for any acknowledgement of the acquisition of professional knowledge through abstraction from experience. The discourses also assume a commonality of experience for these women, which, as their stories suggest, is not always the case. Where there are common experiences they are not always those constructed by the dominant discourses. The developing experiential literature reflects a rather different situation. Read suggests that, although many of the mothers in her study come from a position of 'relative social isolation and powerlessness' and have little formal knowledge of the theoretical model of social construction and disability, their experiences are such that they become:

> convinced through their own experiences that many of the most restrictive features of their own and their children's lives are not an inevitable or necessary consequence of having impairments. They often believe that if only people were to regard it as important enough many of these things could be changed and they and their children could have something different and better.

> (2000: 117)

The stories presented in this book suggest that listening to such experiences can give insights into different understandings and ways of conceptualising difference, SEN and disability. It is suggested that, by reflecting on such voices of experience, professionals might engage with the perceptions of different groups of people within their own practice in order to challenge some of these dominant discourses.

3 Personal and political reflections

It was like a big window, but there was no reflection from the candle. The glass could not be seen, only felt.

(Høeg 1996: 119)

This chapter offers my own personal and professional story from which the study began. The story moves from my growth as a teacher, through the births of my two children and early years of motherhood with a daughter and son with disabilities and learning difficulties, to my personal and professional experiences of inclusion and exclusion. It explores my struggles with 'difference', with the growth of professional and personal tension as competing policies begin to impact on schools, teachers and parents. It outlines my family's struggles to have our voices heard by professionals as decisions were made about the future of our son. The chapter closes by highlighting some of the emergent issues, which will be explored in other stories.

I have two children, Elizabeth, aged 26 and Michael, aged 24. Elizabeth qualified as a teacher and has spent two years teaching in a secondary school in the Midlands but she is not sure whether her future lies in teaching. Michael is now married and studying at a College of Further Education in the East Midlands.

I was not the first teacher in the family. My mother was a primary school teacher and my father worked in commerce. They both came from working-class backgrounds. My maternal grandmother worked long hours in the Lancashire cotton mills to support my mother during her training. She saw teaching not only as a worthwhile career for my mother, but also as a means to betterment for her. My own education was very 'traditional'. I attended a grammar school for girls in the north-west of England. In 1968 I went to Hull University to study history and English and there met my future husband John, who was studying chemistry. In 1971 I opted for a PGCE course at Reading University, largely because my father approved of teaching as a 'suitable job for a woman'.

I started teaching in Reading in 1972 and my first appointment was in a school which had almost 2,000 pupils on role. I was teaching history, English and general studies. My first tutor group was a 'low-ability' fifth-year group (now Year 11) and much of my teaching timetable was with 'lower-ability sets'. One advantage of being a probationary teacher in a very large comprehensive was that there were eight of us and the deputy head had responsibility for our induction. We used to meet on a Monday after school for one to two hours and discuss things such as mixed-ability teaching and differentiation; the design and production (remember 'Banda' machines?) of worksheets (differentiation in the early 1970s); assessment and marking; and, of course, classroom management and discipline. My school 'duty' as a fifth-year tutor was middle-school detention which meant that once every three weeks I had to take charge of the rogues and likely lads, aged between 13 and 16, who had fallen foul of some teacher that week. So onerous a duty was this considered that it meant I was excused from all other morning, lunchtime or evening (bus/playground/corridor, etc.) duties. It was also considered a very serious duty which only senior staff, such as the heads of the middle and upper schools, were supposed to do. These were the days when computers were beginning to be given the job of organising the timetable in very large schools, and it had not been programmed to recognise my complete inexperience. The head of history offered to relieve me of the detention duty but, never one to give up without a fight, I met the challenge head on and completed my year of duty. Needless to say, I learnt a great deal that year. It certainly was not an easy time and was more akin to a complete immersion baptism than a gentle wetting of the brow. I am sure my interest in special needs began then, although this was well before the Warnock Report (DES 1978) and the term 'special educational needs' was still unknown.

Having completed my probationary year, I took a post of special responsibility in an upper school (ages 13–18) near Manchester. Twelve teachers were employed to spend 50 per cent of their teaching timetable with the 'ROSLA' (raising of the school leaving age) students. I was given a post of special responsibility for the fourth year (current Year 10) girls. It was to be a sharp learning curve for me as a young teacher. Many of those boys and girls would have had Statements of SEN today. A number would certainly have been categorised as having EBD (emotional and behavioural difficulties). We 'cared' about the pupils and in various ways spent a great deal of our free time with them on a range of activities and projects. When I got married in 1975, my group came to the church bearing a range of rather odd gifts. It made the day for me.

My husband John and I moved back to the south of England because of his work and I took a job at a College of Further Education in Berkshire. In December 1977 at the age of 28, I had my daughter Elizabeth. I wanted children and really enjoyed being pregnant and secretly hoped for a girl. John was less sure about having children. The pregnancy was not difficult for the majority of the time but towards the end the doctors became concerned. Two weeks before Christmas I was admitted to hospital for a 'few tests'. After an amniocentesis to confirm that the baby's lungs were mature, Elizabeth was induced on 30 December 1977.

I had wanted to have a 'natural' birth, so I was not in favour of induction or the epidural, used in case there needed to be a Caesarean section. As a 'new' mum I felt very intimidated by the whole process and totally unable to counter the recommendations of the medical professionals. I was very much under their control, vulnerable and afraid in case I 'harmed' my baby in any way. When she finally appeared after a labour lasting eight hours, weighing in at 4 lb 2 oz, she was whisked to the other side of the room where a paediatrician was waiting to receive her. She did not breathe for a few moments but soon demonstrated the maturity of her lungs and indeed continued to do so for the next six months! Elizabeth was taken up to the special care baby unit for observation and was supposed to remain there until she reached the magical weight of 5 lb. I remember the feelings of that first night of motherhood. I was very miserable, alone, wired up to various monitors and without my baby.

The next day I was allowed to see Elizabeth. We began to get to know each other over the 'dinner table' so to speak and I slowly began to feel glad that I was a mother after all. I had so looked forward to meeting this little being and imagined that life would be calm and serene; indeed, this was what the magazines and books suggested. This was not to be. The whole experience was dominated by the feeling that at any time I might do something wrong that would cause irreparable damage to this tiny baby. I felt totally unable to cope without medical support, and any notions of 'natural' motherhood seemed far away.

I was placed in the post-natal ward where all the other mothers had their babies in cribs beside their beds during the day. I was the only one whose baby was not there. Every two hours I was called up to the special care unit and it was stressed that regular feeding for a small baby was very important. I absorbed the knowledge. Everything around me in the special care unit was sterilised and scrubbed. Again I took in the information around me. One night while I was up there feeding Elizabeth, one of the babies died. There was a hush about the place. It was a strange moment and I remember feeling so very sad. I looked around at all the 'goldfish bowls' (incubators) with their various blue and pink tags and I was very aware of the battle for life going on in so many of them.

Two days later I was taken to the operating theatre when I haemorrhaged in the middle of the night. For me this was the final straw. When I came round from the anaesthetic, I cried copiously and gave vent to all the fears and emotions which had been bottling up. Elizabeth was brought down from the special care unit five floors above me and the two of us were placed in a side ward. Now I had my baby with me things seemed to improve and two weeks later we both went home, having achieved the magical 5 lb target set for us as 'MumandbabyElizabeth'.

Home contained a dog aged 14 and my mother, who had come to stay to look after all of us and who began to sterilise the house on my instruction. As I had done in hospital, so I continued to do at home. I was even setting my alarm clock every two hours in the night to wake Elizabeth in order to feed her. Elizabeth and I settled to a routine of no sleep and constant crying! At six weeks we had a terrible scare when we discovered her choking in her cot. I was concerned that it might have been a cot death had I not found her in time and became even more unsure of myself as a 'competent' mother. The whole experience of motherhood in the first six months was traumatic. I never felt in control and was convinced that anything I did or did not do was going to be wrong. The hospital experience had undermined me completely.

After six months, Elizabeth started to sleep at night and from then on life began to settle down. I began to relax and consequently so did she and we found ourselves really getting to know each other. The intimacy of the next six months was wonderful and I began to enjoy being a mother as I watched Elizabeth's growth and development with love and fascination.

When Elizabeth was 13 months old I found I was expecting another baby. Ten weeks into the pregnancy I threatened to miscarry and was told to go into hospital for a rest. I declined. John had just started a new job in the West Midlands and there was no one to look after Elizabeth if I went into hospital. So I said the new baby must take its chance; what would be would be. My son Michael arrived on 31 October 1979, weighing 8 lb 2 oz, after a hard but enjoyable eight-hour labour. He greeted the world with a yell and then began feeding. When I awoke next morning, I had my own 'goldfish bowl' by my bed and instantly became the proud mother of a 'bouncing' baby boy. I glowed with motherly pride and happiness.

Having children changes your life. On reflection the births of my two children, while very different, were for me the most wonderful, traumatic, confusing and disturbing experiences. With the birth of my daughter, my first-born, the world became a different place and 'I' a different person within it. The perceived stability surrounding the roles in my life as daughter, woman, wife, lecturer and friend were totally upturned by the birth, after a month in hospital, of my daughter. This tiny baby proceeded to dominate my life for the next 22 months. Relationships with 'others' were filtered through a lens of infant needs and demands. Only in relation to these did I consider my own identity, if I considered it at all through the haze of lost sleep, little food and snatched conversations.

With the birth of my second child the world did not lurch so violently. The baby had read the same books I had read about parental needs (sleep, food, and contact with other adults) and soon fell into a convenient understanding regarding the ways of the world. His needs would be met quickly, simply, lovingly and then he would be content to allow me time to be me; to grow both as a mother and as a new person within this changing identity. I never thought about returning to full-time paid employment outside the home, but threw myself into my new demanding, full-time, unpaid employment at home with my two small children under the age of two. My children were healthy and increasingly fun. The days were spent in the small, essential routines which make up the lives of mothers/fathers at home with young children. These routines began to restore some sense of stability. I was able to think beyond the immediate needs of two small but demanding human beings and regard 'tomorrow' as an inevitable extension of today. Tomorrow would appear and it would, thankfully, be much the same as today.

The shattering of that developing stability occurred on a Sunday morning in late November when we found my son in his cot, deep in a coma. He was twitching slightly but there was no other response. He was 13 months old. He had not been ill; he had shown no signs of anything that might suggest that there was a problem. Over the next few days he remained unconscious and still, except for the strange and disturbing fits which periodically twitched his strong little body. He had suffered a brain haemorrhage but the cause has never really been satisfactorily explained. It seems possible that he had an infantile stroke.

Michael was in a coma for five days and when he did open his eyes a week later we did not know the extent of any brain damage that might have occurred. At 6 months old he had crawled; at 7 months he had walked; at 10 months he was running around; at one year old he had a limited but rapidly expanding vocabulary. Now at 14 months old he could no longer even sit up. The stroke had left my son with a left-sided hemiplegia and epilepsy. We did not know at this stage what level of intellectual impairment had occurred, but over the next few years it became apparent that Michael had a considerable degree of learning disability as well as physical impairment. I have no recollection of feeling any sense of injustice that this should have happened to my son. It had happened and it was now up to us to do the best we could for Michael and to accept that the present reality was now our normality. I was determined that Michael would be 'normal'. Perhaps I refused to accept the extent of what had happened and I confused my normality with that of others. 'Difference' emerges as the perception of normality changes and I may have been reluctant to acknowledge and celebrate such difference.

Certainly our 'normality' changed. Peace was the first thing to go; the peace that comes on a rainy afternoon when a baby is sleeping and a small child is engrossed, playing contentedly. Now our 'normality' included endless trips to assessment clinics, physiotherapy units, hospitals, health clinics. A whole army of professionals now descended on us: speech therapists, social workers and medical professionals. If the house was chaotic, somehow it now mattered whereas it hadn't before. I now felt judged on my performance as a mother. It seemed as though there were queues of people waiting to assess Michael and, by implication, me. How much had *we* done this week? What progress had *we* made? How hard had *we* worked at his physiotherapy?

Michael would try to hide when someone knocked at the door, believing it to signal the arrival of yet another professional bent on prodding, poking or annoying him in some other way. If we decided to go out for a walk or for tea and some therapist called either late for an appointment or unannounced ('I was just passing ... it will save me a visit next Tuesday') it was unsatisfactory and inconvenient all round. The attitude was definitely that as a mother I should be ready and available with my 'poor child' at all times to suit their convenience. There seemed to be little doubt in the minds of the professionals that a 'good' mother of a disabled child would be ready in an instant for the professionals who were coming to 'help'. This was certainly seen as being more important than a walk in the park on a sunny September afternoon, or a game of 'Pooh sticks' from the bridge on a windy October day. Our time didn't seem important to anyone except us. On our first visit to the paediatric outpatients' clinic, Elizabeth, Michael and I waited for four hours to see the consultant.

During the year after his illness, Michael made some improvements. He began slowly to walk again, to climb, and to fall off. He could not use his left arm and this made climbing a hazardous operation but one which he seemed driven to do. As a mother I learnt to sit and watch in a sort of numb anticipation of the inevitable scream. Other mums would rush up and help Michael, when all he wanted was to do it for himself, even if it meant falling off yet again. An understanding physiotherapist fitted him with a special helmet designed for epileptic fits, but it was wonderful as protective head-gear when climbing. The professionals recommended that Michael attend nursery at the age of three. It was really hard to leave him. Elizabeth was with him for a while, but she soon left to start school and he was on his own. I felt his vulnerability or perhaps it was my own. He easily lost his balance and often came home with lumps and bumps because he had fallen and had not had his helmet on. Michael began to show signs of frustration and anger with the other children. He was better with older children and adults who were more tolerant and appreciated some of the difficulties he faced and the effort he made in order to do many things, which others took for granted.

In 1984 Michael began school. I never doubted that he would go anywhere but the local primary school with his sister and friends. At first all went really well at school. The reception class teacher really admired him and, in return, I admired her. She enjoyed facilitating his learning and gave great thought to activities at which he could succeed to build his confidence. She really tried to include Michael in everything the class did. At Christmas, a new intake of children meant that Michael had to move up to the next class and to a very different teacher, who made it clear from the start that, in her opinion, Michael should be in a special school. She set out to prove that she was right!

This was just after the implementation of the recommendations of the Warnock Report (DES 1978) in the 1981 Education Act which introduced Statementing. It was suggested that Michael go through the Statementing process, but it was not clear then how the system would work, nor in whose interest it would be. I was concerned that the head teacher of the school might use it to exclude Michael. There began what can only be described as a campaign of spite against Michael, then a little boy aged 5.

I have since wondered if the campaign was really against me for not just accepting the head teacher's view of the situation and doing as I was told. Any approach to the school brought the response that we were being 'unrealistic' about his abilities and should send him to a special school. I was extremely vulnerable as a mother, very emotional and easily reduced to tears about the whole thing. The frustration and hurt were almost paralysing. I could not understand how professionals could be so dismissive of a child who was doing his best at the age of five to be accepted in the school community. John had to deal with the head teacher. He had a matter-of-fact approach and said that if there were any problems she was to deal with us and not take it out on Michael.

The situation was resolved when in 1985, we moved to a village in Shropshire and both Michael and Elizabeth attended the village school. Michael settled very well. He was with all the village children. There was some minor bullying, but nothing really serious and for the most part he was well accepted. Elizabeth, however, was unhappy and very soon moved to another school where she settled. It meant that Michael was on his own at the school with no big sister to support him. This worried me much more than it did him.

With both children in school I decided to return to teaching. The village was conveniently situated for three LEAs. One of them immediately offered me some work as a home tutor, which I did for two years, before taking a post in the learning support department of a school in a neighbouring LEA. I was the named teacher for a number of students who had Statements of SEN. They were all boys and had specific learning difficulties (SpLD), many with behavioural difficulties as well. I became involved with the work of the learning support department at a time when special needs teaching was beginning to alter dramatically due to changes in education policy and soon I was working almost full time in the school with a range of children with SEN.

By the late 1980s, LEAs were having to become more conscious of the issues surrounding integration and inclusion. The 1981 Education Act was now beginning to impact on schools and classrooms. The unit for pupils with moderate learning disabilities (MLD) in the school was closing and the pupils were being included into mainstream classes with support from a teacher or Learning Support Assistant (LSA). A growing number of pupils were identified as having EBD and dyslexia, the latter of which was just beginning to be accepted as a learning difficulty in the LEA. Pupils in the school who needed support had to go through the stages of Statementing to secure funding and additional support for their identified educational needs. Years 9, 10 and 11 (ages 13–16) were 'setted' for subjects such as mathematics and English. This created 'sink' groups where all the pupils with learning difficulties and disabilities were grouped together. Many of the parents of children perceived as having SEN were now very keen to pursue Statements to ensure support for their children and there were many 'battles' with the LEA. It is worth noting that there were very few children with disabilities in the school, as the LEA had segregated provision for children with physical disabilities, cerebral palsy and cystic fibrosis.

This was around the time of the 1988 Education Reform Act and pressures were being put on us as teachers to 'raise standards' and improve our place in the new league tables. At the same time (late 1980s to early 1990s), funding in the county was being drastically reduced as a result of government cutbacks and it became increasingly difficult to support children with SEN unless they carried a Statement. The LEA, however, was reluctant to increase the number of Statements because of the commitment to funding. Once a Statement of SEN was issued, there was a legal requirement for the LEA to meet those needs. Thus a vicious circle was set up within which parents of children with special needs had to fight to secure funding to support the educational requirements of their children. The situation was also affected by the introduction of the National Curriculum and many children and their teachers were having serious problems with the newly imposed rigidity. Consequently, both teachers and parents wanted children Statemented. However, by this time it was taking over a year to get Statements through and often only then with a tremendous fight from the parents themselves. As teachers we could do little except recommend that a Statement was necessary. At this point the LEA usually refused to continue the process, arguing that the school could meet the needs of the child without further funding or provision. Educational psychologists were the real gatekeepers to funding at this time, for they were the ones who sanctioned the recommendation for a Statement. This made life difficult for many educational psychologists who were employed by the LEAs but who could find themselves called to tribunals by parents to speak out on behalf of the child, effectively against the wishes of their employers, the LEA. Many left the service and for a time we found it very difficult to get an educational psychologist into school to assess a child for a Statement.

By the end of the 1980s I was considering the secondary education provision available for Michael who was now 10, approaching 11. During the whole of his primary school life I had never considered the need for special education. He could 'cope' in the mainstream, certainly at primary level with teachers willing to include and support him. As I watched the struggles of the parents of pupils with SEN at secondary level to secure funding, I became concerned. Perhaps Michael's educational needs *should* be identified through the provision of a Statement. Michael himself was getting further behind academically each year. His understanding of concepts was clearly limited and he often needed a great deal of help to complete basic tasks. How would he fare in the larger, macho environment of the secondary sector?

My concern was increased by my experience as a teacher. I was now teaching at the mainstream secondary school which Michael would, under normal circumstances, attend. While the learning support staff in the school were eager, and inclusion was becoming more accepted in theory, there were considerable strains and stresses developing between the theory and the practice. Support was limited even if children did have Statements. This often meant that breaktimes and lunchtimes were not covered. For many children who present challenging behaviour, or who may be bullied because of their perceived 'difference', these can be stressful periods.

This was also a time when the pressure of conflicting values in educational policy was becoming more apparent. Considerable emphasis was being laid on the need to improve the position of the school in the performance league tables, while at the same time tension was being created by the need to 'integrate' pupils with SEN. Most of my professional work was now done in the challenging 'sink' groups, working with a mixture of pupils who were disaffected, struggling with the demands of the curriculum and who had special educational needs, including dyslexia, MLD and EBD. I was very concerned at the ethos in some of these classes and did not feel that the culture of the school was really supportive of inclusion. It was becoming obvious to me as a teacher, that there were going to be casualties among some of the more vulnerable children, who were after all 'pioneers' of inclusion. When frontiers are challenged and pushed back, there are inevitably casualties. I did not want my son to be one of them.

During his last two years at primary school, Michael became more frustrated and more aggressive. He was becoming increasingly aware of the ways in which his disability limited him in certain mainstream settings. He had little patience with his work and was quick to take offence, often retaliating quickly and inappropriately and, despite the support of the teachers, issues were arising which were causing Michael great distress.

Michael had put great enthusiasm and energy into learning to ride a bicycle. With determination and a number of accidents, he mastered this and was very proud of his newly acquired skill. He attended cycling proficiency lessons after school with the rest of his class, and was looking forward to passing the test. But because he could only hold with one hand, the rules did not permit him to take the test along with all the other children. Michael was distraught. At the age of 20 he still remembered this and the great hurt he had felt ten years previously. He felt excluded, 'different'. As his mother, I too felt his exclusion and distress. Knowing how much he was hurt by situations such as this, I was anxious about his reception in secondary school. I was very concerned about the overall approach to children with special educational needs and especially those with behavioural problems in the school. So in agreement with the head teacher of the primary school, we requested a Statement of SEN for Michael. He was epileptic, had a left-sided hemiplegia, learning difficulties and was displaying challenging behaviour. Additional (funded) support in school seemed to be the answer.

It took 12 months of fighting to get a Statement for Michael. The senior educational psychologist and I clashed on our first meeting. He tested Michael one morning at the primary school and then told me that his recommendation was based on the 'considerable time' he had spent with Michael, by which he meant 20 minutes. His professional opinion was that Michael could attend a mainstream school and that a Statement was not necessary. I was not impressed. He never thought it was worth asking me, as Michael's mother, for my perspective. Nor did he ask me my view as a teacher working in the learning support department of the very school Michael would attend. I was by this time working almost full time, teaching children with special educational needs in mainstream classrooms. I was very aware of the issues that arose every day even with support, which created tensions and difficulties for teachers and children alike. I was increasingly concerned that Michael's complex and multiple needs could not be addressed in a mainstream classroom without adequate support. He would be placed in one of the 'sink' groups and would indeed do just that.

In a neighbouring LEA there was a special school which had a very good reputation for encouraging children to achieve in all aspects of their school life. Michael and I went to have a look at the school and we were very impressed. Michael felt very comfortable and welcome and the 'same as everyone else'. However, overturning the LEA's decision, in the light of the educational psychologist's report, was difficult and we prepared for a fight and an appeal. I spoke to the head teacher of the special school, who agreed to hold a place for Michael. He had experienced these situations before and understood the problems. With only three weeks to go before Michael was due to go to secondary school, and only after threats, verbal battles and long, fraught telephone calls, the LEA agreed to the provision of a Statement and to support our application for a place at the special school. It had been a very traumatic and unpleasant experience for us and especially for Michael. The Statement finally came through in November 1990 by which time Michael was settled at the special school.

It felt very strange to celebrate the fact that my son was attending a special school when I believed in inclusion. I had chosen segregation for my son because I believed that the mainstream school he was allocated was not ready for children like him. But if children such as Michael did not go to mainstream schools, why and how would schools ever need to change? I was aware that I was not being true to my belief that all children should be educated in mainstream schools and that it was the duty of such schools to welcome all children. Although the rhetoric was there, the real commitment to make inclusion work seemed to be missing. On reflection, I have no regrets about the decision as far as Michael and his education are concerned. Michael and I have talked about these issues in great depth. He is older now and has had the chance to reflect on the decisions made at the time, often by people other than himself. He undoubtedly felt 'isolated' from the other children in the village. However, he did make friendships at the special school, which have stood the tests of time and distance. The opportunities he had at the school were very real and he was encouraged to make the most of every opportunity which came his way.

Home–school relations were strong and when Michael's challenging behaviour grew more challenging at home (and for a period of time at school as well), the school proved extremely supportive of John and me as parents, as well as of Michael. There were incidents which would inevitably have led to exclusion from a mainstream school, with all the attendant problems of social rejection that such exclusion brings. Instead, Michael was given space within which to learn how to deal with his own frustrations and disappointments.

Both professionally and personally, 1989 to 1996 was a difficult time for me. I was working with boys who presented challenging behaviour. I spent my days trying to encourage them in their learning. This was no easy task and was often made more difficult by the general culture of the school and the attitude of some members of staff. While far from condoning the behaviour of some of these boys, it was often not difficult to imagine how situations escalated from minor skirmishes to full-scale battles given the inflexibility and lack of understanding by some of the staff. I would go from a day spent working with 'difficult' boys to an evening spent working with my own 'difficult' son. I felt great empathy with the boys and their families. I really tried to like them, to care about them, just as I hoped that the teachers would 'care' about Michael. I have to acknowledge that it wasn't always easy.

Michael was becoming extremely difficult at home and it was suggested that the problem was family-related. We were told that family counselling would help. The social worker, a young woman of 25 with no experience of this kind of work, duly arrived with disastrous results. Her 'professional' expertise was not up to the task and the experience was very harmful to us as a family at that time. I find it interesting to reflect on the fact that these professionals never really considered talking to me as the person closest to Michael. As both a secondary school teacher and the mother of an older daughter, now between 16 and 17, I was well aware of the joys of adolescence. There were other issues at this time, which were exacerbating the situation for Michael. His epilepsy was proving hard to control and the fits were becoming more violent. A number of them hospitalised him as a result of injuries sustained in the fall. One occurred when he had taken Elizabeth's bicycle in a moment of temper and set out on a very dangerous main road. Medication had always been a problem. Michael had tried every frontline drug for epilepsy with varying degrees of success, but had never gained complete control. These are powerful drugs and there were unacceptable side effects for Michael, often relating to behaviour and general awareness. Michael was sent for neurological tests to a senior specialist in Manchester, who recommended that he take a drug with known side effects of aggression, which we were not aware of at the time. We had talked to him about the problems associated with Michael's epilepsy and sought his professional and 'expert' help. When we found out about the side effects of the drug, we felt very let down by the medical professionals.

While I was sure that adolescence was playing its part along with frustration, I also felt that there was more to it than that. I was sure that the drugs and the fits were responsible for much of his challenging behaviour and was determined to keep trying to find the most suitable medication as well as some understanding of the condition and how it might impact on Michael. I began to read about anti-convulsant drugs and realised that there could be side effects which affected behaviour. I had raised this issue before and been told that the drugs were not responsible. Then I read about a drug, Lamictal, which appeared to have few side effects and was considered to be very effective as a frontline drug in the treatment of epilepsy. The consultant agreed that this was a possibility for Michael and changed his medication. The results were amazing. Michael was much more alert and obviously considerably happier. His behaviour began to change. He did not sleep as much in the day; he began to laugh more often and share jokes rather than believe that the joke was about him and react.

However, he was still having fits and his behaviour would become more erratic prior to a seizure. Medically there was evidence to show that 'spikes' from the damaged right hemisphere were also affecting the left hemisphere of the brain. In a subsequent brain scan we learnt for the first time (Michael now being 18), that the right hemisphere had been almost destroyed by the stroke and was serving no useful function at all. When Michael was 19 we met, by chance, a doctor who had trained in Oxford with a brain surgeon who performed hemispherectomies (the removal of one hemisphere of the brain), to 'cure' severe epilepsy. After a series of tests, Michael was offered the chance to have a right-sided hemispherectomy in an attempt to eradicate or at least reduce the seizures.

Michael decided to have the operation. It was his decision and he was quite amazing. His strength, good humour, sheer bravery and determination earned him many friends in the hospital. It also earned him my everlasting respect and admiration. I was so proud of the way he dealt with the whole thing. Michael had the operation in Oxford and was in hospital for two weeks. This was in 1999 and I was studying and teaching at university. During the recovery period I returned to work to teach on a residential weekend for teachers studying for their Masters degrees. I was exhausted and very emotional I am sure, but the complete change of environment, the concentration on something other than anxiety, was almost relaxing. I returned a day later to Oxford and Michael, feeling renewed and able to support him again. I was quite glad to be a working mum.

By 1996, after five years at the special school, Michael felt that he needed a change of environment. The local College of Further Education was suggested but Michael felt that for many reasons it wasn't what he wanted. I had heard of a special FE college in Nottinghamshire which was for young adults from 16 to 19 years of age but which was also a retraining college for people who, because of ill health, had to retrain for a different career. Elizabeth was visiting universities and Michael was keen to visit the college. He was impressed, as were we, and the battle for funding began (again) with the local LEA who were responsible for the application to the Further Education Funding Council (FEFC).

The LEA placed as many obstacles in our way as they could, despite the support from Michael's school. Professionally I knew that absolute determination to 'win' was the only way. It does not make you popular with the professionals and I am sure that my reputation as a 'pushy' and 'unrealistic' and undoubtedly 'selfish' mum was confirmed during the meetings between the LEA, John and myself. I had often told other parents to 'stick to their guns' when they were trying to get a Statement for their child. You have to be the 'immovable force' and this is not easy for parents who are in awe of professionals. Within three weeks we received confirmation that the FEFC would provide the full funding for Michael, and that September Michael began four years at the college.

He really grew up at the college and had many wonderful opportunities. He visited many countries, playing football for the county special football team and on one occasion for England's special team. He represented the college on a visit to Finland and gave a short talk on the visit on his return. He learnt to live in close proximity with others who were not family and to appreciate and respect the feelings and belongings of those around him. He met his future wife at college. They married in 2001 amid tears of joy all round. It will not be an easy life for them, but they are learning to manage things for themselves. They live independently but with support from friends and relatives. They are both continuing their education at the local FE College and hope to find a role for themselves in sports education for people with disabilities and learning difficulties.

1995 was an interesting year at home. Elizabeth was working for her 'A' levels, and Michael was doing four GCSEs and I was trying to complete a Masters degree at university. Tensions ran high and often I did not begin my studies until ten or eleven o'clock at night. Now when I work with teachers doing higher degrees, I am able to understand the demands on them. In 1996 I was given the opportunity to begin a funded PhD related to issues of educational inclusion. I found that much of what I was reading related to my own experiences as either a teacher or a mother in the field of SEN. I chose therefore to do a feminist, qualitative study which involved listening to the experiences of other mothers and teachers of children with SEN/disabilities.

When I reflect on the years working with children with SEN and bringing up a son with SEN, a particular experience comes to mind. I was working with the head of English, Peter, with a particularly 'challenging' group of Year 11 boys. They had tried our levels of acceptance and understanding by some rather extreme and unpleasant behaviour. When the bell rang marking the end of the lesson and the boys left the room, Peter looked at me, sighed with relief and said: 'Aren't you glad you don't have to have your Christmas dinner with that lot?' I said nothing.

My 'little boy' is now a man of 24 and is enjoying married life, so the origins of this story are not located in the tragedy model of disability. However, they do lie within my own experiences as a mother and teacher of children with special educational needs. My own professional and personal experiences since the early 1980s left me with a desire to know whether there were other women who had similar experiences and if there were, what insights our lives might offer into issues related to inclusion, exclusion and constructions of difference.

Personal and political: reflections

In writing this particular account of certain experiences, I am focusing on aspects of my personal and professional life, which connect with the other stories told in the book. Some of these memories are almost 20 years old, but my experiences during that time have only gone some of the way to reassure me that things are really changing for the 20 per cent of children deemed to have special educational needs. I do not seek to lay blame on teachers or other professionals, for clearly changes have been made in policy and practice, but I have yet to be convinced that these changes are making a significant impact on the nature and quality of provision for the majority of these children. Stories I read today, of the struggles of mothers to create normality for their children through mainstream schooling (e.g. McIntyre 2004), still suggest resistance from professionals and anger and bitterness from parents. Why then, after 20 years of inclusive policies and increasing support for SEN, have we not achieved a more inclusive system?

In telling my own story and making the private public, my aim is two-fold. Firstly, I want to place myself firmly in the frame as one of the mother-teachers. I want to identify with them and leave no doubt as to my subjective position. Our stories are not objective accounts but personal, emotional, subjective reflections which are subject to the passage of time and, therefore, imperfect recall. But it is not the detail which ultimately matters, rather the nature of the emotions, the pain, pleasure, excitement, disappointment and hope; what it felt like to occupy certain spaces in time; the caring support from some professionals or the 'orthodoxy' of the rebuttal from others. Secondly, I want to highlight some of the issues which caused me concern during my personal and professional life, and which I felt were not yet resolved; issues which the mother-teachers also raise in their stories. It is for the reader to decide if these issues still contribute to the 'exclusion' of groups of children and their families. What does emerge from all the stories is the complexity of these issues and the contradictions which seem to underpin the whole debate around inclusion and SEN/disabilities. I have attempted very briefly to draw out some of the threads which I feel emerge from the stories, but I hope that readers will relate to them through the lens of their own experience.

Complexities and contradictions

In Chapter 1 I identified some of the perceived barriers arising from contradictions of principle within the two key strands of education policy over this time. Within my own story some of these tensions and contradictions are visible. They emerge again in some of the other stories (e.g. Deborah, Joan and Julia). The issues of SEN and inclusion within mainstream schools are immensely complex and are not confined to policy. They emerge in the ethos and structures of schools and the individuals within them, the processes of assessment, professional perceptions and relationships, the curriculum, the training and support of teachers and in many other areas. Aspects of all these are visible in the stories in different contexts and degrees of contradiction and complexity.

Inter/intraconnections

My own experience suggested that I was not 'either' a mother 'or' a teacher of children with special needs; that the issues were more inter- and intrarelated. The notion that we leave our private experiences at home when we enter the public domain was not the way it was for me, as the example at the end of my story suggests. The other stories also reflect this interconnectedness (e.g. Truda's and Kate's stories). The experiences of the mother-teachers reflect the 'messiness' of lived experience, the struggle to balance personal and professional needs and values. Uncertainties emerge through the emotional nature of these relationships with other professionals as both a mother and a teacher and it is interesting to note in the stories (e.g. Truda, Sonia, Julia and Deborah) how 'emotionally' difficult it is to be a mother-teacher struggling to deal with the perceptions of other educational professionals in relation to one's own children.

Shared understandings

It would appear that despite the discourse of rights and social justice there are still many unresolved issues in relation to inclusion and SEN. While the discourse of inclusion is evident, the discourse of standards and competition prevails, creating tensions for parents and professionals alike. My story charts my own changing awareness of these issues and reflects the moving context around policies of inclusion which is still making it difficult for professionals and parents fully to join forces. They still appear to have different agendas as Todd and Higgins (1998) note. Whether in the home, hospital, clinic or school, the place and agenda may appear to parents to be that of the expert. It is not surprising, therefore, if parents feel that this space represents a place for either submission or resistance rather than for shared negotiation and understanding. All the stories reflect aspects of the 'gap' between parents and professionals to a greater or lesser degree and from both sides (e.g. Sonia, Kate, Truda). However, some also reflect the moments of joy when the gap appears to close even a little (e.g. Julia's story).

Perceptions of difference

The cycling proficiency story was a seemingly small example of the construction of difference which we as adults should have dealt with in a completely different way, but the memory of being excluded from what all the other children were doing remains with Michael to this day. It was a moment which changed my own perceptions as a professional and a number of the other stories reflect similar moments (e.g. Sonia, Deborah, Kate, Truda, Julia). The studies of Read (2000), Russell (2003) and Todd (2003) suggest that much can be learnt from asking parents of children with SEN/disabilities about such experiences. Notions of 'difference' construct tragedy out of disability for these mother-teachers, and many of the *difficulties* of difference tend to arise out of the perceptions and expectations of the professionals as the stories suggest in different ways.

Professional knowledge, power, experience and SEN/ disability

My experiences raised questions for me around what counts as professional knowledge. 'Professional knowledge' in SEN is an interesting issue, as I noted in Chapter 2. 'Expert knowledge' is conferred on those who have usually attended courses, acquired certificates, etc. Yet the whole area of 'training' and professional development in SEN still appears to be somewhat contentious and ill-defined. Many LEAs now offer a range of training opportunities, but claims to professional knowledge in SEN still appear to vary from individual to individual and from context to context. It is argued (Corbett 1996) that the very perpetuation of 'expert' notions of SEN works against inclusion, for as long as expertise is seen as emanating from differently organised and conceptualised training courses for such 'specialists' SEN will be seen as separate and 'different'. The notion of the SEN 'expert' also has to exist within different discourses which see inclusion as part of 'just good teaching practice' or, contra-dictorily, having no place within the competitive policies of the market.

In her recent research with parents about partnership and SEN, Liz Todd asked parents what advice they would give to a friend going through the (SEN) assessment process. The replies resonated with me:

> *Push for everything, don't give up.*
> *Keep an eye on your child. Keep him close.*
> *Grit your teeth and hang on. It's not worth it – hope you get more than we did.*
> *Get an independent report and ask around.*
> *In the early stages try to find out as much as you can. Insist on talking to the people involved.*

(Todd 2003: 290)

My son's educational experiences stretched over twenty years from the early 1980s but the quotes above and the stories of Sonia, Deborah, Truda, Kate, Joan and Julia suggest that the experiences for many children with SEN/disabilities and their mothers may not have changed as much as one might have hoped and expected.

4 Sonia: tragedy or normality?

She said, I didn't ever have to look after him. I can remember standing there thinking, 'What's this woman talking about', you know, because it never entered our heads ... I mean he is our child ...

He was very, very floppy and he still is quite floppy and you have to be very careful picking him up ... However, apart from this and his epilepsy, touch wood, he has no other problems at all.

(Sonia)

When I met Sonia she was in her mid-forties, and lived with her husband Ken, a former social worker, who became a policeman with the local police force, and their two children, Lauren, then aged 14, and Christopher, then aged 11. Christopher is autistic and has profound and multiple learning disabilities (PMLD). He has frequent seizures and attends a special day school. Sonia teaches at a special residential centre which caters for children and adults with severe epilepsy and EBD.

Sonia was born in the north-west of England. Her father was a low-ranking civil servant and her mother did not work outside the house. Sonia had a younger sister but it was Sonia who was considered the 'brains of the family'. However, she chose to leave school after 'A' levels to work with 'mentally handicapped' adults in a long-stay hospital, although she had received no prior training for this. At the age of 24, Sonia made the decision to teach and by 1978 she was teaching in the north-west of England working with adults with learning difficulties. In 1982 Sonia married Ken, then a social worker, whom she had known for some years. In 1984, Lauren was born and Sonia took maternity leave, soon returning to work. Her own mother was very supportive and helped with the new baby, so when Sonia found that she was pregnant again three years later, her aim was to return to work after the birth. Things were not to be so straightforward this time and in 1987 she decided to give up work.

Lauren was a 'normal three-year-old' and very demanding but both Sonia and Ken wanted another child and they hoped that the new baby would be a boy. Sonia had suffered a miscarriage the year before and had been very upset by the loss of the baby at almost 12 weeks. Eight weeks into this pregnancy she had another threatened miscarriage and was ordered to rest. To the relief of the anxious parents, an amniocentesis revealed that the baby was fine, 'completely normal'. The parents were reassured and told 'not to worry'.

Christopher was born with a cleft nose, which apparently is now quite rare. His nose was completely separated by the cleft but it was successfully repaired. Sonia reflected on the implications of the cleft nose and her own lack of awareness of what this could mean. Christopher was not in special care, which she felt surprised many people.

At the age of four months Christopher had a fit and was rushed to hospital where he remained for the next six months. Only at this point did Sonia and Ken begin to realise the severity of Christopher's condition, although it was never really explained to them by the doctors. It was left to the physiotherapist to tell them about Christopher's condition. Christopher was diagnosed as having a split brain, which means that the left and right hemispheres are not connected. The split went right through from his nose to his brain, which means that part of his brain is missing. For the next 12 months Christopher and Sonia were in and out of hospital. The quote at the beginning reflects the view of the health visitor when Christopher left the hospital. Although Christopher is entitled to support from the local authority, which includes up to 82 nights' respite care and a 'home-from-home' service, Sonia has never felt the need to use these services: 'He doesn't have respite care or anything, I mean he is our child and we're quite happy with him and I don't need anything.'

In the spring of 1988, Sonia had to go into hospital to have a hysterectomy and when she came home she was unable to lift Christopher, so she applied for help, 'the one occasion when I asked for support'. The authority offered the services of a nursery nurse to look after Christopher. Sonia laughed ironically as she said, 'I am still waiting for her to arrive! And this despite constant telephone calls. In the event my sister came to stay.'

Undoubtedly, Sonia preferred the privacy of doing things herself for Christopher. She hated the invasion of the public professionals in personal family life:

After all, you don't always want these people trampling through your private life do you? ... If I wanted a Mediloo I would have to be means tested because there would be a social worker involved and I think, do I want all these people coming into my life?

Sonia's husband Ken used to be a social worker with the local authority, but he 'had to get out' once Christopher was born. He couldn't cope with 'doing it all day' and having Christopher as well. Sonia noted:

Ken still finds it difficult to deal with the intrusion of the social services. He hated being visited by his former colleagues from the social services team on which he used to work.

Ken had 'found it really difficult dealing with Christopher', but Sonia described him as 'doting ... being absolutely everything' to Christopher. Sonia explained that Ken also found it difficult dealing with Christopher's school, although he visited it frequently on his rounds while on police duty in the area:

If he sees something he doesn't like he will come home and then go back. He saw him [Christopher] once in his chair in the middle of the afternoon. He was in a pile of rubbish, so I had to ring up and sort of say 'How is Christopher?' and he was found in his buggy at two o'clock in the afternoon. Why wasn't he in his chair at the table with all the other children? ... They didn't do it again ... it stopped straight away.

Since having Christopher, their lives have changed considerably. Sonia was very matter of fact when she said that Christopher has slept in their bedroom since he came home from hospital because of his seizures during the night. He has his own bed in the room by the side of Sonia:

I got fed up of going into another room and coming back to bed again so I just have him by my side now. He couldn't be left as a baby as he was having fits constantly. Now he has about three each night but he doesn't have many during the day. I make sure that he is turned on his side and he's OK and he's not got his arms trapped ... They're quite frightening for him.

Sonia made no other comment on the nightly disturbance except to say that she had got used to it, accepted it and just got on with it. It was part of her normal routine now.

Over the years, Sonia had dealt with many different professionals in relation to Christopher's condition. The doctor who cared for

Christopher in his early days now works at the same centre as Sonia. She noted that 'Doctor N. is not one of my favourite people':

> The GP we've got here is a very nice chap. He tends to let me direct what's going on. If Christopher is ill he'll come immediately and speak to me on the telephone. I feel I am the one in control. When I go to him he will sort of say, 'What do you think?'

Through her professional life at the centre, Sonia has gained both knowledge and experience about the drugs used in the treatment of epilepsy. With this and the knowledge she has gained while dealing with Christopher's condition, she feels able to discuss these things with her GP and is now willing to challenge the doctors if she feels it is necessary.

Sonia has little time for those professionals who, in her opinion, are 'time wasters'. Christopher is assessed as having PMLD as well as physical disabilities. As Christopher grows bigger, mobility is becoming more of an issue for the family and so Sonia and Ken decided to explore the matter of Christopher receiving 'motability' allowance. However, the application was rejected on the grounds that:

> This time next year Christopher could be better. So I sort of said to this chap in Blackpool, that the only way Christopher was going to get better was for Jesus to come and lay his hands on him. You are talking about a severely handicapped child here. But they sent another doctor round to see him and assess whether or not we have been telling the truth.

She recalled the visit:

> This doctor walked in, took one look at Christopher and said, 'Why have I been sent here?' We had a cup of tea and the whole thing was clearly a waste of time from everybody's point of view. Whoever had been dealing with the paperwork had obviously got completely the wrong impression of what Christopher was like. In that respect I was very annoyed. This is where you have to fight. I would not have got that allowance if I hadn't had a real go, even though he is as he is.

The occupational therapist from the authority came in for some criticism as well, although Sonia felt she was being 'unprofessional' by condemning her and saying that she was a 'complete waste of time, effort and space':

> She didn't have anything to offer at all except a bath mat which when she looked in the bath she felt wouldn't fit ... She wasn't any help at all. She

went away and I thought that we had really had a wasted afternoon. I wanted to know what was available to make ours and Christopher's lives easier. It took her ten weeks to get here. I mean what about a ramp for the front door; what about a chair for him to sit on in the lounge, a bean bag even?

Despite his learning difficulties and disabilities, the family had asked for very little, but Sonia was concerned for the future. Sonia felt that her professional experience was not as useful in getting access to aids for Christopher. It had been another mother whom she had met when out with Christopher one day, who had given her some useful information as to where she might get hold of such aids in the local area.

Sonia returned to teaching part time after the birth and her mother looked after Christopher, who continued to have fits constantly as a baby. Sonia worked in a 'rough inner-city school' for the physically disabled and then took a part-time job in an ordinary primary school as an SEN teacher, eventually job sharing with other teachers, 'usually the deputies'. Sonia was explicit in her belief that SEN really meant someone with profound and multiple difficulties and disabilities. She held firmly to the belief that 'children in mainstream schools who cannot read and write, or have English as a second language' are not really those with special needs.

When Christopher was two and a half, he went to a special day school and Sonia began to think about working full time again. Sonia's mother was willing to help with Christopher, so when Sonia heard of a job at a special centre for people with epilepsy she applied. She had previously heard of the centre through her experience with Christopher. It was a large establishment and many of the special schools in the area had connections with it, so Sonia was well acquainted with its work. When she went for the interview she found that she was the only person to be interviewed. She expressed surprise at getting the job:

I don't think there was anyone more surprised than me that I got the job. I didn't think I had enough experience, I haven't got sheets of paper or an SEN diploma ... but I think they valued the experience I had. When I got there most of the other teachers didn't have any special qualifications either.

Sonia had considered trying to get a place for Christopher at the centre, but although Christopher is epileptic, she did not really think this would be a good idea. The centre caters for children and adults who present challenging behaviour:

> They have so many behavioural problems; it's not like an ordinary special school where you just have a few. You are dealing with 50, all with behavioural problems and some very, very severe psychotic behaviour.

Sonia feels that Christopher is too 'docile' and 'vulnerable' and may well be seen as a target by the other children. In many other ways, working at the centre allows Sonia to feel that she is helping Christopher; she is able to keep abreast of the latest drugs and information on epilepsy as well as ask for advice from the doctors at the centre and then relay this back to her GP.

The centre is funded on a charitable basis, but receives pupils and adults who are paid for by the LEAs. While it caters for people of all ages, the school within the 'hospital' caters for pupils aged 5–19. There is also a college for those aged 19–25 and an adult training centre:

> They go till they die really and there's quite a high proportion of residents now. There are about 60 children and I think it's about 40 college students and I would think about a couple of hundred residents who are there all the time.

The children who attend the centre do so on a residential and often permanent basis for up to 52 weeks of the year. Being a parent of a child with disabilities herself, the placing of the children at the centre for such long periods of time elicited strong reactions from Sonia. She spoke of a very diverse group of parents, ranging from those who took their children home every weekend, to others who, in her view, 'abandoned' them. It was perceived by many of the staff at the centre that there were four categories of parents who sought to send their children there. The first group were seen as 'very, very middle-class' parents who wanted to:

> get rid of the child who can't do anything ... We class them [the children] as abandoned and they come on 52-week placements ... [during which time] the child is going to be out of their sight.

The second group consisted of middle-class parents 'who are not coping and are very articulate', working through solicitors and getting reports from psychologists and other professionals to prove that the stress caused by the child on themselves is 'just too much for them to cope with'; 'middle-class Mums who take it on as their challenge to get their children into the centre … for lots of different reasons'. The third group was from 'the other end of the scale', when the intervention was usually from social services to protect the child from aggression within the family, or from the education department who felt that there were very serious special educational needs. The fourth group were those whose children attended on a daily basis. Some of these parents had taken the matter through the courts but usually with support from social services. Sonia reflected sadly on the fact that some of the parents never came to visit their children or take them home:

> We've got one or two children who have been abandoned by the time they are five and the parents never come and we know they're never going to come; they have no contact at all.

Sometimes Sonia found herself feeling resentful towards parents who 'played the system to their advantage, not the child's advantage' and condemned those parents who sent their children to the centre because they couldn't 'cope' or the child 'did not fit in with their lifestyle'. She found this very distressing. On the other hand, Sonia said that there were many parents who came every week and took their children home each weekend.

Sonia clearly felt very strongly about these issues. Her own experience was inextricably woven into her thinking here. She noted with some bitterness how some parents 'are more aware of what they can get out of the authorities and definitely know the system'. She was aware that she judged these parents by her own standards but felt that on the whole she did relate well to parents because they felt that she had empathy with them. The parents 'know I am in a similar situation. They will come to me and say, "We know you understand how we're feeling"'.

She confessed to wondering how some parents actually coped at weekends with some of the children who were so very difficult:

> They [the children] must go in the house and trash the house from the front door through. I mean I know that they pick up the microwave and throw it across the floor because they try and do it at school.

She spoke of the heartbreaking stories of parents trying to cope with their own children and attempting to lead 'normal lives'. Sonia inevitably compared her own experience of life as 'normal' and felt that it was infinitely preferable to the traumas some parents face when dealing with their children. Some of these children are so violent that even the respite care is done at school.

Some parents, however, were perceived as having 'a mission in life': they have made a point of knowing everything they can about epilepsy and 'blind you with science'. Others feel that they have been 'dealt a duff card and that everybody should be jumping to their attention and doing something for them. It's their right to get all these things'.

Sonia believed that the role of the mother was crucial for children with SEN. She cited a case of a young boy she had taught who had been illiterate and who went to a high school with 2,000 pupils. He became lost in the system because his mother 'wasn't articulate':

> If he'd had a more articulate mum she should have been knocking on the doors of the Town Hall saying, 'Just a minute, you are going to do something about this child'.

Sonia's belief was that if the parents didn't 'fight' and 'battle' for their children, then the child would receive less than he or she needed. She maintained that much of the special provision for children such as Christopher was dependent on the mother and her ability to work her way through the system. 'What you didn't ask for you didn't get' was clearly her view, although she herself asked for little. Sonia had not yet felt the need to really fight for anything for Christopher because they had either met the need themselves (within the family) or the service had been adequate. However, she did feel that things were likely to get more difficult as he got older and bigger. Her mother and sister were very supportive when necessary, but on the whole Christopher's needs were met by herself and Ken.

Professionally, Sonia also liked to retain control. She teaches history and geography (Key Stages 1 and 2) and her class usually consists of around eight to ten children aged 5–8. This particular year she had three nursery nurses although normally she only had two. Sonia was a supporter of a system which had been originally designed for use with children on the autistic spectrum, although Sonia now used it with a number of children with language problems as well. The children each had their own individual teaching bays arranged in a 'U' shape. However, Sonia saw her main challenge as accessing parts of the National Curriculum and making it relevant to the needs of the children. She felt there was a contradiction here for her as a teacher. At the centre she was having to 'push maths and English down my children', while at the same time being sceptical of many of the activities demanded by the National Curriculum. Sonia maintained that very often the connections between what the children were doing and the learning outcomes expected by the National Curriculum were tenuous and she welcomed the government's more flexible approach to curriculum for special schools.

The centre did try to establish links with mainstream schools for the children but this was not easy. According to Sonia, there are still too many fears and myths surrounding epilepsy, and many parents and teachers are still afraid of it. Two of the children from the centre had attended a mainstream primary school for one afternoon a week until one of the governors complained on behalf of some of the parents. Sonia noted:

We got the impression you can catch it [epilepsy] like flu – you know, if you touch this child you are going to be epileptic. I felt sad really. I just thought this is just lack of knowledge, lack of understanding, fear of the unknown really.

Exclusion was a real issue for many of the children who came into her care at the centre. Sonia believed that many of the children would not be accepted in mainstream schools for two reasons: the nature of their behaviour and their epilepsy. Yet in her view, the enormous cost of special residential school education was one of the factors which was promoting the drive towards inclusion. If inclusion meant just the placing of children in mainstream schools without appropriate support this could be achieved at very little cost. However, if inclusion were to be done properly it would require a great deal of financial support particularly in the early days and a real change of ethos in many mainstream schools.

The discourse of care was an important one in Sonia's professional and private life. 'Care' was an important aspect of her work and one of the problems for Sonia was the balance between the curriculum and other therapies. Issues of care and education were very important since, as a mother of a child with PMLD, she was concerned that such children were 'cared for properly'. Also as a mother of a child with SEN and as the teacher of children with SEN, Sonia felt the need for 'understanding bosses' who 'cared' about their staff. Despite family support, which was obviously important to Sonia, there were times when as a mother she needed to be with Christopher, such as hospital visits to see the consultant, for instance, or times when he was very poorly. Sonia recalled one occasion when Christopher had chickenpox and her mother was looking after him. Sonia got a phonecall at the centre to say that he was very ill and that her mother had called the doctor, who was on his way. Sonia went to the head of the centre to ask for permission to go home, which he gave very begrudgingly: 'It was sort of well, you know, "Are you coming back?" I thought, well, I don't ask for that much!'

At the centre, Sonia believed that the head saw her very much first and foremost as the professional rather than the mother of a disabled child. However, she felt that there were times when her role as mother suited the head:

> He loves the fact that I have a special needs child because he likes me to sort of help prospective parents look round and he loves for them to say something so that I can bring in the fact that I do know what they are talking about because I've got a child myself. He likes that. I can see him manoeuvring the conversation round especially if we get a parent being a little bit awkward, who has had a long history of battling with the authorities or they've got a chip on their shoulder, sort of 'well nobody suffers like I suffer, nobody understands me'.

Sometimes Sonia wanted to say nothing at all, but if she saw that parents were getting very upset she would tell them about her own circumstances to show she had some insights into at least some of their needs and fears. She lets them know that she understands the effects on home life, the strains at home, especially if she senses that there is anger between the parents.

Parental choice of school had not been a real issue for Sonia, Ken and Christopher. The LEA only had one special school in each sector (primary and secondary), a number of others having been closed. This worried Sonia especially in the secondary phase where the only special school is:

> based on a secondary school model with the National Curriculum with specialist teachers and I don't know how Christopher will cope with that. I have this feeling that eventually Christopher will be excluded within the special school because he will get therapies rather than the National Curriculum. I don't think he will go round with his class. He will be 'siphoned off'.

One afternoon a week Christopher attends the primary department of the special secondary school, but Sonia worried about this as he often comes home injured having been hit by a child with a ruler and Christopher is unable to defend himself from such attacks. Such occurrences confirmed, in Sonia's mind, Christopher's vulnerability and raised concerns about the inclusion of children like Christopher into mainstream classrooms:

> *Even if Christopher was more able I think I would still be very concerned if he went into mainstream. I don't know whether because of lack of facilities, lack of support, the teachers themselves not having the knowledge to deal with these children. I mean you can't just suddenly put somebody with epilepsy into a mainstream class without that teacher having some knowledge of what fits are like, how they are going to cope with what the child is like afterwards.*

Home–school liaison was something which concerned Sonia. While Sonia and Ken were happy with Christopher's school in general, there were times when conflict arose; for example, when the school bought new tables and chairs for Christopher and had not included this information in the home–school liaison book. They were unaware of the change and she felt that, as parents, they should have been invited in to inspect the chairs to ensure their suitability, since they were 'the ones most likely to know Christopher's needs':

> *So I know that next term I shall be putting pen to paper saying, 'When you order these things for Christopher do you not think you should at least contact me and let me know?'*

Details such as this are regarded as important by Sonia as a mother and reflect whether or not the professionals value the child. Sonia maintains that care is a very important aspect of Christopher's education. One of her main concerns is that the school and the teachers 'look after' Christopher and ensure his safety and well-being, preventing anyone from 'thumping' him. As a mother, this concerns her much more than access to the National Curriculum. In fact Sonia was explicit that the educational aspects of Christopher's school life were less important to her than his physical well-being. She felt that it was unreasonable to expect the teachers to give Christopher access to all of the activities in his Key Stage group. She did not expect Christopher ever to know his colours, for example, but she did expect the teachers to be aware of his needs, such as when he needed a drink. Sonia felt it was extremely important that staff learnt his communication skills, knowing that when he clicks his mouth he wants a drink. Christopher 'eye points' when he really wants something and as both a parent and a teacher she considered it important that the staff understood children's needs and means of communication. 'Making life pleasant' for Christopher had to be a priority and in a mainstream setting Sonia felt that issues of care might be compromised. 'Changing his bottom' and dealing with his epilepsy were major issues for both Sonia and Ken:

> Children like Christopher need constant care as well as teaching; they need feeding and cleaning up. This would involve at least two people and I doubt that LEAs or schools would be willing to fund this in different mainstream schools especially in the present climate and push for positions in the league tables.

There were sometimes tensions between Sonia and the other professionals involved in Christopher's care. Sonia felt that very often professionals such as doctors and educational psychologists spoke to her as if she were 'handicapped':

> I've actually had the old head psych from [the LEA] tell me that he has interviewed Christopher for an hour and a half when he was two, and the teacher present sat and looked at the carpet counting the dots on it because she couldn't give me eye contact. He actually asked me what age I thought Christopher should be counting by. This is the head psych! So I did sort of say to him that it would be very nice if he could say 'drink'.

Sonia noted as a mother how the priorities of teachers and parents may be different. She wanted life to be pleasant for Christopher; for example, trips on the bus could be made more enjoyable. However, the staff at the school were worried by the amount of time Christopher spent asleep. This did not concern Sonia. If Christopher is woken up he has a seizure so she has 'come to terms' with the fact that he sleeps a great deal. As a professional she felt it would be very difficult for a teacher in a mainstream school to manage thirty or so other children and 'include' Christopher. Her fear was that it might mean that he would receive

> little provision and be in the far corner of the classroom and ignored. The teacher has enough pressure on her already. I can't see the authority ever funding the caring that would be needed.

As it was she was 'reasonably happy' with the school, and went to work knowing that Christopher was receiving *the best that the school could provide for him. The staff are all SEN qualified teachers and they have a lot of in-service training. What matters most to me is that they know Christopher. I still do not like Christopher to be handled by too many people and I made this an issue with them when he first went.*

As Sonia tells of her professional and private experiences, the interaction between the two is very evident in almost everything she says, but perhaps it appears most clearly when she speaks of Christopher's vulnerability. The death of a little boy during a seizure at the centre had brought home to her Christopher's vulnerability and the uncertainty of what tomorrow might bring:

Then this last term I had a little boy who died and that was very upsetting; that made me realise how vulnerable Christopher was and there but for the grace of God goes him really, you know, because he just went into a seizure and he just died and we've had quite a few this year. We've had three deaths and it made me realise that he [Christopher] might not see adulthood. So I don't write my future if you like because I think we'll see how it goes before I start worrying about what we do when he's 20 and six feet tall.

Tragedy or normality? Reflections

This first story addresses the dominant discourse of disability and SEN, the medical model, which presents the birth of a child with profound and multiple disabilities as a tragedy for the whole family and in particular the mother. While the stories of Joan and Julia also offer perspectives on resistance to this discourse, Sonia's story gives a very clear and particular example of the way in which mothers can and do reject the tragedy model and the 'orthodoxy of professionals' (Sikes 1997: 84). The discourse suggests that mothers with children with PMLD such as Sonia, who show no signs of the tragedy model, are in denial about their child's disability (Roll-Petterson 2001). Sonia's refusal to accept respite care and her pride in managing without support from professionals reflect the lived experiences of other mothers, who, in resisting dominant discourses of disability, refuse to acknowledge their allotted roles as victims and 'just get on and do' (Read 2000, Roll-Petterson 2001).

Sonia's ability to take control in her roles as both mother and teacher enables her to resist the 'debilitating deference' to medical authority

(Oakley 1979: 15), and re-author the discourse by positioning herself in control (Bartky 1990). However, while this control enables her to resist the power of the professionals as a mother, it is interesting to see how she draws on the same discourses of power relations between experts and mothers in her own professional relationships with parents. She uses her own perception of normality to evaluate the perceived normality of other mothers, therefore creating 'difference' in the mothers who cannot 'cope' as well as almost categorising some of these mothers as 'unfit' (Glenn 1994). Her story reflects an interesting juxtaposition of the personal and professional with Sonia eager not to portray herself as she perceives some of the other mothers. Her apparent ambivalence to other mothers and teachers suggests some of the complexities and contradictions of lived experience as opposed to the supposed order and certainty of discourse. Her discussion of the perceived categories of 'other' mothers is an interesting contradiction of the notions of homogeneity suggested by the dominant discourse among the mothers of children with SEN.

Sonia is aware of these contradictions and notes that mothers and teachers may have different priorities for children with disabilities and/or SEN (Armstrong 1995), which again challenges the dominant professional discourse which assumes that their priorities are the same. Normality for Sonia means control over high standards of personal and professional care and prioritising the needs of the children. Sonia is sometimes critical of both mothers and professionals who fail to match these standards. In repositioning herself in this way it could be argued that Sonia places herself within the discourse which constructs mothers as strong in times of adversity (Blackmore 1999, Mirza 1993). Yet, while Sonia is quick to condemn those mothers who cannot cope, she is also very understanding of those she feels face 'genuine' difficulties. Moral purpose seems to count for a great deal with Sonia and moral experience is clearly important in this story. It informs Sonia's personal and professional life, her understandings of SEN inclusion, and other mothers and teachers.

5 Deborah: professionalising motherhood

For a long time I was consciously saying that I must not go in with my teacher's hat on, preaching. I deliberately held back ... Because I was a teacher I held back. ... I thought, I am going to get their backs up.

(Deborah)

Deborah lives in the north-west of England with her partner, David, and their two daughters, Sally, then aged 15, and Lara, then aged 13; Deborah is in her mid-forties. David and Deborah have known each other since childhood, and their families have lived in the area for many years. Sally and Lara both have specific learning difficulties (SpLD) – in this case, dyslexia – and attend the secondary school where Deborah now teaches. It is now known that David also has dyslexia.

Deborah has lived for most of her life in the same village in which she was born and brought up. Her family is well known in the village and she, her brother and sister all did well at school. Her mother worked full time when Deborah was young, due to her father's chronic illness. Consequently, Deborah, 14 years older than her brother, had been very involved in his upbringing. Despite this responsibility, Deborah and her sister went on to became teachers. In 1973 Deborah qualified as a history and geography teacher and in 1975 she married David and settled down to family life. David's mother was also a teacher and was the deputy head of a secondary school in the county, so teaching was well and truly embedded in the family.

Deborah began teaching in a secondary modern school close to where she now lives and remained there for eight years until, in 1981, she left to become head of history at a large comprehensive school also in the North West. She was the only female academic head of department and felt that she was 'bullied out of the position'. When she took maternity leave in 1983, to have her own children, she chose not to go back; even though it was 'a very good job ... [despite the fact that] they didn't like women'.

Sally, her elder daughter, was born by Caesarean section and had 'dreadful' colic for two months. However, it did not put Deborah off having another daughter only 21 months later. Lara also had 'horrendous' colic and the next few years were hard ones for Deborah. She described the frantic, emotional nature of those days with two tiny babies, often one or other of them screaming throughout the night. This was a 'very emotional and trying time ... hell' for Deborah. Sally and Lara were often on antibiotics, which in those days contained colourings and flavourings now known to cause allergic reactions in some people and especially in children. Deborah has come to suspect that the medication may have been responsible for her daughters' subsequent problems. The babies appeared to be much more restless when they were on antibiotics but no one believed her, until one day her mother-in-law witnessed an 'attack':

> It was on that particular day that they began to realise that, no, they hadn't got a neurotic daughter-in-law; there really was something wrong.

By coincidence her mother-in-law had experience of a pupil aged 11 who had been affected by additives in food and medicine and from then on she became more supportive of Deborah. Encouraged by this recognition, Deborah went to her family doctor but received no support from him. Deborah, however, was convinced that both girls were affected by the antibiotics in different ways; in Sally it appeared to act as a depressant and in Lara it appeared to cause hyperactivity.

Having brought up her younger brother, Deborah could not help but make comparisons between him and Sally and she felt concern for her daughter. Sally was also very clumsy as a child and Deborah has since reflected on this: 'if you look at the tick box for dyslexia, she fitted just about every box'. Looking back, Deborah believes that Sally's development was 'textbook' for children with specific learning difficulties but Deborah did not realise this at the time and by the time Sally was three, she was a very real source of concern for her parents. They felt that she was not developing in the 'normal' way in relation to learning skills; for instance, she refused to paint: 'She didn't draw, couldn't draw; didn't paint, couldn't paint; didn't join in, couldn't join in.'

When she did paint it was always in black or very subdued colours. When Sally went to playschool, the experience for Deborah was not a comfortable one:

All I ever had was flak from the teacher. What had I done with my children? (Lara went as well sometimes.) Hadn't I done anything with them at home? Why can't she cut out? Why can't she hold a crayon? I used to get very upset because, well, I mean I was a teacher, my sister was a teacher. I knew they had problems and I had given them all the experience I could. Yet it didn't make any difference ... it was still all my fault.

Deborah clearly felt this very acutely *because* she was a teacher. But she also felt that there was something more. She felt that she was being judged and found wanting as a mother, especially one who was also a teacher and therefore 'should know better':

I've come through it all and I can rationalise it now. I knew all along that it wasn't me. My problem was proving it, getting the immediate family to accept that and getting the school to accept that there was a problem. They saw it as another teacher ... that's how they saw it and that was a huge frustration. They presumed that I was the problem and therefore did virtually nothing to remediate it. It was the same old problem of having a pupil with a teacher as a parent. It blinded them. It's an attitude.

In 1987 Deborah decided to go back to part-time teaching, even though the girls were still preschool and 'life was hell' as the two girls were causing real concern at home. A secondary teacher by training, Deborah found herself 'press-ganged' into teaching at the local primary school, where she became a parent governor. She renewed her interest in special educational needs within the school and was concerned about the long-term effects of LMS (local management of schools) on children with learning difficulties.

By 1988, Sally was ready to start school. The teacher told Deborah that Sally was about two years behind in terms of spatial awareness but not to worry about it. Much to Deborah's relief, Sally's reading appeared to be good. Then she moved into the class of a newly qualified teacher and problems began to emerge, although at the parents' evening, Deborah was told that Sally was doing well. On reflection, Deborah blamed this lack of information to parents on the newly introduced National Curriculum and the reluctance of teachers to admit that there were any problems which might affect the school's reputation:

For two years I was totally ignorant of the fact that there was a severe problem with maths because the books did not come home. All you saw was the beautifully finished work; you never saw the rough material, and as a specialist now I am not interested in what the finished copy tells you. What gives me the information is the raw material, which comes straight from brain to hand.

By the end of Sally's last year in the primary school, it was clear that there was a significant difference between real progress and reported progress, and the severity of Sally's learning difficulty began to emerge. She was reluctant to write anything down and was by this time having migraines and asthma attacks and refusing to go to school. As a parent governor at the school, Deborah was finding this very difficult. This was a distressing and emotional time for Deborah. The last straw was when Sally told her that:

She wanted to die. 'Wanted to die', quote. I thought, enough is enough! I didn't realise what was going on and it absolutely, physically and mentally destroyed me. The learning difficulties were very obvious, very specific. She wasn't putting anything down on paper and the words used when she was later assessed were, 'totally traumatised'.

It was decided that Lara and Sally would move to a different school, where the teacher who would take Sally was a former colleague of Deborah's. They had been through school and their teacher training together so she knew Deborah and 'never saw me as the problem'. Sally very quickly settled into her new school and became a lot happier. Unfortunately 'Lara now went to pieces and all hell broke out! I'd got appropriate teaching for one and now totally inappropriate teaching for the other.' Lara's teacher asked to speak to Deborah, who believed that the teacher blamed her for not working with Lara:

I was, to put it crudely, gobsmacked. They used what I called the 'gobbledygook' system; that is the child wrote anything and then the teacher wrote underneath. If you have specific learning difficulties you write all this gobbledygook and you can't remember what you've written.

Lara was also going wild at home. The tantrums were ... this is emotional. I've got through this now but when I go back it's ... oh ... [Deborah was crying at this point].

Deborah outlined the problems Lara was having and commented that she (Deborah) was the one who was 'diagnosing' the problem, not the teachers. But at this time she had no real knowledge about the nature of the problem:

I could not make head nor tail of it and all I was being told, by a very, very, very experienced teacher, was there isn't a problem; it will come out right. I told myself that I wasn't infant trained. I mustn't presume.

This was a very stressful time for Deborah on account of the fact that she decided she must 'hold back' and not make a fuss with the teachers at Lara's school:

Does that make sense? I thought, I am going to get their backs up. I believed in their experience and their knowledge and that was my mistake.

By doing some supply teaching in the junior section of the school, Deborah got to know the special needs teacher in the school, who was highly qualified and who also had a child with specific learning difficulties. By this time it was acknowledged that Sally needed some help.

Deborah then got a part-time job teaching top juniors history, English and geography in a private school in the area. On the first day the head told her that she had two children with dyslexia in her class and asked her if she knew what it was. Deborah recalled the taboo of dyslexia in secondary schools in the late 1980s and how, when a child she had known had drawn a mirror image of a map, she was told to keep quiet about it: 'You did not discuss it'. The head gave her a book by Beth Hornsby on overcoming dyslexia and asked her to read it. It was then that Deborah began to consider that both Lara and Sally might possibly have some degree of dyslexia.

Deborah got to know two other mothers whose children also had difficulties, and they told her about the Dyslexia Institute. Deborah took both girls for assessment and her fears were confirmed. She now gained the confidence of the special needs teacher at Sally's school, who confided her fears to Deborah about Sally's dyslexia but said that it was still a difficult subject to deal with in schools. However, by the end of that academic year both children were down on the learning support register, although not without a fight, for at this time the LEA was one which did not want to acknowledge dyslexia as a problem:

We did eventually meet the educational psychologist; it took months. They did everything in their power to get out of it and there was absolutely no way that they would consider Statementing for either girl.

Deborah was told that there had to be evidence of two years' learning support before a Statement would be considered. Sally only had two years left at the junior school but before she left the policies in the county changed again. Deborah was aware that what was happening to her was likely to be happening to other parents, who must also be experiencing the same frustrations. As Deborah recounted these events she reflected that when she became a SENCO later in her career, she was 'living her job'. She was able to see the difference in children, i.e. her own, when they had appropriate support. She talked of the failure of traditional reading schemes to address the needs of many children and the importance of using multiple methods and flexibility in teaching to accommodate individual needs:

> *The point is they all need something different: children with pictorial problems, children with memory problems. If you've got a specific type of difficulty that picture might as well not be there. To another child it might be exactly what they need. What they need is a bank of material and flexibility.*

Now sure that the girls were both dyslexic, Deborah began to find out as much as she could about dyslexia. But there was no one within her own family who accepted the girls' dyslexia and Deborah felt increasingly isolated. She became:

> *utterly frustrated, angry and depressed. I was on my own and absolutely totally isolated. My friends were teachers and it wasn't accepted. My own family, my own personal family, who were academic, didn't accept it. Schools wouldn't support me. Nobody would support me.*

The memory of this sense of isolation has remained with her for many years. She was distressed at recalling the memories and said she had spoken to no one since of her unhappiness at that time. These feelings were to be of great importance to her in her later role as a SENCO, however. She decided to do something about her distress by furthering her own personal and professional knowledge and so she enrolled on the British Dyslexia Association (BDA) course:

> *I finished teaching at the private school, cashed in an insurance policy and paid my way through the BDA programme on this diploma course for a year. So I actually gained a very specialised and respected qualification.*

The majority of the people on the course had previous professional experience of dyslexia and specific training already and at first Deborah found it very difficult. But she soon realised that her personal experience was informing her study. While on the course Deborah gradually became aware that her husband was also dyslexic.

Halfway through the course Deborah was approached by a local secondary school to work with a pupil whose Statement actually called for him to be taught by a dyslexia specialist with the very qualification for which she was studying. The school was an 11–16 comprehensive with about 900 pupils and no SEN department. However, there were personal reasons why Deborah took up their offer. Unexpectedly, David had been made redundant with the result that the family had taken a significant cut in income. Deborah had given up her job in the primary school to do the course so this extra money was very useful and allowed Deborah to complete her course. Now the job and the dyslexia course 'went hand in hand' and Deborah spoke excitedly of her success in this new role: 'I went in and turned this boy round. They couldn't believe what we did together. For my part all I did was apply my training.'

The deputy head then asked her to work with a child with severe behavioural problems. This again was successful and Deborah now began to work on a one-to-one basis with a number of children in the school. At this point Deborah had quite a lot of time with each pupil but this was later to disappear. She saw that what she was really doing was raising their self-esteem, which made a significant difference to both the behaviour and the learning of many pupils, particularly those with dyslexia:

> If you raised the child's self-esteem and worked with them one to one then it would have an impact on behaviour and attitude and everything. Children who might have been expelled weren't; they knuckled down and there was a total behaviour change and improvement.

This in turn increased Deborah's confidence and belief in herself as a teacher. (One-to-one teaching (or withdrawal) was seen as the way forward for children with special needs such as dyslexia in the late 1980s and early 1990s, although additional support in the classroom soon became more common.)

It was with teenagers who had special educational needs that Deborah felt her strength lay. The school had been criticised by Ofsted and they were eager to do more for children with SEN. The head of English, who later turned out to be dyslexic himself and had a son with dyslexia, was given responsibility for addressing these issues. He showed a natural interest and became SENCO as the school moved to meet the demands of the 1993 Education Act through the Code of Practice (DfEE 1994), which stated that every school should have a SENCO. But soon there were problems:

> He had a heart attack and this was put down to the stress of being SENCO. It was the stress of taking on the SENCO's role at that time which brought it on when it did.

Things became very complicated now for Deborah, both professionally and personally. The family made an important decision to move to another village. They were very disillusioned with the girls' school and the appointment of a new head teacher at the junior school confirmed their views.

Deborah's school offered her the role of SENCO and she decided that, even though it meant an increase in stress and workload, she would like to accept it. The job would give her the chance to work in an area of education which she enjoyed. But she still felt that it would be in everyone's best interests to continue with the plan to move to another village:

> I'd felt a nobody for years. I had been ridiculed, threatened (by the head of my daughter's junior school – retired). I was local, that's where I was born, families were friends, but I was not allowed to discuss what I was doing at that school with parents. In other words the school didn't want others to be having the same support. I felt on very dodgy ground and wanted to live away from the school.

By the mid-1990s, the role of SENCO was politically sensitive in many secondary schools. Many head teachers were cautious of being seen to be developing expertise in SEN, for, while it suggested a caring school, in the light of policies aimed at raising standards it could send out the wrong message to parents. Head teachers were concerned that a reputation for SEN would attract too many children with special needs, risking the school's position on the all-important league tables.

Deborah's family now called her 'Emily Pankhurst the Second', because of her fighting spirit and her mother became her ally as she realised that the 'fight' for Sally and Lara was real. Deborah, helped by the BDA course at university and the development of her own professional interest in SEN, felt that she had reached a personal turning point. As SENCO she felt that she could 'take the system on without rocking it'. Deborah was also convinced that her professional life as SENCO would directly benefit her own daughters. If she were to be effective for her own and other children, then she would have to be:

very cool, calm and collected. I really do believe in what I am doing, but I cannot stir things up. I cannot be political. I've got to use the system and I've got to do it by proving that what I say works.

In order to manage the job and her children's education, Deborah made the very important decision to move her daughters to her school and become their SENCO:

I had a child who had migraines and asthma. I had a child who could go off the rails and I made a conscious decision to put those children [Sally and Lara] in the same school as myself and that I would have to be their SENCO and therefore manage them round the clock, day in and day out, and yes, it has worked.

Deborah has responsibility for her daughters' special educational needs during school hours as well as at home. She is both professional learning support teacher and mother to her girls, but they all seem satisfied with the arrangement. It allows her to feel in control and to ensure to her own satisfaction that the girls' needs are being met. Deborah acknowledged that many parents would not like such an arrangement, but she was happy that it met both her own requirements as well as those of her daughters.

Professionally, Deborah 'literally started from scratch' in setting up the special educational needs provision in the school and in particular the provision for children with specific learning difficulties, which included her own two daughters. There were only a few children at first as the LEA were reluctant to recognise dyslexia. The educational psychologist would not recommend that children go forward to Stage 5 (the Statement) of the process. But Deborah was 'allowed to make the initial judgement' as to whether children had specific learning difficulties or not:

They respected my training. I mean, I am a specialist and they respected that specialism and allowed me to take pupils on my judgement alone. I had carte blanche.

There were few other 'categories' of special educational need in the school at that time, as most children with SEN attended special schools. Soon there were up to 90 children with specific learning difficulties (of greater or lesser severity) in the school and no real policies to deal with the situation. Deborah was allowed to work with her experience and her 'gut instinct', informed by the fact that she 'worked, ate and slept' dyslexia. Children were interviewed at the beginning of Year 7 as they came into the secondary school and their needs were determined. Lara was one of these children and this helped Deborah to relate to other children as she recognised many of the early warning signs of dyslexia. She also ensured that children with learning difficulties did not feel alone, for she had seen how destructive this could be for both the children and their families.

Deborah also recognised that there were many children who were going into the higher bands (the school was streamed by ability) who had SpLD which had so far not been addressed. She helped the teachers to differentiate their work for the children and provided in-class support for them for several hours each week. The deputy head and Deborah

> hand-picked the teachers we knew would be successful for those bands. And what happened was that the self-esteem of these pupils went up. We put them in the top sets and the teachers accepted that the variety of their work and the standard would sometimes vary. The standard of their work went up. I explained to the rest of the class why some pupils' work varied and the class totally accepted it and there was never a problem. What we were doing was introducing differentiation and proving that these children could succeed.

Deborah assessed all pupils as they came into the school and then discussed her proposed strategies with the pupils and their parents to involve all concerned:

> They knew [the pupils] what their difficulties were and their parents knew. All these pupils now talk openly about their difficulties within a group and tell other people so that if they can't do something they can say, 'Look, I have difficulty with this and I need such and such to get round it'.

Parents were encouraged to become involved and Deborah spent a lot of time in the primary schools getting to know the children and their families:

> I go in each year and talk to the specialist teachers and the class teachers. I see the parents before the start of Year 7 and if they want to talk for two hours I let them. Because what I do is bond with the parents and, once they realise, they are so relieved. They trust you if they

recognise that you understand. They don't expect the world from you. I tell them what I can do and what I can't.

What she attempted to address was the pupils' ability to cope, their strategies and their self-esteem. By working closely with the parents she hoped to allay the family's frustrations: 'I know what all these parents have been through and most of them have been through experiences very similar to those I have described.' She spoke of the relief of parents when dyslexia and specific learning difficulties are identified and the lessening of tension at home:

I firmly believe that if you can remove the tension from the child and the parents and get a good home–school partnership going it's half the battle. One of the things I often have to do is to take the pressure off the parents, which lessens their pressure on the children.

The pain in Deborah's own life is expressed when she talks of parents going through a period of mourning when they recognise that their children are unlikely to do certain things:

If they've fought all the time, they're very angry and very stroppy and many middle-class parents still believe that university is the only answer and therefore their expectations are high and the pressures are high and the tensions are high.

Her own experience as a parent has helped Deborah to understand and relate to other parents with children with similar learning difficulties:

I have one set of very, very professional parents, I mean one very high in education and one very senior lawyer, who gave the primary school hell, but I met them through the Dyslexia Association. She [the mother] met me and realised that her son was coming to me and after about three months I said to her, 'Look, you know me in and out of school. Will you trust me? I want you to back off completely [from the child].' And they did and he has blossomed and they are absolutely over the moon. But what they have come to recognise is that their expectations were far too high and what the child was picking up was, 'I can never deliver what Mum wants!'

Stress on children was seen by Deborah as a barrier to their learning success and she considered it very important that children have space and flexible support to develop strategies for dealing with their learning difficulties. But Deborah felt that she had space and time at the moment, which she did not think she would have for much longer:

To be successful you need time with parents, you need to get to know the family situation and that's what I have been given so far. Given a new head teacher, a new set of circumstances that might not be the case. If they [the government] remove that freedom, I am not sure that I could cope with the job. More and more, certainly this year, time has been taken away and something's going to have to give.

Deborah spoke of other current causes of concern for her in her professional role; the main one, after time and flexibility, being issues concerned with funding:

Funding not coming into school, not coming into SEN in school. We're losing staff and staff are not being replaced and that means taking on more and more work.

Despite the problems, Deborah felt that the impact she had had on specific learning difficulties in the school was recognised. She believed that the school appreciated the importance of the home–school link and that where that existed there was a very good chance of the child making great improvements in both work and behaviour. There seemed to be a pattern (of failure) which centred around the lack of a 'triangle' between home and school and family. If this support wasn't there, then in Deborah's opinion there was less chance of success. One thing which helped her to work through these dilemmas was her ability to empathise with the parents: 'Every time I have a conversation with the parents, I've been there and when I say to them I know what you mean, I mean it.'

She was critical of the National Curriculum, arguing that schools were now facing the 'mopping-up operation' of children who had been unable to cope with it:

I firmly believe that a lot of pupils I've been dealing with, had it not been for the National Curriculum, would not have been so obviously within the realms of SEN. I think they would have coped. Many of these children need more time. Many have not had that early start so they are at a disadvantage. They do badly at their SATs, bring the results of the schools down and so they come under pressure again.

For Deborah as SENCO, other issues were now arising around inclusion. The schools were being asked to include MLD children and children on the autistic spectrum. She now had to fight for more support to help her with pupils who were becoming more aggressive. But she was concerned about the culture within which these changes were occurring. The LEA was going back to more traditional examinations at GCSE level, which in Deborah's opinion did not improve the chances of success for these children.

Tensions and stress were likely to increase in her own context as Deborah's school, an ex-secondary modern, was being amalgamated with an ex-grammar school which was very concerned about its position in the league tables. This might well present problems for SEN in the new school. Prior to this amalgamation Deborah had been told not to advertise her success in SEN too widely, as the school did not want to gain a reputation for such specialism. She envisaged that this situation would get worse after the amalgamation.

For Deborah, the real stress was not in her professional life. The major tensions had arisen around being a mother. She was constructed as a 'neurotic mother' who couldn't cope. Her professional development through the BDA course offered her a sense of fulfilment and belief in herself. It offered her a professional perspective, which others saw as being valuable and which enabled her eventually to gain 'professional' recognition for what she had been saying 'privately' and 'experientially' as a mother:

My biggest problem was that I was bringing up two small children from the day that Lara was born and it was horrendous because no one understood the problems. My husband didn't believe me and every relative I had encouraged my husband to believe that it was me. I felt like a charity ... everyone trying to give me a break, you know ... come with me and do this. I was the problem. He did not realise what I was going through day in and day out with the children.

However, it was clear that, despite the stress of teaching and the workload, Deborah saw her job very positively, both professionally and personally:

I honestly now, retrospectively, think that if I hadn't got that job at the Lodge, my marriage might not have survived. I am not sure that David could have withstood the barrage from Lara. She was so like him. I used to say to him, 'Don't you realise that you are both the same?' I've had to show him the problems and it was the loneliness and the criticism which got to me.

Professionalising motherhood: reflections

Sonia's story suggested that the experiences of mothers of children with SEN and/or disabilities were very different. The second story would seem to confirm this. Deborah's story offers insights into a number of issues some of which are discussed briefly here. Deborah uses the discourse of professionalism to support and justify her experiences as a mother but then draws on her experiences as a mother to inform and support her in her professional role. Through her own professional development she is able to build on her own experiences and use them to inform her increasing professional knowledge. This integration of knowledge and experience is nothing new, but it is interesting to see how the one is used to 'professionalise' the other (by this I mean the fusion of the two roles then incorporated into professional knowledge). It offers a fascinating and particular insight into what might usefully count as 'professional' knowledge. However, it is interesting to note how the discourse retains control, for only as a professional, through the 'articulate professional voice' (Fine 1998: 141), can she convince her family and other professionals that she has something worth saying. Her voice as a mother is ignored. Yet she uses her agency as a mother to move her daughters into her professional arena, where she now acts as their advocate and agent.

Once she has gained the professional 'power', she then finds herself 'caught' by the discourse of professionalism which now constructs her (as a mother) as a powerful professional when she goes to see other teachers. The tension between the role of mother and teacher is highlighted as Deborah seeks to create a balance between the two roles by holding back as the mother (Sikes 1997). Inevitably the struggle between the two roles is an emotional one for Deborah (as it is for Truda and Julia), which is only resolved when she not only mothers her girls but also becomes their SENCO. Deborah's story again reflects the complexity of lived experience, which is not suggested by either the discourse of professionalism or the dominant discourse of motherhood. The power always appears to lie in the professional domain (Fine 1998) and, although Deborah tries to reconstruct it, it silences her private experiences and appears to shift the boundaries to maintain this power (Blackmore 1999).

Like Sonia, Deborah began teaching before the Warnock Report and the development of social construction models of disability and SEN. The relationship between the individual and the developing political and social context is an important dimension in Deborah's story. It is set within the context of growing tensions between conflicting educational policies, and illustrates the increasing tension and stress for both teachers and parents (Warnock 1996, Barton 1998) as well as the creation of a culture in schools which is not supportive of inclusion (Armstrong 1998, Clough 1998a, Barton 1996, 1998). As the SENCO in a mainstream secondary school, and the mother of two daughters with dyslexia, her story highlights the political nature of SEN in the present context and the unwillingness of some head teachers to promote, or even be open about, issues concerned with SEN. She highlights the increasing pressure of her work and notes that because of this she has less time for both children and parents (Davies *et al.* 1998). Her concern about these issues is another reason for becoming her daughters' SENCO.

Deborah's experiences as teacher and parent reflect the way both teachers and parents may have to fight for recognition and support for their children's needs and it highlights the importance of parental advocacy (Bines 2000, Read 2000, Murray and Penman 1996, 2000). The story also supports the importance of making a reality of strong home–school relations, especially for children with special educational needs.

If you show me anything that shows you're trying, I am going to knock myself out to be supportive, to help. It's when they do blatant things like the day I walked in the door and they tell me my kid needs drugs and they've seen my kid three times. You know, that's death!

(Truda)

Truda is in her mid-forties and lives in Ohio, USA with her partner, Jim, daughter Hannah, then aged 15, and son John, then aged 10. John was adopted by the family when he was four. Truda is a university lecturer who works with associate teachers in the teaching of hearing impaired children. I met her while she was visiting an English university with a group of her students. She was interested in my study and wanted to tell me her story. The story is set in the USA, but the commonality of experiences between Truda and the other mother-teachers is considerable.

Truda was born into a farming family in the State of Ohio, in a community in which everyone knew everyone else. She trained as a teacher and specialised in the education of the hearing impaired, which she had always wanted to do. She also did an EMR (Educationally Mentally Retarded) Certificate. Then, while completing her Masters degree in 1981, she met her partner, Jim, at a Church Camp. They were soon married and Truda's plans changed:

He was down from the farm. Well, you know, here I am finishing my Masters ... went to Canada as a student teacher, I am going to go somewhere, well ... then I end up on a farm in Ohio.

After graduation at the age of 24, Truda took a job in a junior high school where the head teacher was desperate for a teacher who could 'teach' children with multi-handicaps in a special unit within the school. Her role was to:

keep the parents happy – this was the line – not a word about the curriculum, but keep those parents happy, because he [the head] didn't want to lose his job. I literally walked into an empty classroom. When told basically that I could do what I wanted, that's what I did.

Soon she gained the support of the staff in the mainstream school and involved the parents. This was quite frightening for Truda at first as she had no experience of parents of children with disabilities, but she was soon meeting them to talk about the work. Some of these meetings caused Truda to question her limited experience:

Here was I, newly married, no kids and she [the mother] was just talking very frankly, I mean we sat in the restaurant for three hours and it became very apparent that Mom and Dad were going to separate, basically over issues around Mike [the son with disabilities]. So I'm sitting here, listening to this. What do I say? How do I respond?

There were to be many similar conversations with parents during her three years at the school. Truda was still moved to tears by the recollection. Her experiences as a parent were to be informed by these earlier encounters:

I mean, what became very clear to me was that no one had a clue what these parents were dealing with, you know, when people use words like 'denial' or whatever. Each kid really did have their own story, clearly we all do, but connecting with families makes you realise the extent of this.

In 1985 Truda discovered that she was pregnant and in August that year Hannah was born. Truda did not enjoy the experience of pregnancy:

The whole pregnancy was a pain ... people talk about it as if it is a fun experience. That is not something I found. The last three weeks they had found this heart arrhythmia and, of course, I knew my kid was either gonna be hearing impaired or visually impaired because that is what I know about!

Although Hannah was not premature, and weighed in at a healthy 8 lb 2 oz, she was placed in the neo-natal unit to check her progress. Truda felt completely lost and inept. As she recounted her story the memory of it still made her cry:

It's hard. I'm sorry. It was real hard. I cried at the hospital. They made me go home without her. This is 15 years ago. They made me go home without her and it was like, what did I go through all that for, because at this point you don't know how fine she is going to be.

Truda vowed she would never go through pregnancy again:

> *I am 27 years old and just falling apart. It was a very … I mean I did that once, I couldn't do it again.*

Despite the early concerns Hannah was fine. However, dealing with her child only added to her sense of total inadequacy. She felt very ignorant about how to handle her new baby:

> *I was the youngest of three, I mean I hadn't been around infants. You sort of watched television and I looked at these magazines. They pretend that women know what to do. That was way off my scale. I contended all along that it was easier to do the PhD than to do this. Not that I want to do that again either!*

Jim on the other hand was the youngest of five, and all his siblings had children so he was 'more equipped, you know, to deal with that'. Hannah soon settled down and, with her mother's help, Truda began to relax. She reflected on her feelings at this time and noted that:

> *I've always been sort of, not a control freak but in control. I am real good at directing things, you know, being in control of things, so this really threw things in my face. It was like, Gee, you're not in control of this one!*

They lived in a farming community where gender role differences were very marked:

> *This is rural gender-separate America here and of course everybody knew that I was 'an outsider'. Everything that I represented flew in the face of what they were. But you see it was like I was brought down a peg or two because I couldn't do this. It was clear in many ways that I wasn't in control of this.*

A friend, who had married straight after high school, was having her fourth child at the same time. The two women would sit and chat:

> *I would just sit in her living room and chat. Here was I with all these academic degrees … I left the farm to go to work, I bought clothes, I did the opposite of the mom thing. She stayed at home. They have a dairy farm. I mean you work hard but she never threw it in my face. She was real strong for me during the pregnancy.*

At first Truda continued teaching, but by November she was beginning to feel the strain and she resigned. Two days later she was offered a job training student teachers. The job did not begin until January so she had time at home to get used to her new baby daughter. She accepted the offer and in January began work on a part-time basis.

Within 12 months the university asked Truda to go full time to supervise student teachers:

This was what I wanted to do. So I started to look around for Doctoral programmes, and my parents knew but nobody else did because there are huge implications based on where we live and ... I mean married to the family farmer ...

Truda soon found a university which could support her in her chosen PhD, but it meant that they had to move. Although Jim was eager to go, despite being in charge of the family farm, the rest of the family was unhappy and blamed Truda, as it meant that Jim's father and brother now had to run the farm. But soon Jim, Truda and Hannah were starting a new life in the city.

Jim had always hoped for a large family but Truda was determined that she was going to have no more children herself. So Jim and Truda began to consider fostering a child and attended classes organised by the social services for those hoping to foster. The courses were designed to help couples understand some of the abuse and neglect which some of these children had suffered. While this process was ongoing, Truda achieved her PhD.

From the beginning the social services viewed Truda as a 'hot commodity' because not only did she have a child already, but also she had a professional interest in special education:

Here was I with a PhD in Special Ed., and it was like, whoa, we have a goldmine here. They have a catalogue of kids, I mean they are literally printed in a catalogue.

This was how they met John:

Actually we saw his picture and it had just been published and he looked like he was this cute little boy who was holding onto a chair to stand up. Hannah was six at the time and our decision had been that we wanted her to be the oldest child. John had been in foster care all his life. He was four.

John was described as 'severely mentally retarded'. He was not potty-trained and had very poor mobility and balance. Truda described her first impression of him:

He had like high-top tennis shoes on, that supported the ankles when he walked. If he walked on grass you could just see him kinda wobbling with his little stick like, oh my gosh! He didn't weigh anything and he seemed small for his age.

John began spending more time with the family as they settled into a new apartment near the university. Soon John was out of nappies and his limited vocabulary began to improve. There were many adjustments for both John and the family but Hannah and John 'became instant siblings':

Here's a six-year-old who is not six. She has been around adults all her life, extremely articulate, thinks she is an adult and now she has a little brother who's just two years younger than her chronologically but is needy, and there were things that were unexplained that we were trying as adults to cope with. I mean we brought an overwhelming need into the home that is clear and how do we try to balance her needs with his needs?

Truda wanted John to go to the church kindergarten that Hannah had attended:

I mean there was this wonderful teacher and 15 children. We literally lived about a block and a half from this place and at this point I went to them and I think I played down what John's needs were.

The school was uncertain, although they agreed to let John come for a period of time. However, things began to go wrong very quickly:

About the third day he was there, and I didn't know about it right away, they'd given him an orange slice and they'd had to call 911 [the emergency services] as he was choking on it. It was that kind of medical thing that started the fear.

John continued to attend part time, but Truda believed that he 'pushed the limits of "at riskness" that they were used to'. So John moved to a 'blended kindergarten' where the children were for the most part typically developing five-year-olds with about 5 or 6 children with learning difficulties and/or disabilities. But John now began to 'do some behaviour things'. It was clearly borne of frustration and was called 'non-compliance'. The extended family was becoming more aware of John's behaviour now. One occasion involved a 26-mile journey so that John could meet Truda's entire family:

Here's this scrawny little kid, like he hadn't been fed, and of course my family is well fed if nothing else. But we are in a new atmosphere ... and I remember a dinner table scene, where, I mean a little thing could just set him off; you couldn't necessarily define it, but a real inability to express needs and wants and fears. He would just scream and his arms and his elbows would go up in the air. His body would contract tightly and it became a sort of thing.

There were 11 of them all in one house on this occasion when John began to scream:

We didn't know what to do, how to deal with anything and everything just posed new situations. Sometimes things would happen which were unintended when he got upset and threw his arms around such as he might knock over a glass of milk, which in someone else's house can be very upsetting. Well here's my sister-in-law as cool and laid back as can be, and my mother saying, 'Well you should spank him'.

Family support could be both a blessing and a trial and often proved to be a contentious issue. Jim came from a family where sons did what they were told by their fathers because 'that was how it was'. John did not understand this and Jim found himself torn between his family traditions and his own sense of how he felt he should approach John. The pressure was increased for Truda because the family thought that she was supposed to be able to deal with 'this stuff' as a special educator. However, she understood that much of this was a 'communication issue for John':

Quite frankly everything has been trial and error. You know we try this, it doesn't work; we try the next thing. I know I've dealt with this with teachers saying there's nothing magical here.

This notion of trial and error was one which Truda found difficult to explain to teachers who felt that, as a special educator and the mother of a child with behavioural difficulties, she must have 'the answers'. She laughed and said that there were times when she just had to tell John to 'go to his room and leave us alone for a minute while we figure this out'.

Truda was at that time conducting research with a teacher as part of a State project on inclusion, and when Jim got a job as a classroom aid in an integrated preschool, their involvement with special education increased. Jim was delighted:

He now discovers that this is what he wants to do for the rest of his life and of course they loved him; I mean to have a male aid with experience of children with disabilities, the quintessential aid! He cooks, he cleans, he builds things, he plays with kids and he's a guy. Gee! How can you beat it! The experience with John helped Jim to get the job, which in the first instance was working with a little boy.

John was now six and a half years old with 'significant delays in skills' although the 'motor stuff had come right along'. Truda wanted him to attend the local school but there was a policy in the county that, while children with mild disabilities went to a segregated school in the home area, children with severe disabilities attended a unit which was some distance away. Truda made it clear that she wanted John to be a part of the community and attend the local elementary school. His first teacher at the school was very traditional:

a little bit older, she's got her rows, you know you sit in your seat, she stands up. This did not suit John or the teacher. People react in different ways. Well this teacher would go ballistic. Every little thing he did set her off.

She was shocked when one day Truda said:

I expect him to be out of my house someday. I want an empty nest. I have to think about life and what each move means. It is about independence. I mean that's what my goal is, independence. He has to be prepared to be in a community, to be out there coping, not segregated.

John's behaviour worried Truda, for she feared that the other children would begin to reject him because they saw him at his 'worst'. Then, one of the other teachers in the school asked to have John in her class. The teacher was not a special education teacher but the fact that she asked to have John impressed Truda:

That was the beginning of something profound, clearly right there. I mean she was just a wild woman. At Christmas she had on a plaid jumper with a turtleneck, with high-top tennis shoes, with a plaid thing with bells on. I mean this was just her personality. John had learnt very quickly that if he acted goofy he could get out of work, but she would just look at him and he would be right back at his desk. It wasn't even always verbal; sometimes she would just start out of her desk – well he was right back at what he was supposed to be doing. Her whole atmosphere of what went on in this classroom was about peers working; it was about establishing routine.

John began to make academic progress but he was partial to 'bolting' from the playground, so the teacher set up a 'buddy' system whereby the children took it in turns to be his playground buddy and they fought over the privilege. Mothers were encouraged to go into the school to help and Truda went in every Thursday morning to read with the children, check spellings and the like. She had little interaction with John, which she felt was a good thing. Truda really enjoyed it:

> *I mean I really did get to know what was going on in the room because I was there every week and saw the development, but it was like a typical mom, not like a professor. I would try real hard to be there for John. It was the most exciting time he and I ever had in school.*

John was enjoying school and beginning to mix well with the other children. The teacher had a holistic approach and encouraged a group of mixed-ability and first and second grade pupils to work well together. There were different teaching and learning styles used and a lot of activity going on all the time. Many of the approaches were adopted by Truda in her own professional role as a teacher educator, because she could see how they were working in this mixed environment.

Meanwhile, Jim was still working in the preschool and he also had responsibility for the home: 'He was the one messing with the house kinda thing, and people did not know how to deal with that. It is a huge gender issue.' Professionally, too, Truda felt there were gender issues. She had her application for tenure (a permanent position) at the university turned down and was very disappointed:

> *I felt not good enough to be one of the boys. Six years' professional work and they say you can't have tenure. Well you are completely humiliated, you are not going to stay and so I really just gave up.*

The department encouraged Truda to fight the decision and suggested that she used John as an excuse:

> *I refused because that wasn't the point. Just because I was a special educator with a child with special educational needs was no reason to use John. They weren't worried about their kids in this way.*

Even though the vote was overturned Truda was determined to leave and she got a job in North Carolina, but the culture shock was 'huge':

> *I mean just huge! Very conservative … religion and that stuff. Even things like stores closed at six o'clock. Schools then were terrible in the State of North Carolina. We had moved from a district that was in the forefront and a teacher who was phenomenal.*

Truda was now doing advocacy work for children with hearing problems and working to include these children in the public system of schooling (the state system). She did not approach the special education service with regard to John's education but went straight to the public school (the state school) and registered him there. By the time the Director ('a wet noodle') realised what was happening it was too late because the school had accepted John, saying they would do all they could to make it work for him even though they had no experience:

> By now the Special Ed. Director clearly knows who I am. I did wonder why you have to get a PhD in Special Ed. to get this for your kid. However, I could sleep at night because I am out there helping other parents get this too. That's what I was doing full time.

Truda praised the school for their efforts with John, who 'was included because they didn't know any better'. But the family felt rather isolated, outsiders in the community. After watching the film *Witness*, which is set in an Amish community very near their home farm in Ohio, both Jim and Truda realised how homesick they were:

> Jim wanted to be Amish. I mean he wanted to farm with horses. I said, 'You want to go home, don't you?' I mean this has been ten years: we were never going back. He just looked at me and I looked at him. Do it! Yeah! So it was time to go home; it was just the weirdest thing.

Truda was now 38. She contacted the local university and found that they had a vacancy in her area: 'It was meant to be. So we got back in July. We were back in Ohio. We were back in the house in which my husband was born.'

Hannah was now 12 and moving into seventh grade. John was 9 going into third grade and Truda made an appointment to put his name down at the neighbourhood school. John was by this time labelled as DH (Developmentally Handicapped), but he had been in mainstream classrooms all his school life. Truda knew the two teachers who were to take the third grade and knew that neither of them had the experience of working with children who presented the complexity John did. The problems began straight away. Every day John had to take the bus to school. During the first week the bus company lost John:

> They didn't listen to the fact that I said you just don't assume that this kid's gonna get off the bus and follow your little line in here, go down

here, up here, go over here in a building. I mean you could just say to another kid to make sure that John goes in the same direction and get help if he doesn't. So he's in a basement room somewhere, they don't know where he is at. An hour into the day they haven't called us.

Through family connections with the school they eventually heard about the problems which were occurring. When a new teacher arrived at the school, matters got even worse and John was eventually excluded from the classroom. Normally it was Jim who went into school if there were things to discuss because by Truda's admission:

I am often somewhere else and it is Jim who goes to the school. I am the Mom with the Special Ed. part and who is clearly more aggressive than my husband. They like dealing with him much better than me because he's not near as ugly as I am, you know. He's very calm and quiet and would never push.

On this occasion both Truda and Jim attended the school meeting, because the school could not agree on the amount and nature of the provision for John. The district was offering one hour per day support and the educational psychologist wanted to change John's 'label' to TMR (Trainable Mentally Retarded), or MH (Multi-Handicapped). Under these categories John would not attend the local school but have to go to school out of town and leave home at 6.30 a.m. Truda refused to allow this. The professionals, however, said that John's IQ was very low and that there were many things that he was unable to do. Truda and Jim decided to take drastic action:

We decided it wasn't worth fighting over and didn't really want to work with these people at all. They didn't want John there. The Principal was a wimp. She turned out to be worthless. So we let them do their thing. They say that John is MH and that he would have to go into town to be educated. So I ask a few little questions to get them riled, you know, about a later bus: 'Oh no! We can't do that; this is the way it's done.'

Truda and Jim made it clear that they wanted John educated in a 'regular classroom'. When that clearly wasn't going to happen they had their reply ready:

No thank you very much; we're gonna home-school John. You could have heard a pin drop. We shocked the ever-living shit right out of them because they had never heard of such a thing before. And so we walked out of the door.

So John began his lessons at home. Truda and Jim tried to work on lifelong learning principles. They took the view that John was on a farm for the first time in his life and there was much learning which could take place through the farm. The family rallied round them and was very supportive but it was not an easy option for John, or for Jim, who was the main 'teacher'. The biggest problem was access to other children and the social aspects of schooling. So after a year of home schooling, they decided to give formal schooling another try. This time John went into town on the early bus with his sister, but it meant him changing buses and waiting outside for 15 minutes, unattended, by a row of 50 buses, morning and night, which was far from satisfactory.

John was now attending a self-contained MH unit, where the Principal was wonderful. John was thrilled because there were other children there, but Truda was concerned as to whether this was the right placement for John as he was the only child who was mobile and able to talk. His behaviour was becoming an issue according to the teacher and it was suggested that John might benefit from taking medication such as Ritalin (methylphenidate). It emerged that John was the only child in the class not taking Ritalin, a drug prescribed to change behaviour and calm children down. Truda and Jim asked for an independent evaluation report on John, which concluded that John was bored with the work and recommended home schooling again.

The matter came to a head when Hannah told Truda that John had 'peed' at the bus-stop on his way to school and was too scared to go into school because one of the teachers had said he would 'go to jail for doing things like that'. There were a number of other incidents which convinced Truda and Jim that something must be done. A meeting was called and the decision was that the school must meet John's needs. The transport problem was addressed and a teacher was chosen who wanted to work with John. A new aid was hired and communication between school and home improved tremendously. The teacher encouraged peer support for John and soon the children were fighting to work with him.

Within a few weeks of this happening, Truda discovered that she was to take a group of students from the university to England and the family decided that they would accompany her. It would be a great experience for both Hannah and John. Jim was to teach John while they were in England and the students would also put their work units into practice. Truda and John would also send things which they collected on their travels round the UK back to John's school and the school would send work to keep John in touch with the class. When I met Truda, this seemed to be working well for everyone concerned.

Truda reflected on the way in which her experiences as John's mother had affected her professional work. She laughed:

> *I say to the hearing impaired educators that I do methods with and student teaching, I tell them: 'You know, I am standing right here on your shoulders. I'm just haunting you out there. See you just remember that in five years because I'll be haunting you'. I am straight with them. 'If you don't want to be there, don't be. Don't be there and say "Sorry". You might have my kid some day.'*

Truda always tried to get the students to understand that the issue between schools, teachers and parents is 'good faith and effort':

> *If you show me anything that shows you're trying, I am going to knock myself out to be supportive, to help. It's when they do blatant things like the day I walked in the door and they tell me my kid needs drugs and they've seen my kid three times. You know, that's death!*

She stressed the importance of the links with parents and acknowledged how much this was due to her own personal experiences, which now informed her professional practice:

> *We now have a course on collaboration and consultation with parents. When the other tutors have them they don't do anything with parents. They don't bring the parents in. They don't see a parent.*

She was adamant that the one thing that being the mother of a child with learning difficulties did was to make her professional life 'real':

> *Ivory towers? You go to my house for 24 hours and don't talk to me about being real. They know I am being straight with them. I'm like, you know you've got somebody's kid here. I would do anything for the students but if they screw up they are out of here because we have too many teachers that don't belong.*

While national and State policies offer rhetorical support, in reality the degree of support for inclusion depends on where you live in the United States as indeed it does in England, but Truda believed that accountability for special education was growing in all States. Despite legislation (including the Education for all Handicapped Children Act 1975 and the Individuals with Disabilities Education Act 1990, renewed in 1997, which gives 'access' to public schools), there are still ongoing debates, as in England and Wales, about exclusion and behavioural issues. Civil rights legislation at Federal level in the United States makes a considerable difference in theory, but this is not always apparent in practice, according to Truda. Some states are more progressive than others and funding remains a serious issue.

Truda considered herself in the role of change agent for other children like John:

> Quite frankly the focus is on John and if other kids ripple the effect then go for it. Other kids will benefit but it needs their parents as well. Often it really is the parents. They [the authorities] are accountable to money not your child. My responsibility is to be accountable for my son.

Truda, as a parent of a child with special educational needs, believed firmly in educating the young associate teachers in her charge to be advocates for the children and to assist parents in their fight to gain access to inclusive education. The 'game' had to be 'played at many levels'. Personal contact with parents was very important to her as both a mother and a teacher. Seeing the parents in school every day allowed issues to be discussed at these different levels without waiting until a situation developed which was more serious and which may threaten a good relationship between home and school. There were some issues which Truda felt were different for herself as a mother because John was adopted:

> You know, it's funny; sometimes I feel guilty because ... I look at some parents and I work with parents so much and I really play down my situation because there is so much I didn't deal with as a parent, you know. I had the anxiety of one pregnancy and then refused to do it again. At some level I don't feel responsible for John. Do you know what I mean? That level of guilt isn't there. There are times when I am very conscious that I didn't have them [the first four years of John's life]: that I didn't give birth to him. I have worked with some parents where the guilt was huge. I have met couples where there is a lot of blame between them. I mean they didn't know why it happened. I believe that at one level I knew what I was getting into when I got John. But I never knew it would be this difficult.

Sometimes Truda felt that she was a 'terrible parent all the way round' because she felt that she had not spent as much time 'being a parent at home' as her mother had and consequently she did feel the 'guilt thing'. Working with families, as she did, she was struck by the way other mothers were amazed at how she coped with work, a family and a child with special educational needs. This clearly embarrassed her. She 'worked real hard to back off' and wondered if John suffered as a result of this. The other parents did not have to work hard at being a special educator:

> They are a parent for their kid and they're good at it. They don't have to be a model. Good Lord, I've done this for 20 years, you know. You can't expect parents to know what I know. I don't want parents to have to know this much to get a good education for their children. So I am always conscious of not raising my situation because I don't want it to look like an example kind of thing.

She talked about the fact that we all have different life choices to make and how these related to our own individual experiences. In her own case she didn't do the laundry or the cooking, as Jim did much of the domestic work. This would change when he returned to full-time work, however. But the work she did outside the home was very visible:

> I do certain things, you just happen to see what I do … I don't, like, hold life together at the farm. I do at some level, you know.

The mix of professional and private could be overwhelming and she sometimes found herself crying as a result of the emotional strain which could result from playing one role at formal meetings about John with the professionals, being calm and rational, while wanting to 'just grab them by the hair', then returning home and the emotion bursting forth as the mother gave way and the tears and anger spilled over.

Being a teacher and a special educator who prepared teachers meant that any challenge to the system was seen as personal. Relationships with schools were important and a teacher educator questioning what was being done in schools and how it related to her own child was seen as a serious criticism of certain teachers and schools. Truda was well aware that 'information was power' and that her professional position and the information she had at her fingertips gave her not only status but real power as a parent. The questioning of everything that John's teacher was doing by a teacher in special education, albeit on a personal level, was inevitably seen as a professional criticism.

But then the issues with John's behaviour increased the stress. Everyone expected Truda to be able to deal with this without difficulty, or so she felt. Any failure to do so tended to bring greater criticism on her than it would have done on other mothers without her professional experience. Truda was very aware that her expertise was in the education of children with hearing impairments and the development of language. However, she felt that many problems that occurred at home were due to inappropriate instruction in school and she was very unhappy about being told how to treat John at home by a teacher who 'failed' in the day. Truda believed that there had to be closer relationships between home and school, closer understanding of the aims for the child, and the needs of the child and the parents. Changes of direction needed time and the people undergoing the changes needed support. Truda recalled the days when children with special educational needs were:

> neglected, abused, picked on. Parents don't want that but they and the teachers don't have the visual concept of these kids in a regular classroom. We educated parents for so long in Special Ed.: 'Give us your poor, give us your disabled, we can help them, we can protect them.' Then we turn round and say, 'Oh, let's put them back into regular ed.' You can't do that. But that, essentially, is what has happened in the US. That kind of neck whipping, you know. So you can't expect parents to just roll over into that kind of thing. The first thing I want to do is to sit down and really talk with the parents long term. It is a persuasive mode from my side. No one is saying 'quick fix' because if you do you are going to be in trouble.

Her final words were about children like John in mainstream classrooms. They reflected her fundamental beliefs as both a teacher and a mother. It was, after all, about beliefs and the kind of future we want for our children:

> People have to believe that all the kids are right there, in the regular classroom. But the continuum or the stretch of a regular classroom is much bigger than we ever allow. You know, you put a kid with mild learning difficulties in it, a kid with a little bit of gifted ability, and if we want to stretch it a little bit more then we can put in a kid with more significant disabilities. John stretched them. They'd never worked to stretch that far before. But finally he had a teacher who took it on as a positive thing and now this is what we are after: it takes the notion of the pioneer at some levels.

Power, resistance and negotiation: reflections

Truda's story connects the experiences of mother-teachers of children with SEN/disabilities in two countries: the UK and the USA. Although there may be differences in the social context, there are also many similarities in their experiences. While the stories offer insights into the ways in which individual lived experience can challenge and resist dominant discourses, Truda's story also highlights the way in which dominant discourses around women and mothers 'resist' the resistance. Coming from a very particular social context within 'gendered' America, Truda's story illustrates her challenge to powerful 'traditional' discourses of gender and gender relations as well as to discourses of motherhood, professional knowledge, special educational needs and inclusion. Hers is a story of ongoing struggle to resist these discourses which construct women in many areas of their lives (Boris 1994, Glenn 1994, Nelson 1994, Segura 1994, David 2003). The story offers insights into how women collude with dominant discourses to retain power and control within 'traditional' areas of women's lives, such as childbirth, where their 'ways of knowing' emerge through experience. Truda and Jim challenged it again when Jim stayed at home to teach John, and Truda went out into the professional and public world. Truda's story illustrates the struggle for control between the individual and dominant discourses in other ways. Despite her clear position on the professional and public side of the boundary, the discourse of the professionals positions Truda as the outsider when it comes to the issues of tenure. The gendered nature of the public, professional discourse, just like the one on parents and schools, is not overt and only surfaces when the discourse is challenged. The story illustrates the importance of the local context within the broader picture, as well as the restrictions of dominant discourses which silently work to 'other' women. By leaving her home and family to follow her own academic career, she is clearly challenging the 'common sense understandings' (Blackmore 1999, Gramsci 1971), which construct women's lives as on the private and domestic side of the divide. Resistance, on many levels and areas, is a large part of the story told here as Truda challenges other dominant discourses around the individual and notions of professional identity, inclusion, disability and SEN.

In matters of inclusion, the story reflects the orthodoxy of the powerful discourse of professionals who construct difference and difficulty for families such as Truda's. It makes explicit how feelings of vulnerability and uncertainty make resistance more difficult for individuals. When individuals feel in control, resistance is made easier. For Truda there are a number of challenges where these issues surface.

Her partner Jim also resists dominant discourses of gender in a number of fascinating ways, such as following Truda in her pursuit of a career, teaching John at home and living within the private and domestic domain usually associated with women and mothers. Their adoption of a little boy with emotional and behavioural difficulties and their subsequent struggles with professionals, who put every barrier in their way, raise many issues and challenges around dominant discourses of mothers, teachers and SEN.

The plea within the story is clearly one for better understanding between professionals and parents and a more open approach to inclusion and special educational needs. 'Good faith and effort' seems to be the underlying principle on which Truda bases her approach to inclusion as both a parent and a professional.

Power and negotiation are also important aspects of the story. Power shifts are visible as different individuals or groups take control and the complexity of professional–parent relationships emerges as Armstrong suggests (1995). Negotiation is an important aspect of this story, reflecting the need for professionals and parents; professionals and professionals; and professionals, parents and children to share perceptions and understandings around values, needs and expectations.

7 Kate: knowledge, experience and understanding

I used to say quite glibly, 'Oh your child needs to be on the special needs register ... and not worry really about what they were going to think or feel about that. Whereas it must have been devastating for a lot of them ... I would definitely think more carefully now as a SENCO.

I just didn't know how to be a mother and all I'd wanted all those years was to be a mother. I had to do all these other things first, so I still didn't have the knowledge of how to be a mother.

(Kate)

Kate lives in the south-west of England near Exeter. She is in her late-thirties and lives with her husband, Martin, and their two daughters, Kirsty, then aged 3, and Mollie, then aged 3 months. Kate's own mother and father had divorced 'quite a few years ago' but the divorce had proved difficult because they were a devoutly Catholic family. Kate has an older sister, two brothers and a younger sister. Kate did not read until she was 'quite old, about eight'. There was competition with her brother who was only a year older than her and who 'always seemed brilliant at school. It was really hard work following in his shadow'. Consequently, Kate said she was 'your worst student ever' until she made the decision to become a primary school teacher: 'As soon as I got into teaching college and I was doing teaching, I did really, really well; I was focused and I enjoyed it and I was good at it.'

Kate is from a family of teachers. Her mother is a retired primary head teacher; her father was a teacher and her sister and brother were also teachers:

Lots of my cousins are teachers. It's just a bit of a, you know, in some families it's other traditions, well in ours it's teaching.

She began teaching in the early 1990s in a mainstream primary school in London and soon became interested in special educational needs. She wondered if her own failure had something to do with this interest. Going into special needs was like:

going into a glove, really, you know, it was just me, it suited me. I felt good at it and I got notice for it and acclaim and all those sorts of things. So I went on quite a few courses, got more and more interested in it.

Her interest and developing expertise in SEN soon became noticed in the school and other teachers used to ask for her advice with children in their own classes. With the introduction of the Code of Practice in 1994, Kate felt it would be useful to find out more about it and how it was going to work so she enrolled on a course run by the LEA which offered a Diploma in Special Educational Needs. Successfully completing the course meant that she was one of only ten people in the authority

who knew the ins and outs of the Code of Practice, so I was in a really good position. It felt really exciting at the time to be involved with it.

Kate was now 32 and was hoping to start her own family:

Nothing happened and nothing happened and it was getting more and more traumatic and we had to go for tests and while we were going through all these tests and all the things I needed something for me, alongside it, so I thought, well I'm going to do this study alongside it so that at least I have achieved something if I don't achieve having a child.

Martin, Kate's partner, was also a teacher and head of mathematics at a local comprehensive school. They had met at college:

We just sort of bumbled along together really, you know, and broke up and got back together again and broke up, you know, the usual sort of long-term relationship. I had been travelling for six months with two girlfriends and I'd got back and the relationship was still intact and so we decided to go for it.

Neither felt the need to get married but they decided that they did both want children at about the age of 30. It was therefore a considerable blow when, after six years of tests trying different treatments, Kate was told that she would never have children:

They said I was having an early menopause and that I'd never have ... and the chances of me having children were, well, non-existent.

Kate was terribly upset. They tried IVF treatment, which didn't work. This was a real blow to Kate who found herself hating every single woman who was pregnant, including her friend Anna at school, who had also been undergoing fertility treatment and who had, at last, become pregnant. They shared a class together so Kate was literally watching Anna's pregnancy develop. Kate was asked to do the duties like the games lessons, which increasingly Anna couldn't do. Things got so bad for Kate that she and Anna 'fell out badly' although they are friends again now. For 'her sanity's sake' Kate decided to focus on special needs at school:

> Either you do that or you roll over and play dead don't you. I was mad, I was really mad. School kept me together. The Code of Practice had come in and I could completely and utterly absorb myself in setting up the systems in school, which was brilliant. I was by now (1994) officially the SENCO. I set about it really and got it all running how I wanted it. I was going for IVF, which is so traumatic, and I went on from the Diploma to the Masters course in special needs at a nearby university.

The school was a large primary in a rather deprived area of London. There were 500 children in the primary school and 20-plus staff. There were many children with special educational needs although only about 4 per cent actually carried a Statement. There were many children on the 'at risk' register and there was 'a lot of neglect'. The Statements were mostly for learning difficulties:

> which then gave attributable emotional and behavioural difficulties ... I am a firm believer that you tackle everything through the curriculum in school ... you know it's their self-esteem. People go on saying you've got to raise their self-esteem. How do you raise their self-esteem? They are in school and they want to be good at something, that's all any child wants really at the end of the day, is recognition for something.

Fortunately Kate and the head teacher worked well together as the SEN team. However, the school began to get a reputation for being 'good' with special needs children and they began to attract children who were excluded from other schools. This brought its own problems in that many of the teachers did not want to deal with more children with SEN. But Kate found the work exciting and fulfilling.

Kate and Martin decided to have a last attempt at IVF treatment. It was a costly and emotionally draining experience for the couple, who had, by now, spent £6,000 on fertility treatments. One single sperm was now injected into a single egg under an electron microscope. They managed to get three eggs fertilised in this way. As they both came from very devout Catholic families, they were careful about how they approached these issues with their families. They had told Kate's family about the treatment but not Martin's. However, when they later told Martin's family what was going on, as both Kate and Martin were in such a terrible state,

> they were brilliant, absolutely brilliant. We decided after the failed IVF attempt that we were going to get married anyway ... having gone through all this brought us much closer together. So we decided to get married and we told the family everything.

Their families were thrilled. Even more so when it became apparent that one of the three embryos had taken and Kate was pregnant:

> It was incredible after being told that I would never have children. The consultant said the odds were like putting all your money on a three-legged donkey to win the Grand National. I was seven-months pregnant with Kirsty when I got married, which in the Catholic Church ... well the priest was brilliant ... Of course the families were delighted to have a Church wedding and all the rest if it. But then Kirsty was born and she had all these problems.

Kirsty was born five weeks early. Kate was due to start her maternity leave the day the school's Ofsted inspection began. This meant that because she was not going to be there to 'hold her flag up', she wanted everything ready before she went:

> I thought, I can't let it go any longer. It was five weeks to go [before the birth] and I was knackered. I was having to have a Caesarean as well because the baby was breach. But I had to have everything ready [for the inspection] even though I really felt that I couldn't go on much longer. Anyway, on that Thursday ... I had a bit of bleeding. So I went to the hospital and then had an emergency section because I had haemorrhaged.

When Kirsty was born she was taken to the Special Care Baby Unit because she was small and she was a bit cold and that was all. There were no other problems apparently. Kate was 'out for the count' as she had had a general anaesthetic. It was the next day before she became acquainted with her daughter and was allowed to dress her and feed her. Kate described her feelings at that time: 'I was absolutely euphoric, absolutely over the moon, completely so excited.'

It was two days before the first signs of something amiss appeared. Kirsty's system did not appear to be functioning normally. She had not passed the meconium and the hospital was concerned. Kate felt lost:

I mean I didn't know anything. I didn't know what this meant. You don't know anything do you and they said that she needed some tests, so you sort of go drained. You know, we have just had this child and she's going to be snatched away from us. So we went up to Great Ormond Street. She was at death's door.

Kate was clearly distressed as she recalled this time and she still could not understand how they had not realised the seriousness of Kirsty's condition. Kirsty underwent an emergency operation at Great Ormond Street, as there were very serious complications with her digestive system and particularly her liver function:

It was touch and go because she was so sick and I just remember us sitting there thinking we don't even know her; we don't know what her personality's going to be like and that was the hardest thing, thinking she's here but we're not going to know her.

But, day by day, Kirsty got a little stronger. Kate and Martin set targets for themselves: 'I mean that was my special needs training coming in.' After five days Kirsty was out of intensive care. Then came another blow. The doctors said they wanted to test for cystic fibrosis. Kate and Martin didn't know much about the disease at that time so they found some old literature which 'scared us terribly because you know she is going to die within a few years at best'.

However, after proper information and counselling, they realised that the prognosis was much better than it had first appeared, so when they were told that Kirsty did indeed have cystic fibrosis they were more prepared for the news and felt able to meet this new challenge. Kate was reassured that there were things which she could do, such as physiotherapy, and new more effective medicines. At this point Kate felt more able to cope than Martin:

I took the lead, definitely, and I had to say to him, because his parents wanted to come down to be with us, 'I can't cope with that', because his mum means well but she takes over your pain ... If we were going to do this together we had to be completely strong for each other, nobody else dissipating that at all.

In the end, Kate's mother came to look after her because, as Kate remarked, although she and her mother

fought tooth and nail, my mother is very practical in those situations and she could come and look after us without taking what we needed from each other away.

The rest of the family were all devastated:

*because from the outside it looked a horrendous situation. We tried so
hard to get pregnant; we finally got pregnant, then the baby had to have
an operation straight away and the chronicle of events – you'd think, my
God, that's terrible but we were just so happy that we had a baby.*

Then there were all the issues about guilt and fault to deal with. Kate
was very clear about this though. Although they wondered if they had
pushed the notion of pregnancy too far by using IVF treatment, they
both accepted that even if they had not needed 'help' they would have
had a child with the condition 'regardless'. Cystic fibrosis is genetic, a
'recessive inheritance' so both parents have to be carriers of the gene.
There could be no portion of blame to either party. This again helped,
for they saw it as the 'two of us together'. However, it proved a
different matter for the two families:

*I think the families found that harder because they were both saying,
'Who is it on our side of the family?' Because Martin's gene is a more rare
gene – I've got the common one – his family are saying that our gene isn't
as common as that gene. I think there is no competition in this.*

However, for both families this had been a difficult experience. Kate
and Martin's brothers and sisters all wanted children and had decided
to be tested for the gene. Two of Martin's four sisters proved to be
carriers and Kate's sister also found that she was a carrier. Her two
brothers had not yet been tested, although one of her sisters-in-law had
been and was a carrier so her brother was about to have the test as
well. Kirsty's birth, therefore, had considerable implications for the
rest of the family.

When Kirsty was three weeks old Kate and Martin were able to bring
her home from the hospital. Kate was 'scared stiff'. She had to 'do
physio on this tiny little thing', as well as give her a great deal of
medication:

*I think if she had been a second child it would have been really difficult
to do. If you had a 'normal' child first then having to do all that to a
second baby would have been completely alien; you'd think, I can't do
that, whereas her being first was all we knew so we just got on with it.*

Kate never missed a single session of physiotherapy, which meant
every morning and every night, and if Kirsty had a cold it meant three

times a day, but Kirsty had never had any chest infections to which cystic fibrosis sufferers are so prone:

> If Kirsty has a cold it means that I have to take her in immediately for cough swabs so they can match what bacteria she is growing with the antibiotic it needs. It's that specific. We just do it; it's routine. She knows nothing else; nor do we. All her dolls and toys get physio.

Kirsty also takes special enzymes to aid her digestion and has to have a very high-fat and high-protein diet. This means that her food costs a lot more and she also has to have a lot more nappies, as she cannot absorb food as well.

Kate returned to work when Kirsty was seven months old. Kate's mother looked after her but Kate insisted on doing all the physiotherapy before she went to work and when she returned at night. She intended to work for a limited period only, but when she returned it was working out quite well, so she decided to work part time, sharing a class. This she found very hard to do after being so involved with the school. She once again took on the role of the SENCO, which meant that she did two days in the classroom and then concentrated on special needs:

> It was much harder now because I was the mother of a child who had more needs. I couldn't put as much into the job as I had previously done because I had to get home to do her physio and to give her the medicine and all those sort of things, so I couldn't give all the reviews and all those sort of things with parents the same time as before. That was really hard. But then there was all the experience I had had with Kirsty. Now being in the classroom with children with special needs was much easier to manage ... I had a different perspective on it, you know, and, it was, how can I put it, it just made you realise what was important. I could meet with the other parents and they knew I had a child and it was different, a different scenario.

Kate now took 'observable notes' of the children so that when she met their parents she was working from these rather than relying on her own 'subjective ideas'. This marked a considerable change in her thinking. Having her own child, especially one who needed such close attention, made her aware of how much can be learnt from close observation and talking to parents. She was also aware of listening to parents more and of how difficult it was for some of them to get to school for an 8.30 a.m. meeting, when they also had two other children to get to school. Before having her own daughter she would *glibly give out these early meetings for reviews and then be sniffy because they'd turn up late with a child in a buggy who'd drop toast or whatever all over my floor. Now I recognise that just getting there at all for anywhere near that time, and actually being worried enough to get there in order to have the review, can be a considerable achievement.*

As a very independent person, Kate found that being a mother did not come naturally. Because she had waited for so long to be a mother and had wanted it so much, she believed that it would 'just come to her':

I thought I was going to be a natural at it but I've had to work hard at it because I am so used to doing my own thing, and I am not a clucky person in the respect that if I see a baby I don't want to go 'goo goo goo' at all. In a lot of respects I've had to teach myself how to do it. People don't really give women that scope though. They expect you to just get on with it don't they?

On a practical level, however, Kate quickly became comfortable with being Kirsty's doctor, nurse and physiotherapist, but being a mother was very different. Kate wanted to be 'just a mother', but it seemed so elusive:

It has probably taken me a good year or so to actually be a mother first, then all these other things second. Because of her special needs, I probably saw them as being ... you see Martin's much better at being a mother than I am, although he's supposed to be the father. He is more naturally adept at being the mother in that respect. My practical side sees that we have to get all these needs sorted out first and then she will be fine.

She now believes that this early perception of hers was wrong:

It was how I came to terms with things because, of course, I can still be a mother first and still do all those [medical] things.

Now she realised that Kirsty was

just a normal baby who needed a bit of extra something at the beginning and end of each day in order to make her day completely normal. She does everything that all the other children do.

Things had been very different when her second daughter, Mollie, was born. When Kirsty was one year old, Kate found that she was pregnant. At first she could not believe it, but as the doctor later told her, 'These things sometimes happen after one pregnancy. It seems to sort everything out.' Mollie did not have cystic fibrosis, nor was she a carrier. Kate and Martin were delighted. For Kate, things were different from the start:

I was just her mother and it was so nice. I was comfortable with it, doing all the things that I had had to wait a year to do with Kirsty. I thought, she's not going to die; she's just not going to disappear on me. I don't have to do anything except feed her, change her nappy. With Mollie I put her in her cot and she goes to sleep. I just didn't think that was a possibility with Kirsty.

Kate was aware of the difference between herself and Martin when dealing with the children:

Martin is brilliant at playing with Kirsty. There can be chaos and debris everywhere and he'll just play with her. I have to have things in order before I can relax and play with them. I shouldn't worry about the chaos but that is something I have to come to terms with about myself. I think that is definitely from being a special needs teacher and a SENCO because you have to pigeon-hole everything so much all the time in order to keep on top of everything. Unless you do that, nothing would ever happen.

But when she had Mollie, it seemed as if

I was just playing at being a mother. It all seemed so easy. When Mollie was born, I just sat and fed her and looked at her ears and looked at her fingers and her toes and looked at her belly-button and there had been none of that with Kirsty whatsoever. I had no time to do the niceties in the first place. I took her [Kirsty] to baby massage when she was little because I thought it would be good to have that sort of touch as opposed to physio. But I didn't take her just for the pleasure of having a baby massage; it had another connotation. When I took Mollie it was just a gorgeous baby massage that she 'goo, goo goos' at. Whereas with Kirsty it was frantic; I was thinking, right I have got to do something to counteract the physio because we are having to hit her hard and I wanted her to have a gentle touch as well. I didn't realise I could be gentle with her just as a mother.

Kate acknowledged that this was probably a lot to do with first and second babies. But this itself caused concerns. Because of the nightly routine of physiotherapy for Kirsty, Kate and Martin placed greater emphasis on this than they did on Mollie's bedtime, which they both recognised could be a problem as Mollie grew older. They were aware that they would have to ensure that Mollie, too, had her 'special time scheduled into the day'.

Now Kate felt that her approach to Kirsty as a baby had been wrong, but it was how she came to terms with the danger Kirsty was in at the time. She was used to being practical and she wondered if this helped her to think that she wasn't getting too close to Kirsty in case something happened. She drew on her professional strength to help her to deal with her personal crisis. The stressful situations in school with difficult children had given her strength which went beyond that required in many other types of jobs. Being constantly creative and having to find alternative ways to deal with situations and children had given Kate a different perspective.

It was Kate's aim that Kirsty would go to a mainstream school and have 'normal schooling'. She wanted the school to be willing and able to help Kirsty with her medication. It was seen as important that Kirsty had the space to be 'normal' at school without it 'being an issue'. There are a lot of problems for children with cystic fibrosis in mainstream schools at the moment. Many schools are refusing to administer the necessary medication in case they are held liable in any way for any problems which might occur. This caused Kate some stress as she felt that such things could be made much easier for the children, their parents and their teachers if schools really wanted to support them:

> The whole thing with CF [cystic fibrosis] is to train them [the children] to be as independent as possible from an early age. Kirsty will start doing her own physio, her own medication and all that sort of thing from an early age. She already does the blowing exercises, things like that, to get the air going.

Kirsty was a pretty girl and Kate believed, sadly, that this was very much in her favour in matters of inclusion:

> Looking normal and pretty may mean that she will have fewer problems. This is a terrible thing to say but in the great scheme of things that's what happens in schools.

Kate found that it was better not to mention the cystic fibrosis until people had got to know Kirsty and had accepted her:

> If I said it to them at the beginning they would treat her differently. They are going to know her as Kirsty and then realise her needs beyond that.

Returning to work was not seen by Kate as a problem, insofar as it was a problem for any other working mother to balance a private and a professional life. Kirsty's health concerns would always be there but it was possible to develop a pattern. Knowing her child was very important to Kate, for it was the only way to keep her healthy. It was important that other professionals recognised this as well. When Kirsty got a cold, it led to a cough but as long as they found out what the 'bugs' were in the cough, the antibiotic could be given and within two weeks Kirsty was better. The whole process lasted about five weeks from the first sniffle to the end of the cold. So far, Kate and Martin have managed to keep Kirsty's chest clear. Inevitably they were learning more and more about their daughter's response to various antibiotics and treatments. The doctors had worked well with Kate and Martin until one occasion:

> I went to the GP down here and I said, 'this is what she needs, this is the pattern' and he would not give her what I wanted. He gave me what he wanted. I haven't come across this because all the other doctors I've been to take the parents of a child with CF as experts because you work with it and deal with it daily and we are more medically aware because we have to be. The hospital actually wrote to him after doing a cough swab and told him that what she needed was what I had originally asked for. The next time I went to see him I thought, 'egg on your face', you know.

In Kate's view it was important for all professionals to 'keep all avenues open and not think, "I'm the professional in this avenue, I'm going to pull rank"'. She recalled multi-professional meetings when one particular professional wanted to be the most important person there, 'for their own merit as opposed to what the child needs'. The child's needs had to be paramount:

> The child should have what she needs, regardless of the funding, regardless of the red tape and the bureaucracy and all the rest of it that's tied in with special needs and education.

Because she had struggled so hard to have a child, Kate felt that her own fight was easier:

> All the trouble we had getting to the point that we had Kirsty made us such a close unit together so that if someone had said, this is the child you are going to have and these are the problems she's going to have, the year before, we would have snatched at their hand and said yes please, yes please. So in a certain respect, us having Kirsty with her needs was a lot easier than other parents having Kirsty with her needs because we were able to deal with it, you know.

Kate was in no doubt that she would 'fight' to get a Statement of SEN if she had to for Kirsty, so that she could have physiotherapy and to have someone who could give her the medication at school:

> because it would mean that she would have a completely normal life without me having to run to the school every lunchtime to give her physio and her medicine, which would automatically stand out that her mum comes down every lunchtime to do this. If she had a welfare assistant at school who she just went to, to have her physio and her medicine, then it could be done within school. It's about her independence, that's what's really important.

Having knowledge of the system from a professional perspective as a SENCO helped Kate to deal with many aspects of it:

> I know how it works and I'm not scared of it. I think as the mother of a child with special needs and because I know the system I will be able to get her what she needs. As both a parent and a teacher in that situation it makes it easier, makes it better for the children really.

However, she was concerned that the educational psychologist would not see Kirsty's needs as she was 'bright'; Kirsty knew all her colours and her speech was perfectly normal for a two-year-old. If Kirsty was in the 'average range' then Kate feared it would be difficult to get a Statement. She was aware of the power she could have as a parent. As a SENCO Kate had written so many letters 'on behalf of parents challenging every single Statement', sending them back 'for clarification of the specific needs and just got them [the parents] to sign the challenge'. Many of these parents did not turn up for meetings and appointments possibly because they 'abdicated' the responsibility for their children to the professionals. They did not appreciate the power they could exert if they wanted to, although Kate always told them that they had far more power than she did as a teacher in this respect.

The power of medical professionals in educational settings was something that was increasingly worrying Kate. She had witnessed a growth in the use of Ritalin (methylphenidate) to 'treat' ADHD (Attention Deficit Hyperactivity Disorder) and control behaviour. Because the drug was prescribed by general practitioners, parents felt it was a medical issue and beyond their control. Inevitably parents wanted their children to behave, and if Ritalin calmed them down then parents found it hard to question the use of the drug. Kate was very critical of this 'medical intervention' in educational matters, for she maintained that it masked the educational issues around the curriculum and the school environment. As the mother of a child who would be on medication for life, she argued that any 'unnecessary' medication should be avoided. She felt increasingly strongly that more and more children were unable to cope with the structures and the pressure of school. Recent changes had resulted in loss of flexibility in both the curriculum and teaching methods, but as long as there was a medical 'solution', the educational environment would not be significantly challenged or changed and the children and their families would continue to be pathologised. The mere existence of special schools within the LEA would mean that she would have to fight to get Kirsty into a mainstream school, although the school she wanted Kirsty to attend was a Catholic school 'with a really good caring ethos'.

Although Kirsty was still very young, Kate was already aware of her own roles as mother and teacher. At the toddler group Kirsty attended, the teachers did not know yet that she was a teacher:

I haven't said anything because I am just getting on with it as a mother. I know a situation will arise at some point.

She reflected on the idea of attending school parents' evenings as a parent and thought it could be difficult:

Because, well, as a teacher, if you have another teacher coming to see you, you can be a bit defensive, especially if the child has special needs.

There were already indications that both medication and gene therapy would offer hope for the future and Kate hoped that medical developments would be such that Kirsty's condition would become easier to manage. There was 'talk of just having a couple of pills a day which would cover everything'. Even in the late 1990s the outlook for children born with cystic fibrosis was not good:

It was still a horrendous disease, or rather condition. I prefer to call it a condition rather than a disease. It does affect people's perception of it. The label approach matters a great deal. I prefer no labelling. Would you want to be labelled? I wouldn't!

Looking back Kate felt that, having suffered some considerable stress as a parent, she would be more likely to understand the pressures which other mothers of children with special educational needs might feel, rightly or wrongly. Now she understood that it was how they felt as the quote at the beginning of the story suggests. She was adamant that parents must 'stick to their guns' and fight if necessary to get what they believed their child needed. If parents were *not* strong then the LEA would 'just dismiss you. He who shouts the loudest gets the most, an awful situation but true.' Kate admitted that she would do anything to get what was needed for Kirsty. This shouldn't be necessary if children had their needs met properly:

> It's about finding a balance between the philosophy and reality; then we might get it right for the kids.

Knowledge, experience and understanding: reflections

Ball (1998: 78) writes that, 'We have too much knowledge and not enough understanding'. Kate is a professional with a high degree of training in special educational needs, and as such has particular professional knowledge. Her story illustrates the need for both professional 'understanding' as well as knowledge. It highlights how drawing on and acknowledging personal 'moral experience' (Polkinghorne 1995) can offer professionals a means of developing such understanding; a particular lens through which to view what might otherwise become the certainty and 'orthodoxy' of professionals (Sikes 1997). This is another story where experience and understanding undermine or challenge that orthodoxy, only in this story the challenge happens within the mother-teacher herself. Kate's story offers insights into the interrelationship between public, professional knowledge and personal understanding; how the former supports the acquisition of the latter and is then fundamentally changed by it so that what counts as professional knowledge is changed forever. As a professional she relies on the 'certainty' of knowledge. As a mother she has to come to rely on the gradual development of understanding through experience. Before she has Kirsty, professional knowledge means being in control; but being a mother means learning gradually, experientially. Professional knowledge offers Kate an alternative way to construct and value herself through the 'valued' public discourse of being a professional. However, when she becomes a mother, her understanding of the meaning of that professional role changes in the light of her own personal experiences (*ibid.*).

Todd and Higgins (1998) and Armstrong (1995) suggest that the balance of power and powerlessness between professionals and parents is not as straightforward as it is often presented in the literature, and that the boundaries are much more blurred than is usually claimed. The story of Kate supports this complex view of the relations between parents and professionals and Kate herself acknowledges the power she can have as an articulate parent who knows the system.

The complexity of the personal–professional (inter- and intra)relationship and the interaction between knowledge, experience and understanding is expressed for me in the simplicity of this comment of Kate's:

> *I didn't know how to be a mother because I had never been one ... I had been very much in control as a SENCO. I could set my targets and I could keep things in order ... I know how to deal with all the CF stuff, but how do I make her go to sleep?*

*But you really can't understand what it's like having a disabled child
unless you have one. Your life is not your own. Even though he is 18 I still
have to think what will I do with James then; or how will I pick him up
then? When most children are 18 you don't have to worry about them in
the same way. You give them a key. But I am always on duty for James.*

(Joan)

Joan is in her early fifties and lives with her husband, Joe, a driving
instructor, and two of her three children, Helen, who was 17 when
Joan told her story and still at school; James, 19, who was about to go
to college. Paul, who was 21, worked as a digital designer for a national
broadsheet newspaper in London. James has a rare syndrome, Cornelia
de Lange syndrome.

Joan came from a small, working-class family who supported her
attempts, as they perceived it, to move into a professional, middle-class
occupation such as teaching. Her parents had been very proud of their
daughter when she passed for the local grammar school and then
graduated from university in 1971, with a degree in chemistry. Joan
recently completed a Master's degree and spoke of her mother's
continuing pride in her academic success. She admitted that she had
left university not knowing what she really wanted to do and so had
gone on to another university to study for her PGCE (Post Graduate
Certificate of Education). Her first appointment as a teacher was at a
comprehensive school in the north of England where she taught
chemistry and physics, and hated it. However, this was where her
interest in children with SEN began:

*It took me less than two years to realise that this [teaching] really wasn't
for me. However, I would say that during those two years, that it was with
the children then referred to as 'remedial' that my interest lay. Even when
I was at college, my special project work had been focused on 'remedial'
children. So right from then I was interested in children with SEN.*

Joan left the school and went to work for a bank in the Channel
Islands, where she met her husband Joe and in 1979 they returned to

the UK and were married. Joe is Slovenian and was born in Eastern Europe. While Joan was still working for the bank in England she had her three children in quick succession; Paul in 1980, James in 1982, and Helen in 1984. Paul's birth was straightforward and Joan soon settled into motherhood:

> It was a dream, just delightful. The usual, you know, you can't believe they can wear you out so much but we just adored him.

Things were very different when James was born two years later. During the pregnancy Joan had received many scans and the doctors had persisted in altering the expected date of arrival of the baby. When he was born, almost on time, James was very small weighing only 3 lb 13 oz. A few days after the birth the doctors told Joan and Joe that things 'weren't quite right' with the baby:

> I knew there was something wrong. James had elfin-like features. He had masses of black hair, really bushy eyebrows and he didn't have that round chubbiness that newborn babies usually have.

The doctors told her a few days later that James had a rare disorder, Cornelia de Lange syndrome. The paediatrician had seen very few cases before but he had recognised James's features. There are no tests to diagnose it and the doctors told the new parents what they knew, which wasn't an awful lot:

> The doctor was matter of fact, although he did have this, 'I am afraid, this is how things are' sort of approach. This was 18 or so years ago. I couldn't believe it. I thought things like this happen to other people. I couldn't take it in at all. It was Joe who was tremendously supportive, and he said it didn't matter what. He was our son and that was the most important thing about him. All I did was cry all the time.

It was three weeks before Joan could summon up the strength to tell her parents:

> I think it was partly shame and partly because I knew they would be tremendously disappointed and upset. By the time he was three weeks old, I had sort of got a handle on it as it were.
>
> My mum just wanted to know how on earth I would cope and I just said, 'Mum that is how it is; that's what has happened and this is how things are. We are going to make life as good as we can.' I think it is fear; it's something you don't know anything about and you're frightened of what's

in store really, what's in store for you, not at that point what's in store for your child.

A doctor in the special baby unit told her that James's development was likely to be very slow and that he might be small, perhaps not making five feet in height. He also told her that James would probably have to go to a special school, as he was likely to have severe learning difficulties:

I think that was the first time I thought that James was going to be 'mentally handicapped'. I was able to gather these bits of information as we went along and at the same time get to know James, so that I knew him as a person.

Joan and Joe decided not to say anything to Paul about the syndrome. They would just present James as he was. They took the view that:

This is James and this is how he is and Paul has just accepted him. He loves his brother. No problem. He talks about his brother being disabled. It's not that he doesn't know and he has asked at times why certain things happened, but we just told him and he accepted it. He's just part of the family and I am glad that is the way the children have treated him. They have been so supportive.

About three weeks after the birth, James neared the magic 5 lb in weight and so he and Joan were allowed home. Once at home, the professional visits began. The health visitor came to check James's weight and to bring oceans of sympathy, a sentiment Joan did not want:

I didn't need sympathy. It drove me mad. I got really irritated with her because she was so full of sympathy. I liked the paediatrician at the local clinic. She told me things, positive things. She told me that I had to work hard at talking to him for when he was asleep he wasn't learning anything. She told me to keep smiling at him. It was a really positive thing I could do for my child to help to bring him on.

Joan's parents were very supportive, although they lived some distance away. They regularly came to baby-sit and often took the other two children home for the weekend. But James had not been to stay on his own with his grandparents. Joan wondered if this was because she had been overprotective:

I don't know whose fault it is. Perhaps it is mine. It is my fault I suppose because I enjoyed spending time with him and he likes being with me.

When they discovered that Joan was expecting her third child, Joan and Joe were very happy. However, Joan asked for an amniocentesis and was surprised to learn that she was at no greater risk of the baby having the syndrome than any other mother. Joan remembered how she was very much against abortion and became really pro-life in those days, a view which she said had not changed. In 1984, when James was two, Helen was born, and the doctor came especially to see Joan to tell her that all was well with the new baby.

Joan now had three children under the age of five and she managed to get the services of a home help but it was Joe who stayed at home to look after the children when Joan returned to work after each maternity leave:

> *Joe must have done quite a lot in the house. I don't think I could have gone to work all day and come home and done the housework. I did the washing and stuff like that. Joe is from Eastern Europe and they have a clear distinction between women's work and men's work. I don't think that Joe told his parents that he was doing the housework, because it's not a manly thing to do in Eastern European culture.*

Joe's parents had been told about James. In their culture 'it is shameful to have a child with a disability, but they have been great with James':

> *They know him and love him as their grandson. Joe's brother thought that James was small because we weren't feeding him properly and he gave us a few tips on how to feed him up.*

As soon as James arrived home from the hospital, the family was 'sucked into the system, a special needs conveyor belt', which at the time Joan and Joe felt reassuring, but there was a serious downside:

> *There's no need to worry because things will be taken care of. So we were going to the Child Development Centre for this; you go to all these different places for that, but I ask you, how does that fit in with work. I didn't have time off work. Joe took him although I went a lot during my maternity leave.*

At the various centres, Joe, James and Joan met a range of professionals:

> *I took in all that they said and treated it as gospel. I was in awe of these experts and did everything they told me to do. I wanted to do whatever was necessary to give my child every chance.*

Joan was happy to accept the advice of the professionals who were trained and therefore 'knew' their job. Her view was very much that there was no point in asking the advice of the professionals and experts if you then ignored it:

> I am not very good at challenging. I don't feel I am in a position to know better. Equally so, if I say something as the professional at school, I don't expect people to tell me that I am wrong. Whenever I am challenged, I take it personally.

When James was two, the question of Statementing was raised. Joan read as much as she could about the process because she found the thought of it terrifying. The emphasis on parental involvement worried her initially:

> I was led to believe that I was going to be consulted and able to choose the school we wanted for James and I found that really scary, so I wanted to know all that there was to know about the process. The truth was that they go through the motions. They already know what they have decided and what they are going to do. He was going to go to the special school. It was ever so easy to persuade me, after all, that is where the money is, the facilities. He has had a very positive school career but I don't know if it was the right choice. We will never know.

At the age of two, James had gone to the assessment nursery; then at five he had gone to school and on to a special secondary school. His school life, however, had been varied and he had experienced a number of inclusive opportunities over the years, sometimes attending mainstream school for one day a week. The family had lived in a village at the time and the school was small and his brother was known there. But when they moved, the head of the new mainstream school was 'not receptive':

> Although she said yes, she meant no. She dillied and dallied and um'd and ah'd and things weren't right and we lost. It took about a year before she had the courage to say 'No, we don't want James at our school'! This was for an integration placement, not a full-time place, perhaps a morning or a day. We got another placement but it would have been nice for him to go there, as that was where all the other local children went.

For Joan, one of the problems of being a working mother was that time went by too quickly, there being too many things to do. This sometimes meant that she didn't chase things up when she needed to. She felt very irritated that the professionals involved with her son often asked what they as a family would like for him, and then set about telling them why such a course of action was not appropriate or available. The method of their approach was often wrong in her opinion:

> *I wanted him to have all the opportunities that everyone else had really. I wanted him to be seen as just normal.*

The mainstream placement was eventually agreed at a school where the head teacher already knew James from a previous school and was committed to encouraging children with learning difficulties. However, when he left that school the difficulties really began. Travelling to a special school away from the school of his brother and sister and the other children around him left James isolated. His school friends lived a distance away. Arranging for his friends from school to come back with him was often difficult:

> *He would never be able to organise it himself and with me working it is difficult. I don't have to organise Helen's friends to come round. They can just come, but for James it is very complicated. I don't know the other mothers and they might not want their children to come. I mean you have to look after them and they don't know me.*

The reason Joan had wanted James to go to a mainstream school was so that he could be part of the community. She felt that segregated schooling led to segregated adult life.

In 1992 Joan took voluntary severance from the bank. Wanting to continue with some kind of employment, however, she wondered what she should do. During her time at the bank, she had taken a City and Guilds course on Continuing Professional Development with an emphasis on SEN. In order to increase her knowledge of what was available for James, she now enrolled on the City and Guilds SEN course for teachers: 'I wanted to find out more. If anything was going, then James was going to have some.'

Having completed the course, Joan at first thought that she might work with adults with learning difficulties and she did some voluntary work at a Social Education Centre as well as some at a nearby special school, where she came to know the head teacher very well. Soon she was persuaded to go on the supply list for the county and within a few days found herself teaching at the special school. She was terrified of returning to the classroom:

I was really scared. I had been in school a little but I wasn't exactly confident. I remember it was an art lesson. I was an 'ex'-chemistry teacher teaching art. It was an all-age school but these children were about 15 or 16; my very first class after the best part of 20 years ... I suppose I got the job because the head knew me and knew I had a son with learning difficulties.

Joan also worked at a school for children aged between 8 and 16 where she supported a small group of children with extremely challenging behaviour. She had to cover all subjects with very little guidance. Soon Joan was in demand at a number of SLD (severe learning difficulties) schools in the county. She found that she was working only in special schools but she was happy about that. After two years she got a job with a neighbouring authority totally 'committed' to segregation with:

all its 11 special schools in nice, neat little categories: primary, SLD; primary, EBD; secondary, EBD; physical disabilities and so on.

The school is the only secondary SLD school in the authority. There are about 95 children and a staff of about 50, full and part time. Joan has been there for seven years now and works full time with Years 10 and 11 at present (ages 14–16). She is the science co-ordinator for the school. Sometimes parents found out that she had a disabled child, when they met her with James outside school, but occasionally Joan told them herself. She felt that these issues were very complex:

I used to think that having James put me in an extremely exclusive position, but then I realised that any parent wants the best for their children. But you really can't understand what it's like having a disabled child unless you have one. Your life is not your own ... So when parents say to me, 'you don't know what it is like to be on duty 24 hours a day', I do. And it's hard. As parents you have a huge emotional involvement, which teachers don't have. You are in a different position when you have a child with special needs. I think it does increase my credibility with the parents.

It was very easy for teachers to be critical of parents. Joan felt that teachers were sometimes very hard on parents who could be experiencing difficult times themselves. She felt that she was probably a 'difficult' parent, who, despite her earlier reservations about challenging professionals, now felt able to challenge educational experts. After seven years working in a special school, she felt that she too had expertise as both a teacher and a parent. She was very aware that she did not like being criticised as a teacher, although she felt very able and willing to challenge teachers as a parent herself. Although Joan acknowledged the complexity and interrelatedness of the two roles, she felt that the more important role was that of the parent:

I think I can understand a parent's point of view. I think this helps me in the way I treat parents, because I do understand what it is like. I do understand that, in general, parents want the best for their children.

To illustrate the difficulties and the complexity of the inter/intrarelationship between the two roles Joan gave one example from her own experience. One day Joan and James had been in the supermarket, when James, who sometimes behaved inappropriately, walked over to a little child and smacked the child hard. Joan was 'mortified' and 'marched James out of the shop and home'. James asked why they were going home:

I was expecting too much from him. I was expecting things that I wouldn't expect from the children at school. If you were taking the pupils at school shopping you would talk about it for a week and then you'd talk about it some more and plan it very carefully. I should have used my professional knowledge at home. It was a lesson for me. Works both ways I suppose. But somehow home is different, where you do what you feel like.

Respite care was a growing issue for Joan and James. NHS respite was very 'institutionalised' and Joan had had a 'long-running battle' with social services about the system. She had been encouraged to use the system in the early days when she went back to teaching, although she had 'stumbled across it by accident really'. At first it was as 'after-school care'. James was to be picked up from school and taken to the respite centre for tea. This was to take place on two or three occasions each week, to enable Joan to work. However, the care was cancelled at the last minute on a number of occasions, which caused Joan considerable concern and difficulty:

They said they had an emergency admission but it put me in a state of emergency! So I got really angry with them. Things went from bad to worse over a period of six months and in the end I wrote to the MP. The end result was that my name is known in social services offices all over the town, but nothing happened. We are absolutely no further on than we ever were. He had one night a week, which really didn't suit me.

One suggestion was that James should have 'shared fostering', which would mean that he would get to know another family with other children, which usually meant sharing a bedroom. James was now 18 and needed his own bedroom. He was also offered respite in a children's placement, but on more than one occasion Joan returned to find him in the sand pit. James needed to see himself as growing up. He was small and appeared young for his age so people tended to treat him as very young anyway. Joan felt he needed to be with older people so she asked for a placement in an adult respite centre. The problem then was that the placements were all over the authority and not in one centre, so there was little continuity and James would not have got to know people at any one centre. Joan felt it was lamentable that few people seemed to care about James's need to make friends as a young adult and have people he knew around him.

Finally, Joan had to pay someone to look after James after school till she got home. Even this was not easy, as it was difficult to find one carer and James now has a range of carers after school. He finishes at 3.00 p.m. but Joan's day doesn't finish till 4.00 p.m. at the very earliest. Things were so difficult at one stage that Joan felt that she would have to finish teaching altogether:

> I spoke to the social worker about it and she said to try to hang on. She told me that other families experienced the same problems. Anyway we are still struggling. We have some support and the rest I plug the gaps with people I pay. They just don't meet the needs of families. I have even had a person come to my house and say that we all have to make provision for our families. I did point out that that was for children who were 5 or 6 or even 10 or 12, but not for adults of 19!

Joan felt the tension at school very much as she had to leave school on time. Being in a special school meant after-school care duties, which Joan had to avoid. The pressure of collecting James was every night, unlike her daughter, who may need meeting after some sports event or after-school activity. Helen helps whenever she can but she is now 16 and so won't be at home forever. Joan describes the after-school care as 'a nightmare':

> It's a sort of balancing act and because we have a very complicated system now, I am afraid I will get it wrong. If one small thing goes wrong the whole thing comes falling down.

Transport is also a concern for the family. At present James gets transport to and from his school but he leaves this year and the situation at college will be different. Sometimes Joe can pick James up, but as a driving school instructor he has to be available when his clients want him and many young learner drivers prefer the hours immediately after school, so it is inevitably a busy time for him.

There is a self-help group for people with Cornelia de Lange syndrome and their families, but Joan and Joe did not wish to join. They were prepared to wait and see what the future might hold all in good time. Only time would tell what lay in store for them. Meanwhile they wanted to get on with the day-to-day issues, rather then be 'waiting for something to happen all the time'.

In the late 1990s Joan had been seconded to a neighbouring LEA where all five SLD schools had senior management posts specifically for integration (as it was then termed), to see various innovative practices in inclusive education. Her remit was to find out about this role and exactly what the job entailed. Largely as a result of this, she had been appointed as Inclusion Co-ordinator in her own school. The post was a senior one and her task was to promote inclusion, but Joan expressed concern about how this might be effected. One of her plans was to maximise the mainstream experience for the pupils in Years 10 and 11. Some of the local sixth-formers came to the school on community work placements but Joan considered this rather an unequal arrangement:

They're doing their community service on us. So there's sort of an, mmm, well is it an equal thing? I don't think they see themselves as equal. Rather than let them just come and 'do' their community service on us I try to bring a bit more equality into it by encouraging a self-advocacy group among the students here, but I am not sure that it has made any difference.

Joan had also tried to set up links with another school, but all these things were slow to take off. One of the issues which was giving her cause for concern was the 'selection' of students who might be 'suitable' for inclusion:

I had a word with our head about this. We send the very best students; the ones who are going to fit into the mould of normality. I am very concerned about that ... The head thinks that children with profound and multiple learning difficulties gain nothing from being in a mainstream school. He thinks that other children gain from them and I would agree with that. I might do some research into what benefits children with

PMLD might gain from being in the mainstream. However, I do think that the head feels that they are better in the segregated setting where they can benefit from all these wonderful facilities. He doesn't give the support I want, which is to exchange ideas with people, although there's nobody to exchange ideas with. I felt very isolated really. I sort of feel that I have been set up to do inclusion because it is the trend and has to be seen to be done.

Joan felt very strongly that James would have gained a great deal from more mainstream experience. While she felt that he had had a 'very happy, safe, secure, stable schooling' his experience of inclusion had not been very positive; it had brought out the 'worst in his behaviour':

I mean there have been occasions when he's just gone to his mainstream school and they have just sent him back because they just can't cope with him, his behaviour has been so bad; ripping other children's books and work. The dinner ladies have complained, well, he couldn't cope with the change in environment just for one day or less a week. The ed. psych. asked why they were sending him. She said she watched him once and he was 'fizzing like a little firework'.

James used to go to the mainstream school on a Tuesday, and often on a Monday he would tell Joan that he was not going to the school today. She thought he was confused with the days but in fact she later realised that what James was really saying was that he did not want to go at all:

He was saying 'I don't want to go', and I failed to hear him. My fanaticism for inclusion made me want him to go because I thought it would be good for him. I think that is one of the reasons why they probably kept sending him even though he didn't want to go, because they knew how I felt about inclusion.

Plugging the gaps: reflections

The dominant discourses of women, mothers and particularly mothers of 'special' children construct women as selfless, loving, unpaid carers in the home (Read 2000). The discourse makes no mention of the fact that many mothers of children with SEN/disabilities try to work, or the problems they face in doing so (Dowling and Dolan 2001, Read 2000). Discourses of mothers and disability suggest that the greatest period of difficulty is when the child is young or at particular times of development (Roll-Petterson 2001). There is an implicit assumption that, as with other children, age brings independence. There is no mention in these discourses of the difficulties for both the young adult and the parents increasing as the children get older; difficulties which are often created by professional constructions of difference such as segregated schooling provision and family support. This reflects how professionals, and consequently service provision, underestimate the support needed by young people and their families, and the nature of that support (Read 2000, Roll-Petterson 2001).

The notion of themselves and their children as independent beings who can lead separate lives does not appear in the discourses of mothers or disability, making it very difficult for such women to work outside the home, or for their children to have any degree of independence or social interaction with others outside the family (Read 2000). The degree to which this social interaction of the young person depends on the mother is evident here, along with the feelings of guilt which can be created through the power of the discourse of mothers as carers. Such a discourse does not acknowledge that mothers may have two jobs (Sikes 1997).

The story suggests the disparity between the reality and the rhetoric surrounding the discourse of the working mother and it is not surprising that relatively few women with Joan's private responsibilities go out to work (Read 2000). For working mothers like Joan, there are still barriers to working outside the home unless there is considerable family support (ibid.). It is hardly surprising, therefore, that so many families with children with SEN/disabilities are economically disadvantaged (Dowling and Dolan 2001).

The story illustrates the difficulties of matching the needs of mother *and* child, in contrast to the notions of the dyad of 'motherandchild' (Everingham 1994) created in the dominant discourse. While the story highlights how the educational segregation of children and young adults from their peers in the local community can create a sense of isolation and difficulty for the development of a social life for young people as they grow older, it also illustrates the difficulties for the mother as agent for her child. It often falls to her to arrange this, which can be a time-consuming and difficult exercise for a mother who is working (Read 2000) and possibly an additional source of guilt.

9 Julia: eating the elephant

Question: How do you eat an elephant?
Answer: In small bites!

> *They [the professionals] were perhaps a bit like a wedge between me and natural friends really. I became very isolated actually when they were both very young ... I felt quite isolated from other mothers and families. I did feel that we weren't invited like other people for some reason. It might have been something to do with something I was giving off. Or maybe I just wasn't part of it all because we were going to clinics.*

> *They said they would love to have him. It was the first time we felt welcome I think. And that first year he was there it was just wonderful. He was a different child, a completely different child.*

(Julia)

Julia lives in the suburbs of a city in Yorkshire, with her husband, Brian, and two sons, Martin, aged 17 when Julia told her story, and Stuart, aged 15. Both boys attend the local comprehensive school: Martin has Down's syndrome and Stuart is deemed gifted and talented. Julia, now in her early fifties, works as a teacher at a nearby special, secondary school for children with profound and multiple learning difficulties (PMLD).

Julia described herself as from the 'aspiring working class'. She said that her home life in a council house in South Wales was 'quite traumatic in a way', with lots of tensions mainly because her mother had a nervous breakdown and found life 'quite difficult'. The family was not 'particularly academic' and Julia's older brother left school with only basic qualifications, although he has since done an MBA. Julia passed her eleven-plus and attended a local co-educational grammar school.

As she moved into adolescence, Julia remembered feeling that her education was of little importance to her parents, because of her mother's illness and her father's preoccupation with keeping the family together. Having done 'O' level GCEs in four years, Julia decided to stay on another year in the sixth form where she was taking modern foreign languages and economics. Out of desperation, her father encouraged her to go to university and, as her friends were all applying, Julia decided to apply for one near where her grandparents lived in Wales, where she took German with French and History of Art. Julia enjoyed the social life of university and the year abroad, common to all students of modern foreign languages.

By 1975 she decided to go into teaching because 'there didn't seem to be a lot on offer for arts or language graduates and I thought this will be something useful to fall back on'. Julia went to London to do her PGCE and, on completion, got a job teaching modern languages in a boys' school in London in the late 1970s. It was virtually an all-male environment, and even the few female teachers were referred to as Masters. While in London she met Brian who was a graduate of the London School of Economics and in 1978 Julia and Brian married. After a period in Greater London and two years travelling around the world, they finally settled in a city in the north of England. Brian took a job in the Civil Service and Julia took various temporary jobs in and around the city, teaching mainly languages. In 1984, at the age of 31, Julia had her first child, Martin:

> I was teaching full time. They did ask me to go back, actually, after I'd had Martin and I went back part time. Then I had Stuart. There is very little between them, two years and two months. I stayed at home till Martin was between four and five and he'd gone to nursery.

Julia remembered how her perception of children had changed:

> When I was teaching before, I thought I knew about people and children and things, but since I've had my own children it seems quite different. Quite a different perspective really. They suddenly became human beings. I saw them completely differently. It gave me a different insight, more understanding. Not necessarily more tolerant or patient.

Martin was delivered by Caesarean section and Julia was not told about her baby son's condition straight away. The midwife had picked up that something was wrong and Martin was taken away for tests:

> He had done really well on the test and got fairly ordinary scores apparently, but he was a bit floppy or something. I had done all the natural childbirth things although the birth hadn't been very natural, but I was determined to breast-feed him, but they kept taking him off me. They would sort of patronise me and say that I would be better getting

my sleep. They said he was a bit jaundiced and that they would give him some water. But anyway they took him and fed him and things like that.

One day when Julia was on her own, a doctor told her that Martin had Down's syndrome:

She sat there, looked very official, I think she had a suit on or something and she sat there just tapping a foot, that kind of approach, and I thought, you've come in and you've told me this thing about … how can you say that? He's beautiful, you know my baby; how can you say that?

Shocked and emotional, Julia had to tell Brian and her parents: 'I felt desperately for my parents; they really wanted a grandchild. My father went home and cried.' As first-time parents Julia and Brian never suspected that anything was wrong. Brian had not really wanted children and Julia now wondered how he must feel having a son with Down's syndrome. She needn't have worried; after a period of time to reflect, Brian was so positive:

It was one of the best things that happened to us really.

Once the family was over the initial shock everyone 'rallied round', although her mother kept bringing 'awful stories' from the daily newspapers:

about how they could do wonders these days with children with Down's syndrome and how you can have cosmetic surgery to make them look normal. I remember getting really cross with her because I felt this was about her needs and not mine. I told her that I didn't mind; he looks fine to me, thank you very much. I was the most ungrateful child because all she was trying to do was to help me.

Most of the support they were offered at the time was medical. When Martin was six months old, Brian and Julia were offered genetic counselling. They were feeling extremely positive about their family. Of course, they had gone through the usual new-parent traumas of watching Martin's weight, 'as do all new mums, especially those who breast-feed'. But, as proud new parents, they were firmly of the opinion that their new baby was

the bee's knees, the apple of our eye, and everything. He was just a wonderful baby. He was lovely and full of fun. We went for this genetic counselling and took six steps back because suddenly we were made to think that it was all doom and gloom. We had this child with Down's syndrome and we were reminded how imperfect this child was and did we want to go on repeating this by having any more children.

A simple test revealed that Martin's Down's syndrome was not hereditary but there was still a considerable risk of them having another child with the same syndrome. The professional who imparted this information, the geneticist, spent much of the time telling them about his own dreadful experiences with a child with diabetes, and suggested how awful their lives were going to be when their children were older and no longer 'cute'. Julia remembered how depressing it had been because 'he just painted this awful picture'. While Brian, Julia and Martin were at the clinic, they were asked if they would mind some photographs being taken. They were horrified for, as Julia described it, 'it was like he was having his photo taken for prison'. The photographs were for a medical journal so that people could be shown the physical characteristics of a child with Down's syndrome. They could have refused but felt too vulnerable at the time. Julia came away from their 'counselling' session crying.

Before Martin was two, Julia found that she was pregnant again. An amniocentesis test revealed that the baby, a boy, was fine and in 1987 Stuart arrived. There was a lot of pressure now from the professionals to send Martin to nursery school and he duly went for two days a week. Julia found this very difficult: 'It was horrific; traumatic! He seemed ever so young really'. The nursery was a social services 'integrated' day nursery, so they had 'normal' children there as well, but Martin did not immediately take to it. Although he normally enjoyed his food, he did not enjoy dinnertime at the nursery and Julia still feels guilty about those days and is haunted by the memory:

> His tiny face crumpling up, starting to cry. Oh I was beside myself. It was breaking my heart. It was like something out of the Victorian age.

Julia felt that if he had been her second child, she would have taken him home, but as a first-time mum she felt that others must know better than she did:

> I didn't know what motherhood was about. I didn't know what babies were about. I certainly didn't know what disabled babies were about. I didn't know anything. It even took a while for me to stand up to my own mother and say, 'Look, Mum, we're going to make lots of mistakes but we've got to make the decisions here.' It took me a while to build up my confidence and to go on my own instincts.

Martin and Stuart began to develop a 'very typical' love–hate, sibling relationship. There were awful scenes in the double buggy when they 'terrorised the neighbourhood'. Julia felt that they were not really meeting local children and their mothers, so the educational psychologist suggested that Martin should attend the local nursery. Until then, Julia was unaware that he was entitled to go there:

> I had no idea. I never knew a thing about special educational needs or the latest legislation or the Warnock Report or anything like that. We never looked back since that advice and I do know we're privileged because I know most parents don't get this sort of proactive advice.

Martin was assessed at the age of one and it was discovered that he needed to wear spectacles and that he had a hearing impairment. They now became 'part of the system' and as soon as he was two, he received a Statement of SEN. Julia became friends with the various therapists, the 'army of support people' who worked with Martin, for 'they were the people I saw most'. Making friends with other mothers was not easy because of all the visits to clinics and the visits of professionals. Julia's isolation is expressed in the quotation at the beginning of the story and again here:

> I think I had some post-natal depression after Stuart's birth, which wasn't diagnosed, and I went through a very hard time when Stuart was about one and Martin was about three.

The visits to the various clinics were particularly hard on Stuart, who was not proving an easy baby at all. It was Martin who was usually the centre of attention when people did call.

The local school agreed to take Martin, who was now six. He missed out on the Reception class, which is generally considered to be a very important stage for all children. The school had a large percentage of Asian children, who were very friendly towards Martin, but he was teased by many other children. He had a support teacher for the deaf, who often withdrew him from lessons at the request of the teacher. His behaviour was deteriorating as he took on the role of the class clown. Julia and Brian also felt that they were not being involved as much as they should be. As they became aware that things were not right, Julia found herself turning this onto Martin:

> When I picked him up from school I would blame Martin for the things that had gone wrong and it was horrible. Suddenly I thought, hang on, this isn't fair. He is getting a double dose; things were going wrong at school and then it was going wrong for him at home.

Julia tried to talk to the teacher about her concerns but felt that the teacher didn't want Martin in her class. One of the other 'team' teachers felt that Julia needed to teach Martin to stand up to the bullies and that it was up to the child to deal with the problem. The school 'tolerated' him going into Year 2 but Julia felt that the teachers had decided that he would not carry on after that. They made it quite impossible for him to stay by asking the LEA for a great deal more support, which was most unlikely to be forthcoming. The school then claimed that there were many aspects of his education that they were unable to meet, and that there were certain things which were dangerous. Stuart had by now joined Martin at the school but was not settling very well. He was soon perceived as 'gifted and talented' but at the age of five, this was only suspected.

It was clear that the school was not going to want to keep Martin. Julia then 'sort of came out':

> I think that, looking back, part of my isolation was obviously something that I had internalised and the more problems that occurred at school, the more I retreated I suppose, and it became more and more difficult. I felt alienated from everybody – all these people seemed to be having a nice happy time, all hunky dory for them, and we were going through this awful, horrible time and I didn't like schools. They were awful places.

On the advice of the support staff, Julia and Brian decided to move Martin. Julia talked the situation over with a friend, who was horrified at what was happening and got other parents to sign a petition and an accompanying letter to the authority, in which the parents outlined how Martin ought to be a part of the school and the local community. But the authority was determined to move Martin, and Julia felt that the effort to stay was too great. Martin's hearing impairment was one of the reasons given for refusal. Brian and Julia were 'too disheartened' by this time and thought about moving to another area. Then it dawned on them that they were just running away which was 'just crazy'. Despite feeling isolated and alienated, they decided to apply to other local schools. One of the local schools invited Martin in for a visit. The staff found him charming and expressed their pleasure in offering him a place at the school and said they would love to have him. Things seemed to be changing:

> We went in once, I can't remember why, and saw Martin walking across the playground with a register tucked under his arm, and he saw us and he went cock-a-hoop. He had been given the job of taking the register back and it's such a little thing but so very important to him. That made our day. It was almost like a new start for us.

Martin was in the class of the deputy head, a 'traditional, typically old-fashioned community-type, junior school teacher' who knew how to include children. The whole class 'became a community around Martin, supportive'. Martin dressed up with the others on Viking day and the teacher created opportunities for him to share in the learning and fun of the day. Inevitably, Martin had his ups and downs at the school and in Year 5 he had a 'horrendous' time during which he was bullied. Julia felt that this was not addressed by the class teacher. There was no communication between school and home about this and it was only through a friend that Julia found out what was happening. This later made her realise that she had to learn to listen to Martin himself and trust him. It had also given her real insights into the importance of home–school communication and the need for partnership between parents and teachers:

> I've learnt a lot. He has taught me that I have to listen to him more. I didn't listen to him; we do listen to him now, though, and he is usually right about things. He has taught us that lesson. He has been my best teacher. But, at the time, we were still in the position of being parents in awe of the local authority. There are colleagues who are still quite unkind to parents if anyone comes in and makes a comment: 'What do they know' is often the reply. 'They're questioning my professional judgement' is the view expressed and you can make yourself very unpopular if you stick your neck out.

Unfortunately, there were a growing number of things that Julia felt weren't right in the school, one of which was that Martin was still seen as the problem when things didn't work. Martin's behaviour was not always easy to understand and things 'could get out of hand', but on the whole Julia felt that the school had tried and that individual teachers had gained from having Martin in their class.

However, the 'battles' started when he came to go to the high school. Martin should have had a place at the local secondary school, but he was rejected. They claimed they couldn't meet his needs, despite Julia and Brian working closely with the LEA to ensure that the Statement expressly stated that he should go to the local mainstream school. Julia remembered that a number of parents of children with SEN were becoming more 'vociferous' about their wishes for their children to attend mainstream schools:

> We were all played off actually. The authority would say one thing to the school and another to the parents ... Eventually I managed to get them to

state even the name of the school. But that didn't stop the school still saying it didn't want Martin. They sent a stinking letter back saying there was no way they could meet his needs.

Finally the LEA offered the school another £1,000 to take Martin. 'The bribe', as Julia refers to it, got 'lost in the school coffers, as it does', but even so Martin went there. 'It's not been plain sailing all the way.' The original aim had been to make an integrated resource at the school for pupils with learning difficulties and physical difficulties. The head had sent round a questionnaire in order to get parents and staff to debate the issues. The answers she got back, even from the teachers, were very discriminatory according to Julia. She noted, sadly, that this was never addressed by the LEA. The situation was made worse for Julia and Martin when he was placed into the classroom of a teacher who clearly did not want him. The comments made on Martin's report were described by Julia as 'abusive' and at best 'unsupportive'. Julia and Brian were distressed and angry:

It might not seem important to other people but when he referred to Martin talking gibberish and things like that we were hurt. He said that Martin had to learn to see to his personal care. I didn't know what he meant. Martin is very particular really. Maybe he had a runny nose or something. Such comments are so hurtful really because there is no redress. We did go and talk to the head about it. She said he was a good subject teacher but doesn't understand children. Nothing really happened, but we don't get those reports back now. I think he did actually warm to Martin because in his last report he said something nice, rather grudgingly, about Martin.

Julia and Brian were aware that only a small handful of staff were really positive about Martin being at the school. He was perceived as a challenging pupil, but it was clear to Julia that he was not the only one in his class, although he was frequently presented as the problem. Without a whole-school approach to inclusion, Julia felt that there would be inadequate resourcing and support, which did not make the teachers' lives any easier. The school still operated a withdrawal system of support, which Julia felt did not give ownership of SEN to all the staff but kept it in the SEN department, although signs of change were appearing. The LEA had paid for an educational psychologist with experience of Down's syndrome to come into the school when Martin was in Year 8, and this did offer other teachers a chance to realise that there were things they could do. She suggested, for instance, that as he was doing his own work anyway, he could just as well be in the top set, where there might be more positive behaviour role models. So he went into the top set for science and it proved to be very successful. This gave the school a little more confidence to be flexible, but by Year 9 things changed again because of options choice and the threat of GCSEs.

At this point the educational psychologist came to talk to Julia and Brian to try to persuade them to send Martin to a special school. Julia and Brian listened as the professional talked about the need to improve Martin's independence skills, which could be done at the special school across the city. Julia asked how Martin would get to the school. The answer: 'In a taxi'. He takes his bike to the local mainstream school and has to organise that himself. Being at the mainstream school had undoubtedly offered Martin a range of opportunities he might not have had, as a result of which he now takes the bus to the local youth theatre on his own.

Martin remained at the mainstream school. Stuart attends the same school as his brother, which pleases Julia. Martin is outgoing and, although there is little doubt in her mind that Stuart wanted to 'see the back of Martin sometimes', she felt that the boys were glad to be together. Stuart, however, is regarded as a student who should add to the school's academic results and, as the school is a high-achieving establishment and quite high up in national league tables, this is seen as important. Julia is concerned, though, that he is not having his needs met. He does not easily socialise and is not an easy communicator like his brother. Ironically, Stuart finds it harder to 'build bridges' than his brother.

Julia returned to teaching when the boys were only very young; Stuart was at nursery and Martin just in school. Like many returning women teachers in the 1980s, she took the supply route back. She was asked by a neighbour to do some SEN supply teaching in a primary special school and, despite knowing nothing about primary teaching or special needs teaching, she was persuaded because the teacher argued that she 'must know quite a bit if you have a child with Down's syndrome', even though Martin was only six at the time.

The school was for children with SLD and PMLD and it also had a care unit for young adults up to the age of 23, although this part of the school has since closed. Julia felt that the teachers were not taking things really seriously and was 'damn glad that Martin, warts and all' was attending a mainstream school.

Julia enjoyed the primary experience so much that she decided to do a conversion course, which gave her an introduction to the National Curriculum and the changes which were coming into schools 'fast and furious' at this time around 1991. Having completed the course she got a job straight away in a local junior school. The staff in the school had been there for some considerable time and treated Julia rather like an NQT, who had arrived with new ideas, but Julia did not settle into the school and so when the opportunity came to go elsewhere she took it.

She then moved to her current post in a special secondary school, where she has taught for six years. Julia was concerned about being in a special school and a number of parents she knew were rather judgemental about her being there because of her views on inclusion. She found this quite hard and tried to defend her choice of school in various ways. First, she argued the 'money bit'. Then she said that she enjoyed working with students with learning difficulties and that she would not meet many such students if she were to teach in mainstream. She said she wanted to 'make a difference' and that she could identify with many of the parents of the children at the school. Her professional life has not been an easy one since joining the school. The school went into special measures after an Ofsted inspection and these were only lifted in the autumn of 2000. Julia noted that, until recently, many of the parents felt that their children were not getting a very good deal. They were very angry, although Julia felt that perhaps the school was used as a bit of a scapegoat:

> Perhaps the school was taking the brunt of the feelings and anger that they'd gone through right from the word go. The caboodle of dealing with the authority, dealing with the professionals, all those things that build up inside you and you haven't got real channels to blame, so you blame the staff. There can be one or two difficult parents, I know, but there was no attempt to get behind what they were saying and why, and get at what they might be feeling and why. They were told that their children had to go to special school and there was no choice. People negotiate with the LEA to get the best deal they can. The ones who shout the loudest, the vociferous parents, get what they want. That's what you have to learn to do. Most people don't shout.

The LEA had what Julia referred to as 'a pecking order of special schools' and Julia talked of them 'selecting out' some children depending on the nature of the disability or SEN. There was little real choice in the LEA, although many parents felt that there was and that they had chosen the special schools. Julia's belief was that the LEA did the choosing unless parents really fought for their choice. Some of the schools had integrated resources, which were popular, but many parents felt that their children would be better away from mainstream schools where they might be bullied. One parent had come to see Julia about her teenage daughter:

> It's the hardest thing in the world, isn't it, a teenage girl growing up in a confusing world? It's hard for anyone. A parent couldn't get behind that. All sorts of worries and anxieties about her daughter, things like sexuality and things like that. But more than that, it was worries about herself, her own loss of life. She's had this daughter imposed on her, all those confusing feelings. 'I haven't got a proper life with my husband; and there's no respite now. I am going to take my child and dump her on the social services' doorstep and say, "You have her and see what it is like".' And she's ended up in tears, this parent who had been really difficult. There is so much emotion there really. The emotion is never talked about.

The response of the school was very much one of 'how dare she'. At one parents' evening this mother had come in and many of the other teachers came over to support Julia, as this particular mother could be 'very difficult'. Julia felt this had been very intimidating for the parent, who had come with just her advocate:

> I felt sorry for this parent, not that she would have understood my empathy, because it is still perceived as a them and us situation really.

Many of the parents at the school knew about Martin, but because he was at a mainstream school they felt that he was 'bright'. Julia smiled and reflected that others never knew what we went through:

> My situation is very similar to theirs really, but they think that it is all right for me. They don't realise that the school [mainstream] is always trying to get rid of him because he is not very bright. She [the mother] wouldn't see me as being a sort of ally, or that I was trying to understand her. I think there was a kind of unspoken understanding and she might have felt that I wasn't as bad as some of the others.

There was sadness in her voice as she spoke of the way in which many parents were treated at the time. In her view, there was very little support for them. The whole process left the children invisible:

*Well, they always are [invisible] really, aren't they. I knew what it was
like; I saw both sides. I thought, why does it have to be like this? There
must be another way. However, you can come over as a 'know-all' if you
are not careful. I think I have a good relationship with the parents really
but it isn't as if they see me as 'one of them'. In fact sometimes I think it
is worse really, because they do not see the difficulties Martin has in
school. They think he is in mainstream because I am a teacher and so
they say, 'Oh it's all right for her, she's a teacher. She knows people in the
right places.' They think I get what I want because of that. They don't
think I have worries about the future too.*

Martin leaves school soon. Other people thought that this shouldn't
present concerns for Julia, who must know the system and would
know what to do. For Julia it felt like being in 'no man's land'. The
school Martin attended had never really accepted that they could learn
from having him there. Julia was a governor at the school and knew
that the word 'inclusion' was still a 'dirty' word, which was avoided
wherever possible. Equal opportunities were talked about in terms of
race, for the children of travellers and children considered gifted and
talented, but there was a reluctance to talk about inclusion, as this
would mean:

*taking all and sundry; kids from other parts of the city as well as those
with learning difficulties. There would be no get-out.*

Because of her beliefs about inclusion and her experiences with Martin
at the mainstream school, Julia fought hard for the children and older
teenagers in the special school, to give them more responsibility:

*I feel that we ought to be trusting them more and giving them more
responsibility. I keep going back to that register that day. It's something
that perhaps some mainstream teachers do. There is a fear that children
can't be left on their own in this special school ... in case there are
accidents ... then we are comfortable. But I send them off and you see
children wandering around the school. Other staff then say that they are
out of control if they are out of a classroom. They're not; they are just
acting independently. So it is difficult.*

At home, Martin was encouraged to join in the family responsibilities
for the household. He accepted this responsibility and loved to have a
list of jobs he had to do. There were boxes for him to tick when he had
done the job. He loved having the responsibility to decide his next job
and Julia was about to introduce this into the school. It was clear that

Julia felt very close to the children in the school and she was sure this was because she had her own experiences with Martin:

It's almost like an extended family really. Many of the children are the same age as my children and like many teenagers they enjoy 'sounding off' and being stroppy. I don't necessarily deal with it any better. The children at school talk about their parents and they make the link. Do I talk about my children at school? Probably too much, but the kids love it. They want to know their names. Both my children have been into school. Martin loves going in. It's Mum's work and he gets a good reception.

When Martin goes to Julia's school he talks about his 'work and colleagues'. He talks about 'going to help out' and Julia 'blurs it. I don't make the distinction'.

However, there are some very difficult issues which arise from the present educational context. Physical contact in schools today is very difficult for teachers, and special schools have to be very careful. Julia acknowledged that in many situations, an arm round a shoulder was helpful with a kind word of encouragement. She saw it as a mother might. Many staff did not feel comfortable with this. Julia considered herself more patient at school than at home but admitted that she had relaxed more recently since she stopped trying to 'teach' Martin. Once she had accepted that he too wanted to relax at home, and that she should leave the teacher at school, things were much better.

Brian and Julia were very mutually supportive with regard to Martin and Stuart. Brian could be assertive and even aggressive if he was really concerned about a situation. In the past Brian had challenged the head teacher about attitudes to inclusion, but Julia admitted that, now Martin was coming to the end of his school days, they had perhaps 'run out of energy', especially if they felt that it wouldn't make any difference anyway. Brian no longer attended annual reviews, although Julia felt that she should go 'to the bitter end' and, very definitely, wore her 'parent's hat'.

Inclusion, for Julia, was about opposing forces and she could foresee there being a great deal of resistance, much of it passive, from schools who would just allow it to fail and then the children with SEN would be taken away:

Mainstream schools don't work for a lot of children. It isn't that good for Stuart. They [LEAs and schools] will let parents become disenchanted and then they will take the children away. For others it will be assumed that they could never attend mainstream school. Their parents will never be encouraged to try to send the children to mainstream school, so that the powers that be can say that the parents don't want inclusion. There is a lot of fear among parents and special schools. Both fear that they might lose out to inclusion.

Although Julia believed that Martin had not had an 'inclusive life', she did consider that the opportunities he had were better than he would have had in a special school. But the gap between Martin and his peers had widened, as indeed Julia had expected it would. By Year 11 teenagers are:

Out and about and up to all sorts, probably things I wouldn't want Martin to get up to and I am sure that they wouldn't want to take him with them sometimes. But once or twice they [pupils from school] have called for him and they've always come to his birthday celebration. I think the other kids are quite supportive. I think he has a group of supportive people. He is actually quite self-sufficient. He goes to the sixth form for lunch and has friends there. He had a week in Scotland doing outdoor education with Year 11 pupils, which was great. First time he has been on a school trip. The only time we had ever allowed him to go ... interesting. Hmmmm.

Eating the elephant: reflections

Despite the work of Tomlinson (1982) and many others, dominant discourses of special educational needs and disability still construct 'needs' through a mainly medical and expert model. In this model, difference is constructed through the processes and practices of professionals, both educational and medical (Corbett 1996, Oliver 1996b). Within this dominant discourse, the discourse of inclusion remains largely rhetoric.

For me, Julia's story highlights two issues – exclusion and inclusion – as the two quotes at the beginning of the story illustrate. It offers insights into the construction of 'difference' through professional discourses and highlights the complexity of the reality surrounding inclusion. On one level it suggests that many barriers against inclusion are firmly in place; on another level it gives real hope that there are educational professionals who have the courage, knowledge and understanding to find ways in which all children can be 'included' in some small way which makes a 'difference' to them and their families.

The story makes visible the way in which professionals take control and construct difference in both child and family, placing the child and his or her mother on the 'other side of the track' (Read 2000: 15), and Julia's story highlights the isolation noted by other mothers of children with SEN/disabilities (Read 2000, Roll-Petterson 2001). Although Julia questions whether this is her own doing, her story does raise the question as to why mothers like Julia feel so isolated. It highlights the ways in which the structures and processes, to which children with SEN/disabilities and their families are subjected, combine to isolate them and define them as 'different', excluding them from the social world and therefore the support networks of other young families (Read 2000, Dowling and Dolan 2001, Roll-Petterson 2001). As we have seen before in some of the other stories, as mothers grow in understanding and experience, their confidence develops and they are able to challenge the dominant discourses of professionals.

For me the most important aspect of this story is the way in which it signals how small acts of inclusion make a great deal of difference; the 'difference' a caring school culture and careful teaching (Corbett 1992) can make to a young child and his or her family. Julia's delight when she feels that Martin has been accepted and welcomed into the school community is clear. It offers an insight into the detail and reality of what inclusion means, and demonstrates what can happen if teachers are allowed to 'try', a view also reflected in Truda's story.

Contexts, contradictions, complexities: commitment and consensus

Maybe it is wrong to imagine that contradictions can be explained.
(Høeg 1996: 92)

Introduction

The stories in this book suggest that inclusion is many things to many people in many different contexts. Among the mother-teachers there is diversity of opinion. While they share certain experiences, they are far from being a homogeneous group. But what I feel emerges from the stories is the overwhelming notion that within the grand scale of things, individuals matter, at every level and in every context. Individual professionals make a difference to children and their families, particularly their mothers.

Contexts: political and sociological

Writing about social and educational exclusion Macrae *et al.* (2003) draw on the distinction between 'weak' and 'strong' versions of exclusion (Viet-Wilson 1998). They argue that, while 'weaker' versions try to change the child to 'fit' into the system (square peg, round hole), 'stronger' forms of the discourse emphasise the significance of 'powerful' individual professionals within the processes. These 'powerful' individuals, together with second order (sometimes unintended) consequences of policy, can contribute to the maintenance of exclusion (Macrae *et al.* 2003). In this book I have argued that the juxtaposition of special education and inclusion within policies of competition and the discourses of professionals contribute to the construction and reproduction of difference. Within each of the stories there exists the remembered professional who, through 'careful' practice, makes the mothers and their children feel valued and included. Equally significant are those professionals who are remembered for their obstructive actions or stances, their reaffirmation of difference as difficulty.

As I noted in Kate's story, Ball (1998: 78) maintains that, 'we have too much knowledge and not enough understanding'. Slee (1999) agrees, arguing that the 'disabling process', which works to separate children and adults with SEN/disabilities, is in part caused by too much *professional* knowledge about special needs. Corbett (1996) regards the very term 'special' as part of this 'disabling process' for groups of children. But government, LEAs and schools seem reluctant to move away from notions of 'professional expertise' in SEN; indeed, LEA training courses for SENCOs appear to be proliferating, and recent DfES policies suggest a more formal management and 'expert' role for the SENCO. If my recent conversation with a senior SEN adviser is indicative, there appears to be a move towards the 'professionalisation' of special education and inclusion through this formalisation of 'expert' knowledge. It was an interesting conversation because his vision is one in which all teachers accept their responsibility for teaching all children within a whole-school ethos where SENCOs and SEN specialists act as consultants and advisers. He noted that the reality was a long way from such a vision.

I would argue that we have moved forward some way in the process of inclusion. Since the early 1980s we have seen a proliferation of policies designed to further educational and social inclusion. There are many dedicated and 'caring' professionals in our schools, who remain faithful to a vision of inclusion for all children and work hard to achieve it. There are undoubtedly pockets of truly inclusive education. While it can be argued that funding is still a major issue, there has been funding from a variety of sources (e.g. Education Action Zones, Excellence in Cities, Standards Funds, etc.), although whether this is sufficient or reaches the right schools and communities remains contentious. There are parents who strive hard to support their children in mainstream schools, sometimes in the face of considerable difficulties and even opposition, and others who, while believing in the need to maintain special and segregated provision, care about inclusive practices within this different context. There are many professionals who work hard to eliminate exclusion within special contexts and many excellent examples of outreach work from special schools to mainstream.

Yet the stories in this book suggest that the process has not moved far enough. While they illustrate the complex interrelationship between professional knowledge and the formation of 'knowledge' through abstraction from personal experience, the women's stories reflect the 'expert knows best' theory – the preferring of the professional above the mother. Within the complexities of home–school, parent–professional relationships, they offer insights into the importance of understanding and experience as a part of professional knowledge. Although the stories reveal the ways in which these mothers challenge the boundaries and constructions, they also illuminate the ways in which dominant discourses work to retain control, through the reproduction of professional constructions of 'normality' in the public domain. The collective experiences offered here suggest a greater sense of normality than is presented in the discourse. The mothers' experiences in many areas of their lives, such as becoming a mother and the early years of child rearing, would be recognised by many mothers of children without SEN/disabilities. This is not to say that these mothers experience no problems but that many of these are created by the 'specialness' of the processes and procedures constructed by experts, who are supposed to be supporting them, and by the attitudes of the professionals themselves. They are not the problems presented in the discourses as sources of difficulty.

The stories suggest that inclusion emerges on two different levels: the meta-discourse level of policies and ideologies, and the micro-, 'reality' level of school. In the former, the rhetoric of official documents is about parental choice and 'all' children 'wherever possible' attending mainstream schools with their peers. But there are contradictions which are masked by the rhetoric. The language marking out 'special needs' creates difference and even the language of inclusion has its 'get-out' clauses, such as the words, 'wherever possible' (e.g. DfES 2001). The stories indicate that initiatives for inclusion can come from special schools seeking to further the mainstream opportunities of their pupils and may be resisted by mainstream schools, where cultures of competition are not supportive of SEN/disabilities and inclusion. While the mother-teachers express their support for mainstream schooling and inclusion, there is also recognition of the very valuable support provided in and by many special schools. The relationship between educational and social inclusion is evident in the stories, with the latter very dependent on the former in many ways.

The reality of 'difference' emerges as the young adults and their families struggle to deal with the social isolation which may result from segregated provision.

Yet the stories reflect the considerable joy that small acts of inclusion bring to the children and their mothers. They offer insights into the notion that inclusion is not about grand policies and discourses, but that the reality of inclusion is where a school or an individual professional 'tries'. One small act or expression of welcome, such as 'We would love to have your child at our school', makes a difference. This 'individualising' of inclusion does not negate the responsibility of the State and the government. The responsibility for coherent and compatible policies, for appropriate and accessible funding, for training and professional development and support for teachers, for appropriate and supportive inspection or rather school self-evaluation, lies with government, LEAs and school leadership. But there is also a responsibility for individual professionals to examine and question their own values and beliefs, constructions and assumptions and to reappraise their professional practices, approaches and, where possible, the structures and processes through which their values are made explicit. As the stories illustrate, the mother-teachers have all, in different ways, reconceptualised their own professional practices and approaches to other children and their parents. Within the day-to-day context of everyday lives, such challenges and changes are highly significant; they matter.

The sociological and political changes of the 1980s and 1990s have brought with them changing notions of professional knowledge. What was seen as appropriate practice in the 1980s may be regarded as outmoded at the beginning of the twenty-first century. Such changes should alert professionals to the possible fragility of such knowledge as a power base, making them rather more sceptical to 'easily claim, firstly to know and secondly to blame' (Billington 2000: 6). The educational framework within which many professionals work may be structurally unsuited to inclusion. But even within this framework, the stories suggest there is space for individual professionals to interpret the various processes of assessment, monitoring and evaluation of children and, as an extension of them, their mothers. These 'powerful' professionals, head teachers, educational psychologists, SEN professionals and teachers, LEA advisers, can affect the culture and ethos of schools and institutions and, depending on their personal values and beliefs, make inclusion 'happen'.

The process of inclusion must involve changes and the stories told here demonstrate that individual professionals can influence this process. But this means challenging existing constructions of difference, a considerable risk for professionals who have vested interests in maintaining existing power structures. The experiences of the mothers suggest the complexity of the issues and the need to listen to the voices of people concerned, in order to gain a more particular insight and understanding. Dominant discourses, on the other hand, by presenting a single, ideological 'collective voice', ossify the issues, reduce the complexity and ultimately risk the failure of real progress in the process of inclusion.

Contradictions and complexities

Contradictions and complexities emerge as almost a leitmotif within the book. They appear to abound within and around the stories, emerging from their contextualisation against dominant discourses and conflicting policies. The contradictions of principle within the two key education policy initiatives of the 1980s and 1990s provide a difficult context for many in education, not least for those concerned with SEN, placing market value before 'moral' values, notions of equity and rights. There are complexities around constructions of professional knowledge through competing discourses, some of which make claims for expertise in SEN, while others support the principle of SEN within a more holistic school approach. As an identified area within education, SEN/disability can claim resources, space and status (albeit lowly), supported by 'special' structures and processes. But this must essentially remain a dubious claim, for who wants to be 'special' if it means being marginalised as 'different' (Corbett 1996).

Complexities also exist around personal and professional relationships, between both the mothers and other professionals, and also within their own intrarelationships, their own personal juxtaposition of the two roles. Their own hesitancy to approach professionals within the role of mother, who is also a teacher, is one such example. It is evident from the stories that there are emotional aspects within both the roles. But within the discourses, while the emotional nature of the personal role is acknowledged, the emotions involved in teaching are omitted, even where the professional is seen as 'mother' in the classroom. As mothers, they can challenge the system on a personal level for their individual child but it may be more difficult for them as teachers to do so, even though as such they are more acquainted with, and have access to, the system. While they can use professional knowledge to inform their private actions, as both Truda and Deborah noted, the *teacher*-mother tends to 'hold back' from doing so unless she believes it is essential and even then she finds it very difficult. The emotions of the mother are seen as a negative factor. As mothers they seem to disappear in the discourse of 'care' which defines them as unpaid carers, which creates difficulties for them as working mothers, particularly as mothers of young adults when the real issues, such as social exclusion and isolation, may be underestimated by some professionals. While it appears that the boundaries are blurred by the dual role of the mother-teachers, it is as articulate professionals that they are perceived as powerful by other parents. Their role as mothers, despite their own acknowledgement and acceptance of its significance in informing their professional role, is still the more problematical, still the less powerful.

Through their complexity, the stories demonstrate the ways in which the mother-teachers try to blur the boundaries of public and private and their belief that working with parents is an important part of working with the children. I would argue that a greater acknowledgement of personal experiences within the professional role might offer more illuminating insights into some of these complexities and contradictions and help to inform the understanding and development of professional practice. I question whether or not greater specialisation and professionalisation within SEN will achieve this.

Commitment and consensus

What can the voices in the stories tell us that might help to make a difference to the lives of children with SEN/disabilities, their mothers and their families? I hope their stories offer insights into constructions of difference, issues around inclusion and personal–professional relationships. I want to suggest that through the immense complexity, the contradictions and challenges, their stories make it clear that it really is worth trying to make a difference; that professionals, as individuals, can make choices which affect the lives of others, for good or ill. I would like to hope that these stories might encourage professionals and others to reflect on their assumptions, preconceived notions and conceptualisations of children with SEN/disabilities, their mothers and their families and perhaps question some of their own practices and procedures.

Amid the agendas of others, these mother-teachers commit themselves to be advocates both personally and professionally for their own children and the 'other' children in their 'care'. They have agency as mothers *and* teachers to interpret the world for their own children, for other children and often their parents. They use their agency to promote inclusive practice, whatever that might mean within any particular context at a particular time. They use their personal values to underpin their professional values. Where there is any contradiction between these values there is personal disquiet. Their role can be viewed as a balancing act; a continual moving between different agendas, where issues of power are difficult and complex but have to be negotiated. Through their stories they emerge as neither powerful professionals nor powerless parents but as mothers with particular agency as well as significant agents of change, for within their professional contexts they all actively pursue inclusive strategies in some form.

While there is no apparent consensus around inclusion, the stories suggest that a commitment to the principle of inclusion is important, even though this may sometimes be within specialist provision. In some cases there is a real sense of a commitment to the more specific struggle for inclusion within mainstream contexts. But there is also a strong sense that these mother-teachers feel there is a cost to this struggle. Their language suggests, as did that of the mothers in Todd's study (2003), that getting recognition for their children, and even some degree of inclusion, is a 'struggle', a 'fight', a 'battle', more reminiscent of carnage than care! So what are the costs of this struggle and for whom? Truda suggests that the children are in many ways 'pioneers' in this process. But how can professionals and parents ensure that these 'pioneers', who are already vulnerable, do not pay the costs for the failure of others? If the language of SEN is reminiscent of 'battle', how can we ensure that the casualties will not be the children? As I stated earlier, it is evident from the stories that there are considerable differences around perspectives on, and definitions of, special needs and inclusion and I would argue that such differences are inevitable for some time to come. However, where we do need consensus and commitment from professionals and parents alike is around who should be the standard bearers in the struggle: the politicians, professionals, parents of the children or the children themselves?

If children with SEN do not go to mainstream schools, how will the schools ever change to meet their needs? How can we ensure that the children and their families are not the victims? The vulnerability of both the children and their mothers comes through in each of the stories. Sonia's concerns focus around the daily 'care' her son needs, which she feels would not be forthcoming in a mainstream secondary school. Joan is deeply hurt by the words of the head teacher who tells her, 'We do not want your child at our school', even though this is for one day a week at a school which takes all the other local children. Kate is prepared to keep her daughter's cystic fibrosis hidden until her child is accepted for herself. Deborah takes her daughters into her own professional care to ensure their needs are met at school and Truda even removes her son from the education system for a period of time because she believes it is failing to support him. Julia wages a continual battle against the LEA just to give her son the education she believes he is entitled to, namely an education with his peers at his local school.

The stories in this book suggest that it is vital that professionals, at all levels and in all contexts, listen to the experiences of mothers of children with SEN/disabilities, for they have much to offer to powerful policy-makers and professionals. They make explicit the difficulties of being a mother in a society which views that as one of the most natural things. Their stories offer insights into private, personal and, therefore, often hidden complexities in relation to understanding how constructions of difference impact on the lives of their children and families. They reveal the numerous ways in which these mother-teachers interpret and reinterpret the world for 'their' children.

This book developed from my own experiences of inclusion and exclusion. I have had to explore these and place them in the public domain along with the stories of the other mother-teachers. I have offered aspects of the stories to educational professionals within my work and a number of women have come to me afterwards offering their own experiences as mother-teachers of children with SEN/disabilities. They are relieved to be able to acknowledge that their experiences are at the heart of their own professional knowledge. They are both comforted and, they suggest, empowered by the knowledge that there are many stories to tell, many more than I ever realised when I began the research. I now frequently hear, 'I thought I was the only one'. I recognise that thought!

When the study began, I declared an empathy with the mothers and a responsibility to them in relation to the stories they entrusted to me. Having worked with their stories, read them, reread them, written and rewritten them, I have come to have a sense of a part of the lives of these women, and I feel that responsibility very keenly. As the book is brought to its conclusion, I can do no better than to leave the last words to one of the mother-teachers.

Kate, the efficient professional, in her story talks about her difficulties in being 'just' a mother. She maintains that it involves learning by experience, by getting to know your children, through listening, observing and thereby gradually learning about them. For Kate:

> *Just being a mother is the hardest job I've ever done, definitely. And I admire the mums who deal with lots of different difficulties.*

I agree completely with this sentiment and I would like to suggest that listening to the experiences of mothers of children with SEN/disabilities might be one way in which professionals can help to ensure that our children are not the victims of inclusion, or its martyrs, but respected and valued pioneers, working with their mothers, their families and 'caring' professionals to knock down the boundaries of discrimination, prejudice and exclusion.

Suggested further reading

Policy context

Armstrong, D. (2003) *Experiences of Special Education: Re-evaluating Policy and Practice Through Life Stories*, London: Routledge-Falmer.

Armstrong, F. and Barton, L. (eds) (1999) *Inclusive Education: Policy, Contexts and Comparative Perspectives*, London: David Fulton Publishers.

Clough, P. (ed.) (1998) *Managing Inclusive Education: From Policy to Experience*, London: Paul Chapman Publishing.

Sociological context

Armstrong, D. (1995) *Power and Partnership in Education: Parents, Children and Special Educational Needs*, London: Routledge.

Billington, T. (2000) *Separating, Losing and Excluding Children: Narratives of Difference*, London: Routledge-Falmer.

David, M. (2003) *Personal and Political: Feminisms, Sociology and Family Lives*, Stoke-on-Trent: Trentham Books.

McIntyre, L. (2004) *The Time of Her Life*, London: Jonathan Cape.

Read, J. (2000) *Disability, The Family and Society: Listening to Mothers*, Buckingham: Open University Press.

Sikes, P. (1997) *Parents Who Teach: Stories from Home and from School*, London: Cassell.

The International Journal of Inclusive Education (Taylor and Francis)

Disability and Society (Carfax)

Methodology

Armstrong, F. and Moore, M. (2004) *Action Research for Inclusive Education: Changing Places, Changing Practices, Changing Minds*, London: Routledge-Falmer.

Atkinson, D. (1997) *An Auto/Biographical Approach to Learning Disability Research*, Aldershot: Ashgate Publishing Ltd.

Clandinin, J. and Connelly, F. M. (eds) (1995) *Teachers' Professional Knowledge Landscapes*, New York: Teachers College Press.

Clough, P. (2002) *Narratives and Fictions in Educational Research*, Buckingham: Open University Press.

Coffey, A. (1999) *The Ethnographic Self: Fieldwork and the Representation of Identity*, London: Sage.

Erben, M. (1998) *Biography and Education: A Reader*, London: Falmer Press.

Goodson, I. and Hargreaves, A. (eds) (1996) *Teachers' Professional Lives*, London: Falmer Press.

Goodson, I. and Sikes, P. (2000) *Life History Research in Educational Settings*, Buckingham: Open University Press.

Plummer, K. (1993) *Documents of Life: An Introduction to the Problems and Literature of the Humanistic Method*, London: Routledge.

References

Abberley, P. (1992) 'Counting us out: a discussion of the OPCS disability surveys', *Disability, Handicap and Society*, 7(2), 139–55.

Ainscow, M. (1995) 'Special needs through school improvement: school improvement through special needs', in Clark, C., Dyson, A. and Millward, A. (eds) *Towards Inclusive Schools?* London: David Fulton Publishers.

Allan, J. (1999) *Actively Seeking Inclusion: Pupils with Special Educational Needs in Mainstream Schools*, London: Falmer Press.

Archbald, D. and Porter, A. (1994) 'Curriculum control and teachers' perceptions of autonomy and satisfaction', *Educational Evaluation and Policy Analysis*, 16, 21–39.

Armstrong, D. (1998) 'Changing faces, changing places: policy routes to inclusion', in Clough, P. and Barton, L. (eds) *Managing Inclusive Education: From Policy to Experience*, London: Paul Chapman Publishing.

Armstrong, D. (1995) *Power and Partnership in Education: Parents, Children and Special Educational Needs*, London: Routledge.

Armstrong, F. and Barton, L. (eds) (1999) *Inclusive Education: Policy, Contexts and Comparative Perspectives*, London: David Fulton Publishers.

Ashdown, R. (1996) 'Providing support in the special school', in Upton, G. and Varma, V. (eds) *Stresses in Special Educational Needs Teachers*, Aldershot: Arena.

Bagley, C. and Woods, P. (1998) 'School choice, markets and special educational needs', *Disability and Society*, 13(5), 763–83.

Baker, K. (1988) 'More replies from the Education Secretary', *British Journal of Special Education*, 15(1), 6–7.

Baldwin, S. and Glendinning, C. (1981) 'Children with disabilities and their families', in Walker, A. and Townsend, P. (eds) *Disability in Britain: A Manifesto of Rights*, Oxford: Martin Robertson.

Ball, S. J. (1998) 'Performativity and fragmentation in "postmodern schooling"', in Carter, J. (ed.) *Postmodernity and the Fragmentation of Welfare: A Contemporary Social Policy*, London: Routledge.

Bartky, S. L. (1990) *Femininity and Domination*, London: Routledge.

Barton, L. (1999) 'Market ideologies, education and the challenge of inclusion', in Daniels, H. and Garner, P. (eds) *Inclusive Education: Supporting Inclusion in Education Systems (World Yearbook of Education, 1999)*, London: Kogan Page.

Barton, L. (1998) 'Markets, managerialism and inclusive education', in Clough, P. and Barton, L. (eds) *Managing Inclusive Education: From Policy to Experience*, London: Paul Chapman Publishing.

Barton, L. (1996) 'Sociology and disability: some emerging issues', in Barton, L. (ed.) *Disability and Society: Emerging Issues and Insights*, London: Longman.

Batho, G. (1989) *Political Issues in Education*, London: Cassell.

Benn, C. (1989) 'Preface', in DeLyon, H. and Widdowson Migniuolo, F. (eds) *Women Teachers: Issues and Experiences*, Milton Keynes: Open University Press.

Beresford, B. (1995) *Expert Opinions: A National Survey of Parents Caring for a Severely Disabled Child*, Bristol: The Polity Press (in association with the Joseph Rowntree Foundation and Community Care).

Billington, T. (2000) *Separating, Losing and Excluding Children: Narratives of Difference*, London: Routledge-Falmer.

Bines, H. (2000) 'Inclusive standards? Current developments in policy for special educational needs in England and Wales', *Oxford Review of Education*, 26(1), 21–33.

Birkett, D. (2000) 'Count me in', *Guardian Education*, 12 December, pp. 2–3.

Blackmore, J. (1999) *Troubling Women: Feminism, Leadership and Educational Change*, Buckingham: Open University Press.

Booth, T., Ainscow, M., Black-Hawkins, K., Vaughn, M. and Shaw, L. (2000) *Index for Inclusion: Developing Learning and Participation in Schools*, London: CSIE.

Booth, T. and Booth, W. (1996) 'Sounds of silence: narrative research with inarticulate subjects', *Disability and Society*, 11(1), 55–69.

Boris, E. (1994) 'Mothers are not workers: homework regulation and the construction of motherhood 1948–1953', in Glenn, E. V., Chang, G. and Forcey, L. R. (eds) *Mothering: Ideology, Experience, and Agency*, New York: Routledge.

Bortolaia Silva, E. (1996) 'The transformation of mothering', in Bortolaia Silva, E. (ed.) *Good Enough Mothering? Feminist Perspectives on Lone Motherhood*, London: Routledge.

Bowers, T. (2000) 'Cold comfort in the Code', *British Journal of Special Education*, 27(4), 203.

Bowlby, J. (1963) *Child Care and the Growth of Love*, Harmondsworth: Pelican.

Brown, P. (1990) 'The "third wave": education and the ideology of parentocracy', *The British Journal of the Sociology of Education*, 11(1), 65–85.

Bryne, E. A., Cunningham, C. and Sloper, P. (1988) *Families and Their Children with Down's Syndrome*, London: Routledge.

Cantwell, P., Baker, L. and Rutter, M. (1978) 'Family factors', in Rutter, M. and Schoppler, E. (eds) *Autism: a Reappraisal of Concepts and Treatment*, New York: Plenum Press.

Carpenter, B. (2000) 'Sustaining the family: meeting the needs of families of children with disabilities', *British Journal of Special Education*, 27(3), 135–44.

Chodorow, N. (1989) *Feminism and Psychoanalytic Theory*, Berkeley, CA: University of California Press.

Clough, P. (ed.) (1998a) *Managing Inclusive Education: From Policy to Experience*, London: Paul Chapman Publishing.

Clough, P. (1998b) 'Balancing acts: policy agenda for teacher education and special educational needs', *Journal of Education for Teaching*, 24(1), 63–71.

Clough, P. and Barton, L. (eds) (1998) *Articulating with Difficulty: Research Voices in Inclusive Education*, London: Paul Chapman Publishing.

Collins, P. H. (1994) 'Shifting the centre: race, class and feminist theorizing about motherhood', in Glenn, E. V., Chang, G. and Forcey, L. R. (eds) *Mothering: Ideology, Experience, and Agency*, New York: Routledge.

Corbett, J. (1998) *Special Educational Needs in the Twentieth Century: A Cultural Analysis*, London: Cassell.

Corbett, J. (1996) *Bad-Mouthing: The Language of Special Needs*, London: The Falmer Press.

Corbett, J. (1992) 'Careful teaching: researching a special career', *British Educational Research Journal*, 18(3), 235–44.

Corker, M. and French, S. (eds) (1999) *Disability Discourse*, Buckingham: Open University Press.

Coward, R. (1992) 'Lash back in anger: have feminists fired a war in women?' *The Guardian*, 24 March.

Cox, C. B. and Boyson, R. (eds) (1977) *Black Paper 1977*, London: M. Temple Smith.

Cox, C. B. and Boyson, R. (eds) (1975) *Black Paper 1975: The Fight for Education*, London: Dent.

Croll, P. and Moses, D. (2000) *Special Needs in the Primary School: One in Five?* London: Cassell.

Croll, P. and Moses, D. (1998) 'Pragmatism, ideology and educational change: the case of special educational needs', *British Journal of Educational Studies*, 46(1), 11–25.

Dale, N. (1996) *Working with Families of Children with Special Needs: Partnership and Practice*, London: Routledge.

Dale, R. (1989) *The State and Education Policy*, Milton Keynes: Open University Press.

Daniels, H. and Norwich, B. (1996) 'Supporting teachers of children with special educational needs in ordinary schools', in Upton, G. and Varma, V. (eds) *Stresses in Special Educational Needs Teachers*, Aldershot: Arena.

David, M. (2003) *Personal and Political: Feminisms, Sociology and Family Lives*, Stoke-on-Trent: Trentham Books.

David, M. (2000a) 'A feminist sociology of family life: family and education in [academic] women's lives'. Paper presented at the British Educational Research Association Annual Conference, Cardiff University, 7–9 September 2000.

David, M. (2000b) 'A personal reflection on research on mothers and education'. Paper presented at the ESRC-funded research seminar series *Parents and Schools: Diversity, Participation and Democracy*, Bath Spa University College, 18 October 2000.

David, M. (1998) 'Involvements and investments in education: mothers and schools', *Journal for a Just and Caring Education*, 4(1) January, 30–46.

David, M. (1993a) *Parents, Gender and Education Reform*, Cambridge: Polity Press.

David, M. (1993b) 'Parents, gender and education', *Educational Policy*, 7(2), 184–205.

David, M., Davies, J., Edwards, R., Reay, D. and Standing, K. (1997) 'Choice within constraints: mothers and schooling', *Gender and Education*, 9(4), 397–410.

Davies, J. D., Garner, P. and Lee, J. (eds) (1998) *Managing Special Educational Needs in Mainstream Schools: The Role of the SENCO*, London: David Fulton Publishers.

Davis, H. (1998) 'The benefits of psychological support for parents', *Opportunity*, 16(2), 1–5.

Dearing, R. (1994) *The National Curriculum and Its Assessment: Final Report*, London: School Curriculum and Assessment Authority.

DES (Department of Education and Science) (1988) *Draft Circular [1/89] Revisions of Circular 1/83: Assessments and Statements of Special Educational Needs; Procedures within the Education, Health and Social Services*, London: DES.

DES (Department of Education and Science) (1981) *Circular 8/81: The Education Act 1981*, London: DES.

DES (Department of Education and Science) (1978) *Special Educational Needs: Report of the Committee of Enquiry into the Education of Handicapped Children and Young People (The Warnock Report)*, London: HMSO.

DES (Department of Education and Science) (1967) *Children and Their Primary Schools: The Plowden Report*, London: HMSO.

DfEE (Department for Education and Employment) (1999) *Parent Partnership and Special Educational Needs: Perspectives on Good Practice*, Nottingham: DfEE Publications.

DfEE (Department for Education and Employment) (1998a) *Meeting Special Educational Needs: A Programme of Action*, London: DfEE.

DfEE (Department for Education and Employment) (1998b) *Home–School Agreements: Guidance for Schools*, London: DfEE.

DfEE (Department for Education and Employment) (1998c) *School Standards and Framework Act*, London: DfEE.

DfEE (Department for Education and Employment) (1998d) *National Literacy Strategy Framework for Teaching*, London: DfEE.

DfEE (Department for Education and Employment) (1998e) *National Numeracy Strategy Framework*, London: DfEE.

DfEE (Department for Education and Employment) (1997a) *Excellence for All Children: Meeting Special Educational Needs*, London: DfEE.

DfEE (Department for Education and Employment) (1997b) *The SENCO Guide*, London: DfEE.

DfEE (Department for Education and Employment) (1997c) *Excellence in Schools*, London: DfEE.

DfEE (Department for Education and Employment) (1994) *The Code of Practice on the Identification and Assessment of Special Educational Needs*, London: HMSO.

DfES (Department for Education and Skills) (2004) *Removing Barriers to Achievement: The Government's Strategy for SEN*, London: DfES.

DfES (Department for Education and Skills) (2002) *Special Educational Needs: A Mainstream Issue*, London: Audit Commission's Report.

DfES (Department for Education and Skills) (2001) *Special Educational Needs Code of Practice*, London: DfES.

DiQuinzio, P. (1999) *The Impossibility of Motherhood: Feminism, Individualism and the Problem*, New York: Routledge.

Donzelot, J. (1979) *The Policing of Families*, London: Hutchinson.

Dowling, M. and Dolan, L. (2001) 'Families with children with disabilities-inequalities and the social model', *Disability and Society*, 16(1), 21–35.

Dyson, A. (1993) 'Do we need special needs coordinators?', in Visser, J. and Upton, G. (eds) *Special Education in Britain after Warnock*, London: David Fulton Publishers.

Ehrenreich, B. and English, D. (1978) *For Her Own Good: 150 Years of Expert Advice to Women*, London: Pluto.

Elliot, J. and Iredale, W. (2003) 'Housewives go backwards in status race', *The Sunday Times*, News, 1 June, p. 6.

Everingham, C. (1994) *Motherhood and Modernity: An Investigation into the Racial Dimension of Mothering*, Buckingham: Open University Press.

Fine, M. (1998) 'Working the hyphens: reinventing self and other in qualitative research', in Denzin, N. and Lincoln, Y. (eds) *The Landscape of Qualitative Research: Theories and Issues*, London: Sage.

Firestone, S. (1970) *The Dialectic of Sex*, New York: Bantam Books (republished 1993 by Morrow).

Flude, M. and Hammer, M. (1990) *The Education Reform Act 1988: Its Origins and Implications*, London: The Falmer Press.

Foucault, M. (1979) *Discipline and Punish*, London: Allen Lane.

Foucault, M. (1973) *The Birth of the Clinic* (trans. A. Sheridan), London: Tavistock.

Friedan, B. (1963) *The Feminine Mystique*, London: Victor Gollancz.

Fulcher, G. (1999) *Disabling Policies? A Comparative Approach to Education Policy and Disability*, 2nd edn, Sheffield: Philip Armstrong Publications.

Fulcher, G. (1989) *Disabling Policies? A Comparative Approach to Education Policy and Disability*, London: Falmer.

Gewirtz, S., Ball, S. and Bowe, R. (1995) *Markets, Choice and Equity in Education*, Buckingham: Open University Press.

Gilbourne, D. and Youdell, D. (2000) *Rationing Education: Policy, Practice, Reform and Equity*, Buckingham: Open University Press.

Giroux, H. (1991) 'Postmodernism as border pedagogy', in Giroux, H. (ed.) *Postmodernism, Feminism, and Cultural Politics*, Albany, NY: State University of New York Press.

Glendinning, C. (1983) *Unshared Care: Parents and Their Disabled Children*, London: Routledge and Kegan Paul.

Glenn, E. N. (1994) 'Social constructions of mothering: a thematic overview', in Glenn, E. V., Chang, G. and Forcey, L. R. (eds) *Mothering: Ideology, Experience, and Agency*, New York: Routledge.

Glenn, E. V., Chang, G. and Forcey, L. R. (eds) (1994) *Mothering: Ideology, Experience, and Agency*, New York: Routledge.

Gramsci, A. (1971) *Selections from the Prison Notebooks* (ed. and trans. Q. Hoare and G. Nowell Smith), New York: International.

Grumet, M. (1988) *Bitter Milk: Women and Teaching*, Amherst, MA: The University of Massachusetts Press.

Hanafin, J. and Lynch, A. (2002) 'Peripheral voices: parental involvement, social class and educational disadvantage', *British Journal of Sociology of Education*, 23(1), 35–49.

Handy, C. (1995) *The Empty Raincoat: Making Sense of the Future*, London: Arrow Books Limited.

Hargreaves, A. (1994) *Changing Teachers, Changing Times: Teachers' Work and Culture in the Postmodern Age*, London: Cassell.

Hartnett, A. and Carr, W. (1995) 'Education, teacher development and the struggle for democracy', in Smyth, J. (ed.) *Critical Discourses on Teacher Development*, London: Cassell.

Helsby, G. (1999) *Changing Teachers' Work*, Buckingham: Open University Press.

Helsby, G. and McCulloch, G. (1996) 'Teacher professionalism and curriculum control', in Goodson, I. and Hargreaves, A. (eds) *Teachers' Professional Lives*, London: The Falmer Press.

Helsby, G. and Saunders, M. (1993) 'Taylorism, Tylerism and performance indicators: defending the indefensible?', *Educational Studies*, 19, 55–77.

Hewett, S. (1976) 'Research on families with handicapped children: an aid or an impediment to understanding', *Birth Defects*, X11, 34–5.

Hewett, S. (1970) *Families and the Handicapped Child*, London: Allen and Unwin.

Hillgate Group (1987) *Reform of British Education: From Principles to Practice*, London: Claridge Press.

Høeg, P. (1996) *Borderliners*, London: Harvill Press.

Hood, S. (2001) 'Home-school agreements: a true partnership?', *School Leadership and Management*, 21(1), 7–17.

Hood, S. (1999) 'Home-school agreements: a true partnership?' *School Leadership and Management*, 19(4), 427–40.

Kaplan, E. A. (1994) 'Look who's talking, indeed: foetal images in recent North American visual culture', in Glenn, E. V., Chang, G. and Forcey, L. R. (eds) *Mothering: Ideology, Experience, and Agency*, New York: Routledge.

Kaplan, E. A. (1992) *Motherhood and Representation: The Mother in Popular Culture*, London: Routledge.

Kauffman, J. M. and Hallahan, D. P. (eds) (1995) *The Illusion of Full Inclusion: A Comprehensive Critique of a Current Special Education Bandwagon*, Austin, Texas: Pro-ed.

Lawn, M. (1990) 'From responsibility to competency: a new context for curriculum studies in England and Wales', *Journal of Curriculum Studies*, 22(4), 388–92.

Lawn, M. and Grace, G. (eds) (1987) *Teachers: The Culture and Politics of Work*, London: The Falmer Press.

Lawton, D. (1980) *The Politics of the School Curriculum*, London: Routledge and Keegan.

Le Grand, J. and Bartlett, W. (eds) (1993) *Quasi-Markets and Social Policy*, London: Macmillan.

Lewis. J. (1992) *Women in Britain since 1945: Women, Family, Work and the State in the Post-War Years*, Oxford: Blackwell.

Lindsay, G. (2003) 'Inclusive education: a critical perspective', *British Journal of Special Education*, 30(1), 3–12.

Lipsky, D. K. and Gartner, A. (1998) 'Factors for successful inclusion: learning from the past, looking forward to the future', in Vitello, S. V. and. Mithaug, D. E. (eds) *Inclusive Schooling: National and International Perspectives*, Mahurah, NJ: Lawrence Erlbaum Associates.

Lunt, I. and Evans, J. (1991) *Special Educational Needs under LMS*, London: Institute of Education.

MacDonald, M. (1981) 'Schooling and the reproduction of class and gender relations', in Dale, R. (ed.) *Politics, Patriarchy and Practice*, London: Falmer and Open University Press.

Macrae, M., Maguire, M. and Milbourne, L. (2003) 'Social exclusion: exclusion from school', *International Journal of Inclusive Education*, 7(2), 89–101.

May, D. (1996) 'Stress in teachers of children with special educational needs: past, present and future', in Upton, G. and Varma, V. (eds) *Stresses in Special Educational Needs Teachers*, Aldershot: Arena.

Mayall, B. (1996) *Children, Health and the Social Order*, Buckingham: Open University Press.

McConachie, H. (1997) 'Do UK services really support parents?', *Opportunity*, 15, 1–2.

McIntyre, L. (2004) *The Time of Her Life*, London: Jonathan Cape.

Millet, K. (1970) *Sexual Politics*, New York: Doubleday.

Mirza, H. (1993) 'The social construction of black womenhood in British educational research: towards a new understanding', in Arnot, M. and Weiler, K. (eds) *Feminism and Social Justice*, London: The Falmer Press.

Mitchell, J. (1975) *Psychoanalysis and Feminism*, Harmondsworth: Penguin.

Mitchell, J. (1971) *Woman's Estate*, Harmondsworth: Penguin.

Moore, M., Beazley, S. and Maelzer, J. (1998) *Researching Disability Issues*, Buckingham: Open University Press.

Munn, P. (ed.) (1993) *Parents and Schools: Customers, Managers or Partners?*, London: Routledge.

Murray, P. and Penman, J. (eds) (2000) *Telling Our Own Stories: Reflections on Family Life in a Disabling World*, Sheffield: Parents with Attitude.

Murray, P. and Penman, J. (eds) (1996) *Let Our Children Be: A Collection of Stories*, Sheffield: Parents with Attitude.

NASEN (National Association for Special Educational Needs) (2000) *Proposed Revision of the SEN Code of Practice and Accompanying Guidance on SEN Thresholds*, Tamworth: NASEN.

Nelson, M. K. (1994) 'Family day care providers: dilemmas of daily practice', in Glenn, E. V., Chang, G. and Forcey, L. R. (eds) (1994) *Mothering: Ideology, Experience, and Agency*, New York: Routledge.

Newson, E. (1981) 'Parents as a resource in diagnosis and assessment', in Brechin, A., Liddiard, P. and Swain, J. (eds) *Handicap in a Social World*, London: Hodder and Stoughton, in association with The Open University.

Nias, J. (1996) 'Thinking about feeling: the emotions in teaching', *Cambridge Journal of Education*, 26(3), 293–306.

Norris, C. and Lloyd, G. (2000) 'Parents, professionals and ADHD: what the papers say', *European Journal of Special Needs Education*, 15(2), 123–37.

Oakley, A. (1986) 'Feminism, motherhood and medicine: who cares?' in Mitchell, J. and Oakley, A. (eds) *What is Feminism?* Oxford: Basil Blackwell.

Oakley, A. (1980) *Women Confined*, London: Martin Robertson and Company Limited.

Oakley, A. (1979) *Becoming a Mother*, Oxford: Martin Robertson and Company Limited.

Oakley, A. (1974) *Housewife*, London: Penguin Books.

Oliver, M. (1996a) *Understanding Disability: From Theory to Practice*, Basingstoke: Macmillan.

Oliver, M. (1996b) 'A sociology of disability or a disablist sociology?', in Barton, L. (ed.) *Disability and Society: Emerging Issues and Insights*, Harlow: Longman.

Olshansky, S. (1962) 'Chronic sorrow: a response to having a mentally defective child', *Social Casework*, 43(April), 190–3.

Ouston, J. and Hood, S. (2000) *Home-School Agreements: A True Partnership? Report of a Research Project for the Research and Information on State Education Trust* (RISE), London: Rise.

Parker, I. (1992) *Discourse Dynamics: Clinical Analysis for Social and Individual Psychology*, London: Routledge.

Peters, S. (1996) 'The politics of disability identity', in Barton, L. (ed.) *Disability and Society: Emerging Issues and Insights*, Harlow: Longman.

Polkinghorne, D. E. (1995) 'Narrative configuration in qualitative analysis', in Hatch, J. A. and Wisniewski, R. (eds) *Life History and Narrative*, London: The Falmer Press.

Pratt, M. (1985) 'Scratches on the face of the country', in Gates, H. (ed.) *Race, Writing and Difference*, Chicago, IL: University of Chicago Press.

Pugh, G., Aplin, G., De'Ath, E. and Moxon, M. (1987) *Partnership in Action: Working with Parents in Preschool Centres, Vol. 2*, London: National Children's Bureau.

Ranson, S. and Tomlinson, J. (1986) *The Changing Government of Education*, London: Allen and Unwin.

Read, J. (2000) *Disability, The Family and Society: Listening to Mothers*, Buckingham: Open University Press.

Ribbens McCarthy, J. (2000) 'Mothers' involvement in their children's schooling'. Paper presented at Bath Spa University College, 18 October 2000.

Rich, A. (1976) *Of Woman Born: Motherhood as Experience and Institution*, New York: Norton.

Rogers, R. (1984) *Crowther to Warnock: How Fourteen Reports Tried to Change Children's Lives*, 2nd edn, London: Heinemann Educational Books.

Roll-Petterson, L. (2001) 'Parents talk about how it feels to have a child with a cognitive disability', *European Journal of Special Needs Education*, 16(1), 1–14.

Ruddick, S. (1989) *Maternal thinking*, New York: Ballantine.

Ruddick, S. (1982) 'Maternal Thinking', in Thorne, B. and Yalom, M. (eds) *Rethinking The Family*, New York and London: Longman.

Russell, F. (2003) 'The expectations of parents of disabled children', *British Journal of Special Education*, 30(3), 144–9.

Russell, P. (1990) 'The Education Reform Act: the implications for special educational needs', in Flude, M. and Hammer, M. (eds) *The Education Reform Act 1988: Its Origins and Implications*, London: The Falmer Press.

Sayers, J. (1991) *Mothering Psychoanalysis*, London: Penguin.

Sebba, J. and Ainscow, M. (1996) 'International developments in inclusive schooling: mapping the issues', *Cambridge Journal of Education*, 26(1), 5–18.

Segura, D. A. (1994) 'Working at motherhood: Chicana and Mexican immigrant mothers and employment', in Glenn, E. V., Chang, G. and Forcey, L. R. (eds) *Mothering: Ideology, Experience, and Agency*, New York: Routledge.

Sharpe, S. (1984) *Double Identity: The Lives of Working Mothers*, Harmondsworth: Penguin.

Sikes, P. (1997) *Parents Who Teach: Stories from Home and from School*, London: Cassell.

Silver, H. (1990) *Education, Change and the Policy Process*, London: The Falmer Press.

Skidmore, D. (1996) 'Towards an integrated theoretical framework for the research into special educational needs', *European Journal of Special Needs Education*, 11(1), 33–47.

Slee, R. (1999) 'Policies and practices? Inclusive education and its effects in schooling', in Daniels, H. and Garner, P. (eds) (1999) *Inclusive Education: Supporting Inclusion in Education Systems (World Year Book of Education, 1999)*, London: Kogan Page.

Slee, R. (1998) 'The politics of theorising special education', in Clark, C., Dyson, A. and Millward, A. (eds) *Theorising Special Education*, London: Routledge.

Slee, R. (1996) 'Inclusive schooling in Australia? Not yet!', *Cambridge Journal of Education*, 26(1), 19–32.

Slee, R. and Weiner, G. with Tomlinson, S. (eds) (1998) *School Effectiveness for Whom? Challenges to the School Effectiveness and School Improvement Movements*, London: The Falmer Press.

Smart, C. (1996) 'Deconstructing motherhood', in Bortolaia Silva, E. (ed.) *Good Enough Mothering? Feminist Perspectives on Lone Motherhood*, London: Routledge.

Smith, D. (1987) *The Everyday World as Problematic: A Feminist Sociology*, Milton Keynes: Open University Press.

Smyth, J. (ed.) (1995) *Critical Discourses on Teacher Development*, London: Cassell.

Spain, D. (1996) *Balancing Act: Motherhood, Marriage and Employment Among American Women*, New York: Russell Sage Foundation.

Stanley, L. (1992) *The Auto/Biographical I: Theory and Practice of Feminist Auto/Biography*, Manchester: Manchester University Press.

Steedman, C. (1987) 'Prisonhouses', in Lawn, M. and Grace, G. (1987) *Teachers: The Culture and Politics of Work*, London: The Falmer Press.

Steedman, C., Urwin, C. and Walkerdine, V. (eds) (1985) *Language, Gender and Childhood*, London: Routledge and Kegan Paul.

Swain, J. and Walker, C. (2003) 'Parent–professional power relations: parent and professional perspectives', *Disability and Society*, 18(5), 547–60.

Thomas, D. (1982) *The Experience of Handicap*, London: Methuen.

Thomas, G. and Glenny, G. (2002) 'Thinking about inclusion. Whose reason? What evidence?' *International Journal of Inclusive Education*, 6(4), 345–69.

Todd, E. S. and Higgins, S. (1998) 'Powerlessness in professional and parent partnerships', *British Journal of Sociology of Education*, 19(2), 227–36.

Todd, L. (2003) 'Disability and the restructuring of welfare: the problem of partnerships with parents', *International Journal of Inclusive Education*, 7(3), 281–96.

Tomlinson, S. (2001) *Education in a Post-Welfare Society*, Buckingham: Open University Press.

Tomlinson, S. (1982) *A Sociology of Special Education*, London: Routledge and Kegan Paul.

TSO (The Stationery Office) (2003) *Every Child Matters* (Green Paper), London: TSO.

TTA (Teacher Training Agency) (1999) *National Special Educational Needs Specialist Standards*, London: TTA.

TTA (Teacher Training Agency) (1998) *National Standards for Special Educational Needs Co-ordinators*, London: TTA.

Upton, G. and Varma, V. (eds) (1996) *Stresses in Special Educational Needs Teachers*, Aldershot: Arena.

Urwin, C. (1985) 'Constructing motherhood: the persuasion of normal development', in Steedman, C., Urwin, C. and Walkerdine, V. (eds) (1985) *Language, Gender and Childhood*, London: Routledge and Kegan Paul.

Viet-Wilson, J. (1998) *Setting Adequacy Standards*, Bristol: Polity Press.

Vincent, C. (1996) *Parents and Teachers: Power and Participation*, London: Falmer Press.

Walkerdine, V. and Lucey, H. (1989) *Democracy in the Kitchen: Regulating Mothers and Socialising Daughters*, London: Virago.

Warnock, M. (1996) 'The work of the Warnock Committee', in Mittler, P. and Sinason, V. (eds) *Changing Policy and Practice for People with Learning Difficulties*, London: Cassell.

Wearing, B. (1984) *The Ideology of Motherhood*, Sydney: Allen and Unwin.

Wedell, K., Stevens, C. and Waller, T. (2000) 'SENCO forum', *British Journal of Special Education*, 27(4), 204.

Wilson, J. (2000) 'Doing justice to inclusion', *European Journal of Special Needs Education*, 15, 297–304.

Wolfendale, S. (2002) *Parent Partnership Services for Special Educational Needs: Celebrations and Challenges*, London: David Fulton Publishers.

Wolfendale, S. (ed.) (1997) *Working with Parents of SEN Children After the Code of Practice*, London: David Fulton Publishers.

Wolfendale, S. and Cook, G. (1997) *Evaluation of Special Educational Needs Parent Partnership Schemes*, London: DfEE.

Index